WHAT'S NEXT FOR STUDENT VETERANS?

★★★★★★★★★★★★★★★★★★★★★★★★★★★★★★★

MOVING FROM TRANSITION TO ACADEMIC SUCCESS

DAVID DIRAMIO, EDITOR

Cite as:
DiRamio, D. (Ed.). (2017). *What's next for student veterans? Moving from transition to academic success.* Columbia, SC: University of South Carolina, National Resource Center for The First-Year Experience & Students in Transition.

ISBN: 978-1-942072-10-2
Published by:
National Resource Center for The First-Year Experience®
and Students in Transition
University of South Carolina
1728 College Street, Columbia, SC 29208
www.sc.edu/fye

The First-Year Experience® is a service mark of the University of South Carolina. A license may be granted upon written request to use the term "The First-Year Experience." This license is not transferable without written approval of the University of South Carolina.

Production Staff for the National Resource Center:
Project Manager: Tracy L. Skipper, Assistant Director for Publications
Design and Production: Allison Minsk, Graphic Artist
External Reviewers: Sonya Joseph, Assistant Vice President of Student
                             Affairs, Valencia College
                             Phillip Morris, Program Director, Office of Veteran and Military
                             Student Affairs, University of Colorado–Colorado Springs

Library of Congress Cataloging-in-Publication Data

Names: DiRamio, David C., editor of compilation.
Title: What's next for student veterans? : moving from transition to academic success / David DiRamio, editor.
Description: Columbia, SC : National Resource Center for The First-Year Experience and Students in Transition, University of South Carolina, [2017] | Includes bibliographical references and index.
Identifiers: LCCN 2017025521 (print) | LCCN 2017047585 (ebook) | ISBN 9781942072157 (Ebrary) | ISBN 9781942072164 (EPub) | ISBN 9781942072102 (pbk. : alk. paper)
Subjects: LCSH: Veterans--Education (Higher)--United States. | Veterans--Education--United States.
Classification: LCC UB357 (ebook) | LCC UB357 .W52 2017 (print) | DDC 378.1/9826970973--dc23
LC record available at https://lccn.loc.gov/2017025521

ABOUT THE PUBLISHER

★★★★★★★★★★★★★★★★★★★★★★★★★★★★★★★★

The National Resource Center for The First-Year Experience and Students in Transition was born out of the success of University of South Carolina's much-honored University 101 course and a series of annual conferences on the first-year experience. The momentum created by the educators attending these early conferences paved the way for the development of the National Resource Center, which was established at the University of South Carolina in 1986. As the National Resource Center broadened its focus to include other significant student transitions in higher education, it underwent several name changes, adopting the National Resource Center for The First-Year Experience and Students in Transition in 1998.

Today, the Center collaborates with its institutional partner, University 101 Programs, in pursuit of its mission to advance and support efforts to improve student learning and transitions into and through higher education. We achieve this mission by providing opportunities for the exchange of practical and scholarly information as well as the discussion of trends and issues in our field through convening conferences and other professional development events, such as institutes, workshops, and online learning opportunities; publishing scholarly practice books, research reports, a peer-reviewed journal, electronic newsletters, and guides; generating, supporting, and disseminating research and scholarship; hosting visiting scholars; and maintaining several online channels for resource sharing and communication, including a dynamic website, listservs, and social media outlets. The National Resource Center serves as the trusted expert, internationally recognized leader, and clearinghouse for scholarship, policy, and best practice for all postsecondary student transitions.

Institutional Home

The National Resource Center is located at the University of South Carolina's (UofSC) flagship campus in Columbia. Chartered in 1801, the University's mission is twofold: (a) to establish and maintain excellence in its student population, faculty, academic programs, living and learning environment, technological infrastructure, library resources, research and scholarship, public and private support, and endowment; and (b) to enhance the industrial, economic, and cultural potential of the state. The Columbia campus offers 324 degree programs through its 15 degree-granting colleges and schools. In fiscal year 2015, faculty generated $243 million in funding for research, outreach, and training programs. UofSC is one of only 32 public universities receiving both Research and Community Engagement designations from the Carnegie Foundation.

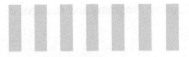

CONTENTS

Tables and Figures..vii

Foreword ix
David Blair

Editor's Preface...xiii

Section I: Student Veterans in the 21st Century: Experiences and Perspectives
Chapter 1 3
Data-Driven Inquiry, Servicemembers' Perspectives, and Redefining Success
Corri Zoli, Rosalinda Maury, and Daniel L. Fay

Chapter 2 25
Opportunity, Inequity, and America's Story: Intersections With
Military-Connected Individuals in Higher Education
Andrew Q. Morse and Dani Molina

Chapter 3 41
The Journey or the Destination: Exploring Engagement Patterns of Disabled
Student Veterans
Amanda Kraus, R. Cody Nicholls, and James S. Cole

Chapter 4 59
Mental Health and Academic Functioning of Student Servicemembers and
Veterans in Higher Education: The Importance of Social Support
Adam E. Barry, Shawn D. Whiteman, and Shelley MacDermid Wadsworth

Section II: Student Veterans in the 21st Century: Programs and Academic Outcomes

Chapter 5 79
Serving Those Who Served: Promising Institutional Practices and America's
Military Veterans
Dani Molina and Tanya Ang

Chapter 6 93
Navigating Toward Academic Success: Peer Support for Student Veterans
*Michelle Kees, Brittany Risk, Chrysta Meadowbrooke, Jane L. Spinner, and
Marcia Valenstein*

Chapter 7 117
Completing the Mission II: A Study of Veteran Students' Progress Toward Degree
Attainment in the Post-9/11 Era
Wendy A. Lang and Tom O'Donnell

Chapter 8 135
Academic Outcomes and the Million Records Project
Chris Andrew Cate

Chapter 9 147
Where Do They Fit? Applying the Conceptual Model of Nontraditional
Undergraduate Student Attrition to Student Veterans
Ryan L. Van Dusen

Chapter 10 163
Essential Practices for Student Veterans in the California Community College
System
Wayne K. Miller II

Section III: Summary, Implications, and Recommendations

Chapter 11 179
What's Next? Charting the Course Before Moving Off the Radar
David DiRamio

About the Authors 191

Index...199

TABLES AND FIGURES

Tables

Table 1.1   Length of Service..6

Table 1.2   Plans to Pursue Higher Education..6

Table 1.3   Reasons for Joining the Armed Services..8

Table 1.4   Most Valuable Sources of Resources and Information.....................................9

Table 1.5   Role of MOS in Promoting Interest in and Preparing for Further Education..9

Table 1.6   Lasting Impressions of Military Service...10

Table 1.7   Key Challenges in Transition..11

Table 1.8   Funding Source for Past, Current, or Future Education....................................13

Table 1.9   Reasons for Sharing Service Experiences at School.......................................14

Table 1.10 Reasons for Not Sharing Service Experiences at School...................................15

Table 1.11 Skills Developed During Service..19

Table 1.12 Reasons for Leaving the Armed Services..20

Table 1.13 Influence of Military Specialization on Employment, Education, and STEM Participation...21

Table 3.1   Student Veterans With at Least One Documented Disability Compared with Other Student Groups..46

Table 4.1   Summary of Hierarchical Multiple Regression Analyses for Variables Predicting Military-Affiliated College Students' Academic Functioning...66

Table 4.2   Summary of Hierarchical Multiple Regression Analyses for Variables Predicting Military-Affiliated College Students' Mental Health.........67

Table 8.1   Student Veteran Sector Migration From Initial Enrollment to First Degree Earned..143

Table 8.2   First Degree Completion by Age Group..144

Table 9.1   Participant Demographics...154

Table 9.2   Variable Regression Matrix Table...157

Table 10.1 Chi-Square Results for the Top Eight Essential Practices..................................164

Table 10.2 CCCS Student Veteran Self-disclosed Discharge Ranks...................................172

Figures

Figure 2.1   Average Adjusted Gross Income Among First-Year
              Undergraduate Student Veterans by Race and Ethnicity.................28
Figure 2.2   Percentage of First-Year Undergraduate Student Veterans Who
              Received VA/DoD Benefits by Race and Ethnicity..........................29
Figure 2.3   Proportion of First-Year Undergraduate Student Veterans With
              Unmet Need and the Average Amount by Race and Ethnicity.....30
Figure 2.4   Proportion of First-Year Undergraduate Student Veterans With
              Unmet Need and the Average Amount by Gender..........................30
Figure 2.5   Proportion of First-Year Undergraduate Student Veterans With
              Loan Debt and the Amount by Race and Ethnicity..........................31
Figure 2.6   Proportion of First-Year Undergraduate Student Veterans
              With Loan Debt and the Amount by Gender....................................32
Figure 2.7   Military-Connected Undergraduates Enrolled in STEM
              Fields by Service Status..33
Figure 2.8   Number of Non-completion Risk Factors for
              Military-Connected Undergraduates by Service Status...................34
Figure 6.1   The PAVE Model of Tiered Roles for
              Training and Implementation..98
Figure 6.2   Elements of the PAVE Program...100
Figure 6.3   PAVE's Partner Campuses..109
Figure 7.1   Mean GPA for Sample Institutions...121
Figure 7.2   Persistence Rates for Sample Institutions,
              Fall 2011 – Spring 2012...123
Figure 11.1   Estimate of Staffing Needs Based on Student Veteran
              Enrollment...181

FOREWORD

★★★★★★★★★★★★★★★★★★★★★★★★★★★★★★★★★★

One of the greatest pleasures of serving today's student veterans is to see them progress year-by-year through a program of major study, take the life-changing walk across the stage to receive a degree, and move into the workforce well prepared for the next chapter in life. As those of us who work with this unique student population know, a student veteran's path through the higher education landscape can be strewn with potential academic and personal landmines. For example, most of these students have been out of school for years, some are married with children, others face formidable challenges associated with physical and psychological injuries, and many are likely to have a combination of several challenges.

Many higher education professionals have roles in a student veteran's collegiate journey, but some are uniquely positioned to advocate on their behalf. As a 25-year veteran of the U.S. Army working with servicemembers for more than 10 years at Mississippi State University and now at The University of Alabama, it continues to be an honor to support student success, especially for the men and women who have served our country in times of conflict and have sacrificed much to preserve our freedom. Those of us who work with student veterans may feel that this is not only our mission, but our solemn duty, as well.

Contained within the pages of this important book are recent research findings in student veteran affairs, presented by many recognizable and prominent scholars in the field of study. As you work your way through this volume, I hope you will grasp, as I have, the significance of each chapter's contribution to the timely topics presented, including the latest in best practices, academic success metrics, mental health measures, and concerns for educational equity and support.

In the past decade, the higher education community has created veterans centers at schools across the country, developed programs and services for student veterans, and helped this population make a successful transition to college. More recent initiatives, like the Department of Veterans Affairs' VetSuccess Program, which has been embedded at dozens of colleges and universities across the nation, are further improving the chances for veterans to succeed. While acknowledging the strides that have been made in veterans education and as someone charged by my institution with continuous improvement, I find myself asking, "Where do we go from here?" and "What is our next step in the development of programs and services to make student veterans' success a common outcome across all institutions of higher learning?"

In my opinion, *What's Next for Student Veterans?* is a must-read for higher education professionals at all levels, from those directly serving this population of students in the campus veterans center to the administrators overseeing these areas to faculty in the classroom. For those considering a career in veterans services, this book is an essential tool that will help guide their future work. Even seasoned professionals in this field will be surprised by the important topics and provocative findings described herein.

Many of us have witnessed the increase of the military population at campuses across the nation. And, as enrollment numbers climb for this cohort of men and women who fought in the wars in Iraq and Afghanistan, there have been noticeable changes and challenges in the higher education profession that are commensurate with that growth. As educators who strive to be catalysts for student success, we are uniquely positioned on campus to be a powerful influence for servicemembers making the transition from the military to college (and beyond). I am often reminded in my role that, much like the original Post-WWII GI Bill recipients helped transform this country in the last century, the group of students we serve today may well be the next "Greatest Generation." Who better to lead our nation in the future than those who served our country admirably in a period of global threats and international conflicts?

As a consumer of research and observer of veterans' issues over the past decade, I am pleased to discover how the latest research and findings presented in this book show the progress that has been made in the study of student veterans in higher education. Moreover, as educators we clearly understand how critical it has become to make evidence-based decisions when allocating resources for programs and services. The findings in this book will assist in that decision process by answering questions about variables, such as persistence, retention, degree completion, employment after college, and myriad other metrics and outcomes. I know these are the questions my supervisor has for me when it comes to measures of program efficacy and the effectiveness of funding certain programs.

I would like to personally thank David DiRamio for his hard work and dedication to the field of student veteran education and student success over the years. Since 2008, I have learned much from David's research, writing, and conference presentations. As a veteran himself, he has devoted significant time in his career to inform higher education professionals across the country about the challenges our servicemembers face in college and how we can better support them on their own personal marches toward academic success, career goals, and personally enriching lives.

In this book, DiRamio and his colleagues explore and provide us with information sorely needed to shape the next steps the higher education community, along with our partners and stakeholders, must take collectively to support our veterans and their families.

David Blair
Director, Veteran and Military Affairs
The University of Alabama
Tuscaloosa, Alabama

EDITOR'S PREFACE

★★★★★★★★★★★★★★★★★★★★★★★★★★★★★★★★★★★★

The first wave of research about student veterans—conducted over the past 10 years—focused mostly on describing the phenomenon of the student veteran and their transition from military service to civilian life and the college campus. Important findings from this period included evidence that peer connections and support are vital for early student success (Ackerman, DiRamio, & Garza Mitchell, 2009) and that colleges and universities should, if enrollment numbers justify it and where practicable, introduce a one-stop shop approach to veterans services (Rumann & Hamrick, 2010). Studies from this period were based mostly on small samples and typically employed qualitative methods. While these studies were data rich and of high quality, the findings were by definition not generalizable and the implications for practice were mostly speculative because they had not been empirically tested.

In early 2014, the release of findings from the Million Records Project, a cooperative research initiative of Student Veterans of America, the National Student Clearinghouse, and the U.S. Department of Veterans Affairs, signaled the beginning of a second wave of research focused on the academic success of veterans in college. Results from this project, which used sampling from approximately one million veteran education, beneficiary, enrollment, and completion records, revealed for the first time how the most recent generation of veterans are performing in higher education. As Chris Cate suggests in Chapter 8 and elsewhere (see Cate, 2014), the findings from this survey are encouraging: Veterans' completion rates are better than any other post-traditional student group and were similar to the rates for traditional college students.

The purpose of this book is to present findings from this second wave of research about student veterans, with a focus on data-driven evidence of academic success factors, including persistence, retention, degree completion, and employment after college. In an atmosphere of tight budgets and scarce resources, it is vital that decision makers are furnished with empirical evidence to make data-informed decisions that benefit students. This volume is intended for the whole of the higher education community, but particularly those tasked with providing programs and services for student veterans and who will carry the mantle forward for the next decade.

Chapters 1 through 4 provide a framework for a deeper understanding of the experiences and perspectives of student veterans making transitions from military service to civilian life, including barriers to academic success, mental health concerns, challenges faced by disabled students, and issues of equity in postsecondary education. Chapter 1, coauthored by Corri Zoli, Rosalinda Maury, and Daniel Fay of the Institute for Veterans and Military Families at Syracuse University, describes key elements of veterans' transitions and shares best practices for research, which emphasizes a multichannel approach to collecting data from student veterans.

In Chapter 2, Andrew Morse and Dani Molina offer a primer for better understanding military-connected undergraduates and key factors associated with access, matriculation, financial need, and degree attainment. Their key theme is educational equity, and their data suggest that a disproportionate percentage of veterans attend for-profit institutions and community colleges. Many also have unmet financial needs and accrue debt while in college despite the educational benefits provided by the Post-9/11 GI Bill.

Amanda Kraus, Cody Nicholls, and James Cole use mixed-methods research in Chapter 3 to investigate levels of engagement for student veterans with disabilities and present findings of interest for the higher education community, including information about the lower perceived gains that these students reported from their collegiate experiences. In Chapter 4, Adam Barry, Shawn Whiteman, and Shelley MacDermid Wadsworth report on their research about mental health and academic outcomes. Among their findings is that positive mental health support from family and friends promotes coping skills and resiliency.

Section II emphasizes programs to support student veterans and key academic outcomes, such as persistence and graduation rates. Chapter 5, coauthored by Dani Molina and Tanya Ang, summarizes a decade of best practice research supported by the American Council on Education to facilitate student veteran success. Michelle Kees and colleagues from the University of Michigan provide details in Chapter 6 about the Peer Advisors for Veteran Education (PAVE) program that they have implemented at more than 40 schools over the past five years. Wendy Lang and Tom O'Donnell in Chapter 7 provide data-driven findings relating to the academic success of student veterans and discuss the creation of their Graduation Probability Index, derived from data gathered by Operation College Promise and its consortium of 23 universities.

Chris Cate, senior researcher at Student Veterans of America, breaks new ground in Chapter 8 by providing details from the acclaimed Million Records Project in which large databases were merged from the National Student Clearinghouse, the premier financial aid-tracking agency, and the U.S. Department of Veterans Affairs. The combined database was used to examine the academic progress of more than 100,000 veterans who have used military educational benefits, including the Post-9/11 GI Bill, to pursue postsecondary education between 2002 and 2010. In Chapter 9, Ryan Van Dusen assesses the validity and usefulness of a familiar model of student retention as applied to the post-traditional, student veteran population. Wayne Miller reveals essential practices, which are detailed in Chapter 10, from his exhaustive mixed-methods study of nearly 500 student veterans enrolled in the California Community College System. Finally, Section III draws on key findings from the volume to make recommendations about the next steps for serving college student veterans.

I hope readers will consider how their own institutions support student veterans beyond their initial transitions to college while keeping in mind that the next step is a focus on academic success metrics (e.g., persistence, retention, graduation, career development, employment). The authors featured in this book provide examples that build upon the higher education tradition of developing research-based programs to support students. Now, more than a decade since the first student veterans began enrolling in college using Post-9/11 GI Bill benefits, many colleges and universities across the nation are indeed making efforts to not only provide services for veterans but also advocate for their academic success. However, for some schools, there is still much left to do for supporting student veterans. Ask yourself how you can provide leadership at your school in order to "serve those who have served." As President John F. Kennedy proclaimed in 1963, "As we express our gratitude, we must never forget that the highest appreciation is not to utter words, but to live by them" (Proclamation No. 3560, 1963, p. 1).

David DiRamio, Ph.D.
Associate Professor, Auburn University
U.S. Navy Veteran (1980–1986)

References

Ackerman, R., DiRamio, D., & Garza Mitchell, R. (2009). Transitions: Combat veterans as college students. In R. Ackerman & D. DiRamio (Eds.), *Creating a veteran-friendly campus: Strategies for transition success* (New Directions for Student Services, No. 126, pp. 5–14). San Francisco, CA: Wiley.

Cate, C. A. (2014). *Million records project: Research from Student Veterans of America.* Washington, DC: Student Veterans of America. Retrieved from http://studentveterans.org/images/Reingold_Materials/mrp/download-materials/mrp_Full_report.pdf

Proclamation No. 3560. (1963). *President John F. Kennedy: Thanksgiving Day, November 5, 1963.* Retrieved from http://www.presidency.ucsb.edu/ws/?pid=9511

Rumann, C. B., & Hamrick, F. A. (2010). Student veterans in transition: Re-enrolling after war zone deployments. *The Journal of Higher Education, 81*(4), 431–458.

SECTION ONE

★★★★★★★★★★★★★★★★★★★★★★★★★★★★★★★★★

STUDENT VETERANS IN THE 21ST CENTURY:
EXPERIENCES AND PERSPECTIVES

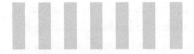

CHAPTER 1

Data-Driven Inquiry, Servicemembers' Perspectives, and Redefining Success

Corri Zoli, Rosalinda Maury, and Daniel L. Fay

Sitting in a makeshift conference room at Fort Drum in upstate New York in early spring 2010, there was little doubt that the soldiers in attendance, many coming off combat rotation in Iraq and Afghanistan, were wondering why it was so important to talk with Syracuse University social scientists about their postservice education plans. However, the diverse men and women, representing a broad spectrum of ranks, military occupational expertise, and battlefield experience, were frank and forthcoming. Many mentioned they planned to use their GI Bill benefits to go to college, either pursuing degrees and civilian jobs that were different from their military occupational specialties (MOS) or training for careers in public service and international work, doing more of what they had been doing and helping societies rebuild (Zoli, Maury, & Fay, 2015b). Others said, "College isn't for me," and went on to explain that they could get all they needed from military schooling and certification programs (Zoli et al., 2015b).

Some interviewees, in turn, asked about specific colleges and universities, the value of for-profit degrees, and whether college admissions would look favorably on their service (Zoli et al., 2015b). Many were appreciative of the opportunity, with permission from their supervisors to take a reprieve from their duties, to talk about college, their futures, and their lives after the military. These were the things they did not have time to reflect on, given the intense operational tempo (Steinberg & Zoli, 2011), and suggests that servicemembers may be unlikely to have an opportunity to develop a plan for successful transition while still engaged in military service.

Talking with servicemembers directly and relying on social science methodologies attentive to individuals in context has anchored our broader data-collection efforts and focused our inquiry on their perspectives of their service, postservice, and education experiences. These conversations—especially as servicemembers' experiences change over time and as new ones are added to the mix—enabled a rich understanding of diverse individuals, including the challenges faced and the strategies many used to move forward, as well as the complex and varied environments that must be managed. At the core of this chapter is the recognition that servicemembers draw on multiple sources beyond the college campus and academic coursework to achieve their education goals and aspirations. This lens embraces a broader notion of academic success than common higher education metrics may capture (e.g., persistence, retention, advancement, degree completion, career placement) to include military experiences (e.g., training, transition). Likewise, a wider trajectory of learning experiences—beyond the academic degree or training program alone—is considered, taking into account the many sometimes-difficult antecedent events that shape transition experiences, education goals and aspirations, and academic success for military servicemembers.

In broadening the scope, such inquiry will offer higher educators increased clarity on military service, the characteristics of those who serve, and the changing security environments that now characterize the present military environment.[1] Veterans' postservice experiences may thus, in turn, help to inform and elevate the national conversations on public service, civic engagement, and the pivotal role of education in military and civilian life, too often taken for granted in the academy. Servicemembers' perspectives can provide a contemporaneous snapshot of the current policies used to ease transition to civilian life, but importantly also assess the institutions, especially colleges and universities, responsible for assisting a large number of transitioning servicemembers. Taken together, these expanded notions of postservice goals, educational aspirations, and academic success, as well as such intervening factors as civic engagement, family commitment and responsibility, and public service following military commitments make for important priorities in what counts as education research on military-connected communities today.

Data-Driven Approach to Veterans' Inquiry

In addition to the servicemembers' perspective, a second aspect of the research on which this chapter is based (Zoli, Maury, & Fay, 2015a, 2015b, 2015c) is the importance of building new, more sensitive and comprehensive

---

[1]Congress found that "service on active duty in the Armed Forces" was "especially arduous for the members of the Armed Forces since September 11, 2001" so that there was a need for an educational assistance program that provided "enhanced educational assistance benefits ... worthy of such service." (S. 22, 110th Cong., U.S. Govt. Print. Off., 2007 [enacted]. p. 1)

datasets, reflective of servicemembers' actual experiences and the heterogeneity of the all-volunteer military. Survey instruments were developed specific to our research objectives, gathering both quantitative and qualitative responses and reflecting servicemembers' stories, interpretations, and explanations of their views. Where relevant for comparative and contextual purposes, information from Departments of Defense (DOD), Veterans Affairs (VA), Labor and Census, Education, and the National Science Foundation (NSF) datasets were incorporated into the analysis, as well as the data emerging academic and think-tank research initiatives (e.g., Pew Research Center, 2011).

In contrast to robust historical research on U.S. military personnel, benefits, education, and postservice success, relatively few national and academic studies have asked veterans about their service experiences or investigated the role of education in their transition to civilian life, especially for recent cohorts. To explore these questions, veterans-serving organizations (VSOs) and community networks, including academic institutes, have been integral to our research. At Syracuse University, the Institute for Veterans and Military Families (IVMF) and the Institute for National Security and Counterterrorism (INSCT) have proactively built communities of practitioners, scholars, and stakeholders on military and veterans' issues. Such community networks were leveraged to develop a multichannel recruitment process to reach out to servicemembers (i.e., active-duty, veterans, reservists, guard, and family members or dependents) across many different social domains (e.g., government, military, and VA-supported networks, academic-veterans communities, IVMF social media, private sector veterans communities). Further, to best engage the responses received, an interdisciplinary approach was used drawing on input from faculty and staff from Syracuse's social science areas (i.e., security studies, public management, and qualitative and quantitative analysis).

We designed a multimethod survey to capture both national representativeness (i.e., demographic, years in college, career choice, and military training courses) and qualitatively rich data. The goal was to establish not only broad-based but also granular and diverse findings and to include individual responses when warranted.

The response to our survey was overwhelming, both by those completing the online tool and by stakeholders wanting to hear about what was learned. The primary dataset comprises more than 8,500 respondents and includes both quantitative and qualitative information that gives much detail about respondents' reasoning and personal stories behind their answers (Zoli et al., 2015c). The sample consisted mostly of veterans (80%) who served in the recent

Gulf War Era (i.e., 63% post-9/11 and 17% Gulf War I). About 87% had been enlisted servicemembers, 11% were officers, approximately 25% were women, and nearly 2% were the family members (i.e., dependents). Most respondents were also seasoned military professionals, with nearly 80% having had at least four years of service experience and nearly half of that group (40%) having nine years or more in service (Table 1.1). Likewise, the vast majority of our survey respondents had direct experience in higher education, either through past, current, or planned future enrollment (Table 1.2).

Table 1.1
Length of Service (n = 7,209)

Q. In total, how long did you serve on active duty?	Percentage (%)
Less than one year	2
1–3 years	20
4–8 years	40
9–20 years	18
20+ years	20

Table 1.2
Plans to Pursue Higher Education (n = 5,668)

Q. Do you want to pursue higher education or training?	Percentage (%)
Yes, currently enrolled full time	42
Yes, currently enrolled part time	11
Yes, I plan to enroll in the future but not currently enrolled	17
No	4
Unsure about future plans	7
Already completed education goals	19

Results from the primary survey instrument (Zoli et al., 2015c) are presented in the next section, focusing on the role of education in postservice transition, education challenges and barriers, and postservice success. Findings are integrated within a broader discussion of the military-connected community in higher education in order show the value of understanding such a diverse and often overlooked population.

The Role of Education in Postservice Transition

One servicemember commented, "Higher education is at the frontlines of a successful transition." He elaborated, noting that in his experience, many academic administrators and faculty did not realize the pivotal role they and universities play for military-connected students in transitioning from national service. Too many in the academy take for granted the transformative role of education, especially for students moving from fast-paced, cooperative environments into settings defined by self-reflection and intensive study.

In many respects, this study's data affirmed these insights. When respondents were asked, "How much do you agree with the following statement: Education should play a role in postservice transition," 92% agreed or strongly agreed. This contrasts with research on previous cohorts of military servicemembers that assume education is simply a means of human capital development that improves job and earning potential for individual servicemembers (e.g., Bound & Turner, 2002). Our findings offer a more holistic role for educational institutions in the transition process.

Affirming previous research, when survey respondents were asked to rank their top five reasons for joining the armed services, education received the top score at 53% (Zoli et al., 2015b). As shown in Table 1.3 and noteworthy, *a desire to serve your country* and *new experiences, adventure, and travel* took the second and third spots. Many respondents reported other interesting reasons for joining the armed services, including a *sense of purpose, career opportunities, a history of service in your family,* and *defending your country.* Clearly, the value of education proper— as well as broader notions of learning at multiple levels (e.g., adventure, travel, purpose, opportunities)—occupies the minds of many U.S. servicemembers.

More subtly, servicemembers were asked to rate the helpfulness of a range of resources in their transition. While most ranked *family and friend support* first (84%), education-related items were also highly rated: *university GI Bill processing assistance* (72%), *university administration* (69%), and *academic advising* (62%). These supports—help with managing benefits and dedicated individuals and offices for integrating into the campus setting—were continually emphasized throughout the survey. Table 1.4 shows that *personal contact with individuals from college or university* was the sixth most important source of valuable information in their transition (at 42%)—second only to *government websites, VA network, and online sources.*

Table 1.3
Reasons for Joining the Armed Services (*n* = 6,158)

Reasons	Percentage (%)
Education benefits	53
A desire to serve your country	52
New experiences/adventure/travel	49
Sense of purpose	36
Career opportunities	31
A history of service in your family	29
Defend your country	29
Practical skills and training	25
Financial security	21
Leadership	20
Retirement benefits in the future	20
Health care benefits	19
Lack of job opportunities	16
Job security or fulfillment	12
Military community, network, or quality	9
Improve earning potential	8
Promotion or advancement	7
Other	7
Friends enlisted	5

There were also links between respondents' military service experiences and education planning that echoed the value placed on education by service-members. Most of the respondents, as mentioned (see Table 1.2), were enrolled in school (53%), either full time (42%) or part time (11%). An additional 17% planned to enroll in the future, and almost 20% had completed their education goals to date—hence, around 90% of all respondents were working on, planning for, or had completed their education goals. Only 11% of respondents expressed uncertainty about future education plans of any kind. In this sense, the overarching sample was largely poised to partake in education or educational planning.

Respondents also linked their military experiences—training, deployments, and military jobs, including MOSs—with education and life success (see Table 1.5). For MOSs, in general, most (74%) reported that their job played some role

Table 1.4
Most Valuable Sources of Resources and Information (*n* = 4,410)

Source	Percentage (%)
Government websites, VA network, and online sources (GI Bill website)	45
Personal contact with individuals from college or university	42
Family members or friends	37
Information from college or university websites	37
Veterans network or Veteran Service Organizations (VSO)	35
Information from teachers or guidance counselors	14
Military media targeted to military personnel (Military Times)	14
Education liaisons on bases	12
Any additional sources	11
College guidebooks	7
College ranking sources *(U.S. News & World Report)*	7
Advertisement in media	5

Table 1.5
Role of MOS in Promoting Interest in and Preparing for Further Education (*n* = 6,618)

Source	Percentage (%)
MOS promoted interest in education, in general	74
MOS promoted interest in a training, certification, or licensing program	71
MOS prepared for education	68
MOS prepared for civilian job	66

in promoting their interest in education. A similar percentage (71%) reported their MOS responsibilities promoted their interest in a training, certification, or licensing program. A total of 68% of respondents indicated that their military job at some level (i.e., moderately, very, or completely) prepared them for education while 66% of respondents indicated it had prepared them for their civilian career.

In addition, servicemembers were surveyed about the impact of military service on their education, life, civilian jobs, and careers in the STEM fields

(Table 1.6). Overall, 82% agreed that military service left a lasting impression,[2] with 71% of respondents saying service *left a lasting impression* (i.e., moderately and completely) on their ability to *develop skills and attributes* helpful to educational success. Previous studies (e.g., Gade, 1991) have examined educational attainment among servicemembers (as compared to civilian counterparts) in various periods of service, but often failed to explore the veterans' own perceptions beyond correlative data on these matters, especially if they identify the skills and attributes gained in service as translating into interest and success in postsecondary education. The goal here was not to assess the normative impression of the experience, but rather *if* military service had a lasting impression generally.

Table 1.6
Lasting Impressions of Military Service (n = 5,970)

Q. Has your military experience left a lasting impression on you?	Not at all (%)	Slightly (%)	Neutral (%)	Moderately (%)	Completely (%)
In developing skills and attributes that will help you succeed in education	9	9	11	30	41
In training, licensing, and certification programs	21	11	18	25	25
In your interest in science, technology, engineering, or mathematics	28	11	19	24	18
In career goals	13	8	14	31	34
In life	5	5	9	29	53

Transition and Education Challenges and Barriers

In thinking about effective transitions for military servicemembers, it is critical to understand that education may help mitigate or even remedy some of the barriers or challenges experienced by military-connected students. It is for this reason—among others—that it is worthwhile to probe concerns expressed by servicemembers about the education domain itself.

Respondents relayed key barriers faced in their postservice transition when asked to identify "the key challenges in your transition." Challenges encompassed

---

[2] As in the Life Experiences Survey (Sarason, Johnson, & Siegel, 1978), the wording of the item was intentionally neutral, recognizing that some of the most profound influences on a person may involve both good and bad experiences and, thus, allowing respondents to report both negative and positive impressions.

the following categories: getting through the system, employment issues, civilian reintegration, health issues, and education challenges. Table 1.7 ranks responses to specific challenges.

Table 1.7
Key Challenges in Transition (*n* = 4,782)

Challenge	Percentage (%)
Navigating VA administration and benefits	60
Getting a job	55
Getting socialized in civilian culture	41
Financial struggles	40
Skills translation	39
Depression	35
Employment preparation	34
Understanding GI Bill benefits	32
Contradictory information	31
Civilian day-to-day life	31
Disability	31
Using and accessing GI Bill benefits	28
Info about education opportunities	26
Transferring military course credits	25
TAP inadequate	25
Anger management	23
Mental health issues	22
Posttraumatic stress (PTS) or combat stress	22
College or university culture and climate	20
Stigma of being a servicemember	20
Family members, spouse, children, and dependents	19
Academic preparation	19
Education administrative obstacles	17
Physical injuries	17
Getting along with others	14
Other	6
Traumatic brain injury (TBI)	5
Military sexual trauma (MST)	5

Note. Respondents could select multiple answers; total will add up to more than 100%.

In addition to accessing benefits, respondents expressed several concerns related to employment—getting a job was ranked as the second-highest transition challenge (after benefits administration issues). Importantly, this challenge, like others, may be improved by education pursuits, whether in completing a degree or certification program or participating in the career placement and planning process that accompanies many programs.

Likewise, financial struggles, skill translation, and employment preparation—all highly ranked employment challenges—could be aided by education pursuits. These concerns were not just perceptions. As indicated in Table 1.8, while the GI Bill predictably remained the most commonly identified source of funding for all education endeavors in this sample, more than half of the respondents reported that they were *self-funded* when asked to identify the funding sources for their past, current, and/or future education or training programs.

Equally important are respondents' concerns about health issues as obstacles to transition and, therefore, to educational success (Elliott, Gonzalez, & Larsen, 2011). Moreover, research suggests health and wellness issues—depression, disability, anger management—may be addressed to some degree by education programs (DiRamio & Spires, 2009; Smith-Osborne, 2012).

As so many respondents were predisposed toward education, it is not surprising that education challenges were not ranked as highly as other key transition obstacles; however, fairly large numbers identified here and elsewhere concerns about college or university culture and climate (20%) and the stigma and stereotypes associated with service to country (20%). Because these cultural issues pervade responses throughout the survey—both quantitative and qualitative—the next section examines its role in veterans' success.

Transition and Cultural Barriers

In trying to understand climate issues for student veterans, the qualitative data shed light on the different, even antithetical, organizational environments at work in the U.S. military and in civilian and college life. Servicemembers often mentioned that there is a pervasive misunderstanding or even ignorance about what they do; how the military functions; civil-military relations; U.S. foreign policy; and U.S. traditions, laws, and institutions governing the military and national service.

Cited frequently in this study, respondents pointed out persistent myths about U.S. military servicemembers, both on college campuses and in the mainstream media, including the idea of the "broken hero," the notion

Table 1.8
Funding Source for Past, Current, or Future Education (n = 5,117)

Source	Percentage (%)
Post-9/11 GI Bill	65
Self-funded	54
Federal financial aid	49
Military tuition assistance (TA)	34
State-funded aid (e.g., scholarships or grants)	27
Montgomery GI Bill for Active Duty and Veterans (MGIB-AD)	25
Vocational Rehabilitation and Employment (VR&E)	19
Other	11
Employer paid or reimbursement	11
Veterans Educational Assistance Program (VEAP)	9
State specific military tuition support	7
Montgomery GI Bill for Selected Reserves (MGIB-SR)	5
Officer commissioning programs (e.g., West Point, ROTC, West Point Reservist, National Guard)	5
Tuition waivers	2
Spouse and Dependents Education Assistance (DEA)	2
Reserve Education Assistance Program (REAP)	2

that all veterans have PTSD, and the view of veterans as undereducated or less intelligent than their civilian counterparts, among others. Even faculty members, many respondents noted, make a series of troubling assumptions about veterans' identities, politics, experiences, competencies, and education and employment goals. Interestingly, a recent cohort of creative writers who are also veterans have also begun to identify, critique, and complicate many of these myths—often in advance of academic research (e.g., MacKenzie, 2015; Ricks, 2015; Schultz & Chandrasekaran, 2014; Sutherland, 2015; Zoli et al., 2015a).

Some academic leaders and journalists have also painstakingly corrected stereotypes or raised neglected issues, such as the small numbers of veterans recruited to prestigious institutions (Sloane, 2013), the critical role of ROTC programs in training well-educated officers and citizen-soldiers (Neiberg, 2009), the importance of high-quality degree programs for servicemembers (Capicik, 2010), and the helpful role of colleges and universities in picking up the slack when VA benefits are delayed (Scott, 2011). In addition, the work of Zoli and associates (2015a, 2015b, 2015c) has underscored the fact that many eligible GI Bill beneficiaries did not use their hard-earned education benefit—in part because of concerns about campus culture. Some servicemembers reported they would forgo the financial benefits rather than attend an unwelcoming institution.

Addressing the culture issue from another angle, participants were asked whether they felt comfortable sharing their experiences as a veteran or servicemember at their college or university (Table 1.9). The majority (79%) of respondents said they were comfortable talking about their service while also acknowledging that they were *proud of [their] service* (83%) and felt service experiences were *part of [their] identity* (81%). Notably, far less than half of servicemembers surveyed expected that their service experiences would be *well received* by student peers (30%) or by faculty and staff (29%).

Table 1.9
Reasons for Sharing Service Experiences at School (n = 3,347)

Q. Do you feel comfortable sharing your experiences as a veteran or service-member at your school?	Percentage (%)
Proud of service	83
It is part of my identity	81
Expect to be well received by peers	30
Expect to be well received by faculty or staff	29
Friends know me already	20
I get benefits on campus	9
Other	6

More worrisome were the answers provided by those who did not feel comfortable sharing their experiences as a servicemember (21% of this sample; see Table 1.10). When asked why they were not comfortable talking about their service experiences, more than half cited *others' naiveté or lack of familiarity with military service* (63%); *different maturity and worldliness levels of students on campus* (61%); and *stigma, prejudice, or bias* (53%) as sources of discomfort. These were not naive, inexperienced, or unreflective individuals commenting on campus climate—most of the sample had ample college experience. Moreover, many were self-reflective, even self-critical, as slightly more than a quarter reported that their reasons for not sharing their service experiences had to do with their own *internal feelings and concerns about service,* and 21% cited the fact that they wished to make a *fresh start* emphasizing a *new identity.*

Table 1.10
Reasons for Not Sharing Service Experiences at School (*n* = 865)

Q. Why do you not feel comfortable sharing your experiences as a veteran or servicemember at your school?	Percentage (%)
Others' naiveté or lack of familiarity with military service	63
Different maturity levels and worldliness of students on campus	61
Stigma, prejudice, or bias	53
Age differences	51
Mismatch between military and academic culture	49
Conflicting political ideology or worldview with faculty or students	45
Different standards of professional behavior on campus	31
Fear of judgments and repercussions	29
Internal feelings and concerns about service	25
Fresh start or new identity	21
Other	12

As more student veterans enroll in college, these issues may be slowly changing. Yet, if another underrepresented student group preferred to stay silent about their status, identity, and experiences due in large part to others' negative perceptions, there would likely be a concerted effort to change that situation, including reeducating the community on its stereotypes and misassumptions. That such perceptions about national service by both faculty and students can remain—at least in the eyes of one in five servicemembers on campus—indicates that we have not done enough to educate the academic community about a core constituency on campus.

Moreover, that this issue is infrequently identified as a core concern for higher education stakeholders or, more rarely, made the subject of prioritized academic research, gives some indication as to where the academy is at this historic moment on veterans' inclusivity.

Ironically, we seem to have taken a step backward after World War II when a broad spectrum of students poured onto college campuses, including women, ethnic minorities, first-generation students, and students with low socioeconomic status (SES), and changed the face of higher education. Not only did such inclusivity become normalized by academic leaders, it became a prioritized area of inquiry by researchers and received support by federally sponsored initiatives (see for example, Griliches & Mason, 1972; Kleykamp, 2006; Sampson & Laub, 1996; Warner & Pleeter, 2001). The historical record is clear that such changes centrally involved servicemembers who, in large part through GI Bill support, helped to democratize the higher education landscape in America. Our data suggest that for the post-9/11 cohort, higher education communities are not as welcoming as they were to previous generations of servicemembers.

In fact, one of the subtler benefits of inquiry of U.S. military servicemembers today may be in exactly these kinds of links and realizations—that we have become, again, perhaps a highly selective and exclusive system of higher education, one in which economic exclusion is mainstreamed through admissions practices, background and viewpoint diversity are deprioritized, and only certain constituencies are permitted to access higher education under the sign of diversity. In short, as recognized early on by the Bradley Commission on Veterans' Benefits in the United States (March, 1956), Mettler (2005), Segal (e.g., Cooney, Segal, Segal, & Falk, 2003; Segal, 1995; Segal, Bachman, & Dowdell, 1978; Segal & Segal, 2006), Skocpol (1995), and Krebs (2006), among many others, military veterans and national service may well be a key indicator of the robustness of our public institutions in and beyond the academy.[3] Contemporary research should follow in those footsteps, especially as studying veterans may provide pivotal information about higher education access in general.

One helpful way to do this would be for higher education communities to recognize the diversity and heterogeneity of the all-volunteer force—the nation's most demographically diverse public institution—as an asset for higher education institutions, a sector that ostensibly prioritizes diversity (Segal & Segal, 2006). There has been a push for an expanded definition of diversity

---

[3] The U.S. Presidents' Commission on Veterans' Pensions (headed by General of the Army Omar N. Bradley) was established by Executive Order (EO) No. 10588 (Jan. 14, 1955) to study the laws and policies concerning pensions, compensation, and related nonmedical benefits for veterans and dependents. Findings from the commission suggest 51% of all returning veterans (7.8 million) used their education benefits. By 1947, those veterans using the GI Bill comprised 49% of students enrolled in U.S. universities; and by 10 years post-World War II, 2,200,000 veterans had attended college and 5,600,000 had participated in vocational or on-the-job training under the GI Bill (March, 1956).

in many institutions, including colleges and universities. In short, a broader definition would move beyond basic demography (e.g., gender, race/ethnicity) to include geography and background. Among servicemembers this would include areas of professional expertise, branch of service, rank and experience, range of job training and military jobs, and education programs (Zoli et al., 2015a; 2015b). Much of this diversity—demographic and beyond—is embraced in the course of service, not only in expressed norms but in required, servicewide Equal Opportunity (EO) training courses that inculcate diversity as a universal value.

Military Service Experiences: Lasting Implications in Transition

In many respects, one of the most interesting sets of findings from this survey showed the role of military service in shaping servicemembers' experiences of postservice transition and in framing servicemembers' ideas about academic and life success, more generally.

Respondents were asked, "As you reflect on your experiences throughout the course of military service—including negative and positive aspects—how would you describe your service experiences in general?" Most assessed their service in largely positive terms (58%) while about one quarter said it was *somewhat positive* (24%). Likewise, the majority (88%) reported that joining the military was a good decision (*mostly positive* or *somewhat positive*).

Most respondents (79%) also report that their service experiences "played a role in their success." When asked to provide more detail on this question, many explained that they felt the military was a worthwhile challenge; "a lot harder than college"; a place where they learned leadership and discipline, among other life skills; and "formative of my character." Others mentioned they were "very proud of serving this country," despite the "frustrating and nagging bureaucracy of the Army," and they especially valued their learning experiences outside the continental United States. While respondents were not asked to define academic success itself, these factors—character formation, leadership, discipline, and international experiences—emerged again and again in discussions of key takeaways from national service to civilian life and education.

The "amazing opportunities" in commanding hundreds of troops and the learning curve that came along with being held accountable for billions of dollars' worth of equipment was noted by some. Others mentioned the role of the military in stabilizing their personal or home lives, in helping them "get away from the dangerous neighborhood where I lived," and in creating "a sense of self-respect" that they did not have growing up. In addition, the important role of gaining "an identity"—in "wearing the uniform"—and in preserving that identity by "keeping my nose clean, working hard, and going to college" was noted. Still other respondents mentioned the countless difficult experiences they encountered, including while serving in the military, which made them a stronger, more resilient, and capable postservice professional. Some clearly expressed negative experiences due to failings in military leadership, operational tempo, the military bureaucracy, unaddressed health and mental health concerns, morale, and family complications. About 8% and 10% of respondents saw their service experiences in negative or neutral terms, respectively.

Many servicemembers also said they learned from the military how "to take responsibility for my own life early on," which in turn "led to my current success." One respondent described herself as "a confused White girl living on food stamps in a dangerous inner city neighborhood," while now, "20 years later—almost to the day of entering boot camp—I am a Georgetown University graduate and an eight-year employee of the intelligence community." Another participant mentioned that "the Navy was the opportunity I needed to get my life on track," from "merely surviving to thriving in a matter of a few short years." Other respondents said they "use the skills I learned" in the military "every day," so much so that "I am so thankful for my choice to enlist." When asked to identify "all those [skills] that were strengthened or enhanced by your military experience," the top choices, which more than three quarters of respondents selected, were work ethic and discipline, including self-discipline; teamwork; leadership and management skills; mental toughness; adaptation to different challenges; professionalism; and the ability to get things done (see Table 1.11).

These findings suggest military experience provides many of the skills and abilities higher education stakeholders aim to develop among students. From work ethic, leadership or managing large groups of individuals, military service personnel may offer a unique and valuable perspective to other students in and outside the classroom. Faculty, staff, and other university personnel could therefore benefit from knowing servicemember status among their students and encouraging this population to share and develop their identity with the larger campus community.

Survey participants were asked if joining the military was a good decision (70% *completely* and 88% *moderately*) as well as their top five reasons for leaving (see Table 1.12). In ranked order, most said the following: they *lost faith or trust in military or political leadership* (35%); they wished to *pursue education and training opportunities* (32%) outside the military; *family reasons* (31%); *the completion of one's military service obligation* (28%); and *military retirement* (26%). When asked whether they ever found themselves wanting to go back to the military, 59% of the sample indicated that they either always, often, or sometimes wanted to go back into service, while 37% said they either never or rarely want to go back to service.

Table 1.11
Skills Developed During Service (n = 5,915)

Skills	Percentage (%)
Work ethic or discipline	87
Teamwork	86
Leadership and management skills	82
Mental toughness	81
Adaptation to different challenges	78
Self-discipline	77
Professionalism	77
Ability to get things done	76
Training and teaching others	74
Coping with adversity	73
Confidence and self-esteem	73
Perseverance	73
Ability to complete the mission	70
Working effectively with supervisors	70
Dealing with uncertainty	70
Camaraderie and supporting peers	70
Crisis management	69
Making decisions about time and resources	69
Social and communication skills	68
Resilience	68
Time management	66
Moral code and social responsibility	64
Level-headedness and perspective	63
Organization	63
Cultural understanding	63
Delegating responsibilities	62
Goal setting	57
Technical expertise	55

Table 1.12
Reasons for Leaving the Armed Services (*n* = 5,217)

Reasons	Percentage (%)
Lost faith or trust in military or political leadership	35
Pursue education and training opportunities	32
Family reasons	31
Completion of military service obligation	28
Military retirement (20 years or more)	26
Career change or alternative job opportunities	26
Concerns and grievances about services	22
Other medical reasons	21
Military culture, community, and lifestyle	16
Dissatisfied with deployments	13
More marketable to private sector	13
Other	11
Military administration or requirements	10
Achieved top rank and could not advance anymore	10
Disability retirement (less than 20 years)	8
Involuntary separation (forced to retire/leave military)	7
Administrative discharge	5
Operational tempo too difficult	5

Most servicemembers (74%) reported that their military experiences promoted an interest in education to some degree, and a majority (71%) said that it promoted their interest in training, certification, or licensing programs (see Table 1.13). Even more interestingly, a majority (68%) reported their service experiences actually prepared them for their education programs. This link between service and education was also evident in specific disciplinary areas, notably STEM fields, in which 43% (see Table 1.5) of respondents indicated that their military specialization, job, or training was STEM-related.[4] Generally, post-9/11 servicemembers linked their military skills and capabilities to their postservice success, both in the classroom and in their career and employment pursuits.

---

[4] Respondents were asked if their military specialization, job, or training was related to STEM fields (n = 6,625); approximately 43% of respondents indicated it was. Table 1.5 presented findings surrounding how servicemembers' MOS influences interest in higher education. This question probes how military service experience in general influences education pursuits.

Table 1.13
Influence of Military Specialization on Employment, Education, and STEM Participation (n = 6,618)

Q. Did your military specializations or jobs:	Not at all (%)	Slightly (%)	Moderately (%)	Very (%)	Completely (%)
Promote your interest in education?	26	15	21	23	15
Promote your interest in a training, certification, or licensing program?	29	15	19	22	15
Prepare you for your education?	31	17	22	18	11
Promote your interest in STEM?	34	15	20	19	12
Prepare you for your civilian life?	34	18	21	16	11

Taken together, many of these responses show an expressed link—both good and bad—between the role of military experience and higher education experiences, whether positive, negative, or ambivalent. Notably, respondents treated these issues of transition and academic success in broader and more variegated ways than the contemporary discussion in the higher education literature. Academic success takes on a different scope—it means traditional academic learning and continuing education, but also choosing a postservice education and training pathway that takes into account multiple learning experiences (not just academic performance or background). It has multiple associations stemming from servicemembers' broad array of experiences. While most respondents stated their motivations for pursuing education were practical (e.g., get a degree for purposes of a professional career and job placement), many also reported that they prioritized personally motivated intellectual work and as an opportunity to engage in the fun of learning. For instance, servicemembers were asked in an open-ended question, "What are your favorite parts of your academic experience?" The top answers were telling: being with other veterans, exceptional faculty, learning new things, interacting with other students and veterans, the pride of just actually being a part of a well-known or well-established university, making my family proud, achievement, and research and exploration, among others.

In many respects, these views differentiate static and metric-based notions of academic success—in favor of broadened pathways, formal education as a continuing journey, built from experiences far removed from the academy. That dynamic, broad-in-scope, trajectory approach to higher education success is not measurable by numbers alone—it requires veterans' perspectives. Perhaps research on veterans will contribute to this wider notion of academic success and inspire academic leaders to make an organizational and institutional commitment to it and to this subpopulation's distinctive experiences in coming to these standards. It requires, of course, looking at student veterans' perspectives on college campuses in a holistic way—not in solely quantitative or disciplinary-specific terms.

References

Bound, J., & Turner, S. (2002). Going to war and going to college: Did World War II and the GI Bill increase educational attainment for returning veterans? *Journal of Labor Economics, 20*(4), 784–815.

Capicik, L. C. P. (2010, April 24, 2015). *The importance of education to a post-military career.* Retrieved from http://www.americansentinel.edu/blog/2010/12/07/the-importance-of-education-to-a-post-military-career/

Cooney, R. T., Segal, M. W., Segal, D. R., & Falk, W. W. (2003). Racial differences in the impact of military service on the socioeconomic status of women veterans. *Armed Forces & Society, 30*(1), 53–85.

DiRamio, D., & Spires, M. (2009). Partnering to assist disabled veterans in transition. In R. Ackerman & D. DiRamio (Eds.), *Creating a veteran-friendly campus: Strategies for transition success* (New Directions for Student Services, No. 126, pp. 81–88). San Francisco, CA: Wiley.

Elliott, M., Gonzalez, C., & Larsen, B. (2011). U.S. military veterans transition to college: Combat, PTSD, and alienation on campus. *Journal of Student Affairs Research and Practice, 48*(3), 279–296.

Gade, P. A. (1991). Military service and the life-course perspective: A turning point for military personnel research. *Military Psychology, 3*(4), 187–199.

Griliches, Z., & Mason, W. M. (1972). Education, income, and ability. *Journal of Political Economy, 80*(3), S74–S103.

Kleykamp, M. A. (2006). College, jobs, or the military? Enlistment during a time of war. *Social Science Quarterly, 87*(2), 272–290.

Krebs, R. R. (2006). *Fighting for rights: Military service and the politics of citizenship.* Ithaca, NY: Cornell University Press.

MacKenzie, M. H. (2015). *True grit: The myths and realities of women in combat.* Retrieved from https://www.foreignaffairs.com/articles/2015-08-12/true-grit

March, M. S. (1956). President's Commission on Veterans' Pensions: Recommendations. *Social Security Bulletin, 19*, 12. Retrieved from http://www.ssa.gov/policy/docs/ssb/v19n8/v19n8p12.pdf

Mettler, S. (2005). The creation of the GI Bill of Rights of 1944: Melding social and participatory citizenship ideals. *Journal of Policy History, 17*(4), 345–374.

Neiberg, M. S. (2009). *Making citizen-soldiers: ROTC and the ideology of American military service.* Cambridge, MA: Harvard University Press.

Pew Research Center. (2011). *The military-civilian gap: War and sacrifice in the post-9/11 era.* Retrieved from http://www.pewsocialtrends.org/files/2011/10/veterans-report.pdf

Ricks, T. E. (2015). *We romanticize military service—until we see some combat and bury some friends.* Retrieved from http://foreignpolicy.com/2015/09/17/we-romanticize-military-service-until-we-see-some-combat-and-bury-some-friends/

Sampson, R. J., & Laub, J. H. (1996). Socioeconomic achievement in the life course of disadvantaged men: Military service as a turning point, circa 1940–1965. *American Sociological Review, 61*(3), 347–367.

Sarason, I. G., Johnson, J. H., & Siegel, J. M. (1978). Assessing the impact of life changes: Development of the Life Experiences Survey. *Journal of Consulting and Clinical Psychology, 46*(5), 932–946.

Schultz, H., & Chandrasekaran, R. (2014). *Want to help veterans? Stop pitying them.* Retrieved from https://www.washingtonpost.com/opinions/want-to-help-veterans-stop-pitying-them/2014/10/31/1885e088-5eb9-11e4-9f3a-7e28799e0549_story.html?tid=a_inl

Scott, G. A. (2011). *Veterans' education benefits: Enhanced guidance and collaboration could improve administration of the Post-9/11 GI Bill Program.* Collingdale, PA: Diane Publishing.

Segal, D. R., Bachman, J. G., & Dowdell, F. (1978). Military service for female and black youth: A perceived mobility opportunity. *Youth and Society, 10*(2), 127.

Segal, M. W. (1995). Women's military roles cross-nationally past, present, and future. *Gender & Society, 9*(6), 757–775.

Segal, M. W., & Segal, D. R. (2006). Implications for military families of changes in the armed forces of the United States. In G. Caforio (Ed.), *Handbook of the sociology of the military* (pp. 225–233). New York, NY: Springer.

Skocpol, T. (1995). *Protecting soldiers and mothers.* Cambridge, MA: Harvard University Press.

Sloane, W. (2013). *Annual veterans count, 2013.* Retrieved from https://www. insidehighered.com/views/2013/11/11/number-veterans-enrolled-elite-colleges-drops-essay

Smith-Osborne, A. (2012). Supported education for returning veterans with PTSD and other mental disorders. *Journal of Rehabilitation, 78,* 4–12.

Steinberg, L., & Zoli, C. (2011). *Battlefield to classroom: Findings, barriers, and pathways to engineering for U.S. servicemembers*: Arlington, VA: National Science Foundation.

Sutherland, C. D. W. (2015). *5 common myths about veterans and military families.* Retrieved from http://www.huffingtonpost.com/colonel-david-w-sutherland/5-common-myths-about-veterans-families_b_8523670.html

Warner, J. T., & Pleeter, S. (2001). The personal discount rate: Evidence from military downsizing programs. *American Economic Review, 91*(1), 33–53.

Zoli, C., Maury, R., & Fay, D. (2015a). *In search of the post-9/11 veterans' missing perspectives.* Retrieved from http://warontherocks.com/2015/04/in-search-of-post-911-veterans-missing-perspectives/

Zoli, C., Maury, R., & Fay, D. (2015b). *Missing perspectives: Servicemembers' transition from service to civilian life-data-driven research to enact the promise of the Post-9/11 GI Bill.* Syracuse, NY: Institute for Veterans & Military Families.

Zoli, C., Maury, R., & Fay, D. (2015c). *Survey 1: Service member to student survey: Veterans' perceptions of transition, higher education and success.* Syracuse, NY: Institute for Veterans & Military Families.

CHAPTER 2

★★★★★★★★★★★★★★★★★★★★★★★★★★★★★★★★★★★★★★

Opportunity, Inequity, and America's Story: Intersections With Military-Connected Individuals in Higher Education

Andrew Q. Morse and Dani Molina

Opportunity is a commanding theme in America's story. Closely tethered to this theme are our nation's colleges and universities, which empower students through their educational missions to pursue a path to socioeconomic well-being. Indeed, our nation's system of higher education has contributed to the development of citizens who, in turn, use their knowledge and skills to catalyze innovations within a global economy that increasingly demands attainment beyond high school (Carnevale, Jayasundera, & Gulish, 2015; Carnevale, Smith, & Strohl, 2010; U.S. Bureau of Labor Statistics, 2015). Recent projections suggest, for example, that two out of every three jobs in the United States will require a postsecondary credential within the next decade (Carnevale et al., 2010). Yet, the tightening link between educational attainment beyond high school and workforce opportunity is tempered by a litany of evidence that depicts a system of postsecondary education that is out of reach for many Americans. Our nation continues to struggle with unequal access to opportunities that persist along demographic and socioeconomic lines.

Participation in postsecondary education by underrepresented racial and ethnic minority students continues to lag behind that of their White counterparts. Recent data show that 72% of White high school graduates of the Class of 2008 immediately enrolled in postsecondary education during the fall of that same year (Aud, Fox, & KewalRemani, 2010). By contrast, Aud and colleagues (2010) noted that 56% of Black and 62% of Hispanic high school graduates immediately enrolled in a college or university. Looking at participation in science, technology, engineering, and mathematics (STEM) disciplines, researchers have found that, despite a recent uptick in the number of racial and ethnic minorities enrolled in an undergraduate STEM program nationwide, disparities linger between racial and ethnic minority groups and their White peers in terms of the proportion of total participation in these disciplines (Espinosa & Nellum, 2015; Rodriguez et al., 2012). Though women comprise a majority of higher education's undergraduate demography in the United States, Espinosa and Nellum (2015) also noted lower levels of participation in STEM fields among women as compared with men.

For many aspiring college students, the cost to attend a postsecondary institution far outstrips the discretionary income to pursue and attain educational credentials. Low-income Americans have seen the purchasing power of need-based federal financial aid diminish due to longstanding stakeholder disinvestment and steadily increasing costs to attend a college or university (Cahalan & Perna, 2015). A 40-year trend analysis of equity indicators conducted by the Pell Institute for the Study of Opportunity in Higher Education and PennAHEAD, for example, found that the average proportion of tuition, fees, and other costs covered by the federal Pell Grant, which supplies need-based aid to low-income students, declined by 50% between 1974 and 2012 (Cahalan & Perna, 2015). This trend is exacerbated by starting salaries that continue to be outpaced by increased tuition prices and student debt, thereby cutting into discretionary income that may place considerable burdens on borrowers to cover fixed living costs and the long-term repayment of student loans (Cahalan & Perna, 2015; Jank & Owens, 2012). Higher education's increased reliance on tuition and fees will only widen the distance between low-income Americans and access to postsecondary education, perpetuating a cycle of inequitable workforce opportunity.

Family characteristics and employment status add layers to our nation's challenges with opportunity inequity. Data from the U.S. Department of Education's Beginning Postsecondary Survey (NCES, 2016) show that approximately one in five first-time, beginning undergraduates have at least one dependent at the time they enroll in postsecondary education. Further, three quarters of part-time students work 20 hours or more per week while enrolled and approximately one quarter of students who maintain full-time enrollment work at least 20 hours per week (Kena et al., 2014). In their *Time is the Enemy* report, Complete College America (2011) raised the important point that managing the rigorous task of balancing family, employment, and educational responsibilities over time is itself a challenge to postsecondary access, persistence, and attainment among working students who may also have dependents. In fact, analysis by NCES (2015) has identified employment status and dependents as two characteristics associated with not completing a postsecondary credential.

Taken separately, inequities that stem from demographic characteristics or socioeconomic status point to areas of action by leaders in higher education as they construct strategies and support systems to promote postsecondary access and success on their campuses (Bensimon, 2005). Together, these inequities signal the importance of understanding the intersectionality of the whole person in relation to the characteristics and needs of our nation's diverse student demography. Lines of scholarly inquiry and practical consideration have continued to build a rich understanding of the intersections between lingering demographic and socioeconomic inequities and postsecondary access, persistence, and attainment; however, the conversation has yet to encompass the experiences of those with current or prior military service. By examining points of similarity and difference among military-connected students (Molina & Morse, 2015), and drawing upon other facets of their holistic identities that may influence their experiences in postsecondary education, the higher education community will have a deeper understanding of the challenges and successes of servicemembers and veterans on our campuses.

In this chapter, we offer a primer on the characteristics of military-connected undergraduates on key factors associated with postsecondary access, matriculation, and attainment. Further, we draw intersections between military-connectedness and the broader national effort by the higher education community to understand and address lingering inequities in postsecondary opportunity. Then, we offer discussion on this work as it relates to efforts by the higher education community to support the postsecondary success of servicemembers and veterans.

Equity and Opportunity: Considering Demographic Characteristics and Military Affiliation

Our presentation of differences among students with a current or prior connection to the military begins with an examination of the financial aid and income backgrounds of first-year undergraduate student veterans. We analyzed data from the National Postsecondary Student Aid Study (NPSAS; NCES, 2015) to identify points of difference along demographic and socioeconomic lines.

Income characteristics of the first-year undergraduate student veterans in our analysis varied substantively by race and ethnicity. As depicted in Figure 2.1, individuals who identified as White reported the highest average adjusted gross income of $29,167 per year. By contrast, Latino first-year undergraduate student veterans reported an adjusted gross income of $19,671 per year, on average (a 33% difference). These differences are important to consider in relation to

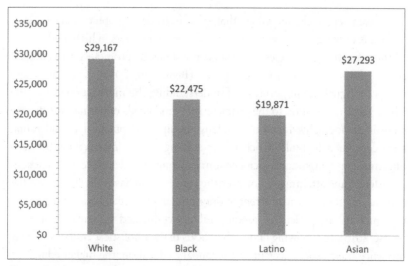

Figure 2.1. Average adjusted gross incoming (AGI) among first-year undergraduate student veterans by race and ethnicity.

today's college affordability discussion, signaling possible disparities in the amount of discretionary income among veterans to cover expenses associated with pursuing higher education. Such differences might also mean that some student veterans may also need to work while enrolled to cover costs associated with attending a postsecondary institution. Though need-based federal aid, such as the Pell Grant, exists and the GI Bill may help address this disparity for military-connected undergraduates who quality, the analysis presented in the next section shows that many servicemembers and veterans in higher education struggle to cover college costs, and that differences by race, ethnicity, and gender add important layers for consideration.

The GI Bill is an educational benefit that has provided financial assistance to qualifying servicemembers, veterans, and their families who enroll in a college or university (U.S. Department of Veterans Affairs, 2016). Since its enactment in 2009, for instance, the Post-9/11 GI Bill has translated to an investment of greater than $53 billion to support the postsecondary educational pursuits of more than 1.4 million eligible recipients (Worley, 2015). This benefit has put higher education in reach for many who may have otherwise not had sufficient resources. In fact, a report by the RAND Corporation for the American Council on Education (Steele, Salcedo, & Coley, 2010) found that roughly a quarter of military-connected students chose to enroll in higher education because of the Post-9/11 GI Bill.

It is important to note, however, that not all who have served in the military receive U.S. Departments of Veterans Affairs or Defense (VA/DoD) education benefits while enrolled in a college or university. Among veterans beginning their college education, those who do not use their earned education benefits may not be aware of their program existence. As Figure 2.2 depicts, for instance, approximately one half of Black and Latino and three in five White and Asian undergraduate student veterans received VA/DoD education benefits their first year enrolled in a college or university. Examining by gender, we also found that three-fifths of male (59%) and female (60%) first-year undergraduate student veterans received benefits. These findings illustrate that not all individuals who have served in the military receive GI Bill benefits but also show differences by race and ethnicity.

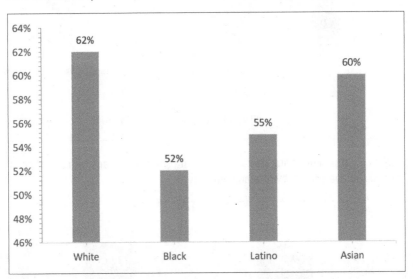

Figure 2.2. Percentage of first-year undergraduate student veterans who received VA/DoD benefits by race and ethnicity.

A majority of first-year undergraduate student veterans had unmet financial need to cover tuition, fees, and other costs to attend an institution, even after all financial aid, including VA or DoD benefits, had been disbursed. In terms of race and ethnicity, Figure 2.3 shows that three out of every five Black and Latino first-year undergraduate student veterans had unmet need that averaged $5,666 and $4,711 during their first years, respectively. Four out of five Asian first-year undergraduate student veterans had unmet need that averaged $5,187. In terms of gender, Figure 2.4 shows that female first-year undergraduate student veterans were more likely to report unmet financial need (64% to 53%) and at average amounts ($6,594 to $4,276) higher than their male counterparts.

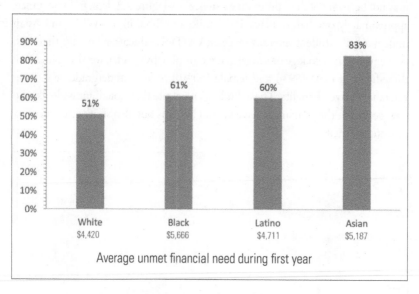

Figure 2.3. Proportion of first-year undergraduate student veterans with unmet need and the average amount by race and ethnicity.

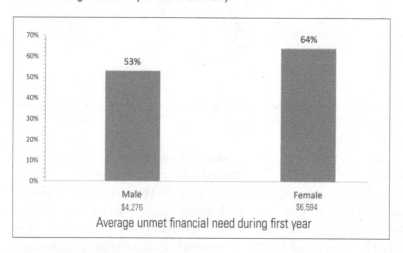

Figure 2.4. Proportion of first-year undergraduate student veterans with unmet need and the average amount by gender.

Though not all of the students in this study used VA/DoD college benefits, this analysis shows a gap between the cost of attendance and the total aid packages among those who do receive their earned education benefits through military service. With an in-state tuition benefit, monthly housing allowance, and a stipend to cover books and supplies, the Post-9/11 GI Bill provides a lucrative source of financial support for eligible recipients (U.S. Department of Veterans Affairs, 2016). Based on their income backgrounds, however, servicemembers and veterans may face additional financial need to cover the costs associated with pursuing and attaining a postsecondary credential. To bridge that gap, military-connected students may take on loan debt.

Figure 2.5 reports the percentage of undergraduate student veterans who received student loans and notes the average amount accrued during their first year. One in five first-year undergraduate student veterans who identify as Asian received a student loan, averaging $2,055. By contrast, more than half (53%) of Black first-year student veterans accrued loan debt that averaged $7,459. Further, nearly 4 of every 10 Latino first-year student veterans accrued an average of $5,275 in debt throughout the year. As depicted in Figure 2.6, nearly 6 in 10 (58%) female undergraduate student veterans accrued debt that averaged $6,235 after their first year. In comparison, 4 in 10 (42%) male undergraduate student veterans received student loans averaging $4,796 after their first year.

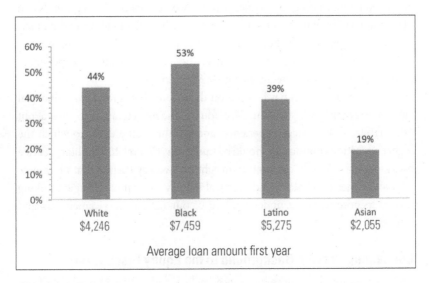

Figure 2.5. Proportion of first-year undergraduate student veterans with loan debt and the amount by race and ethnicity.

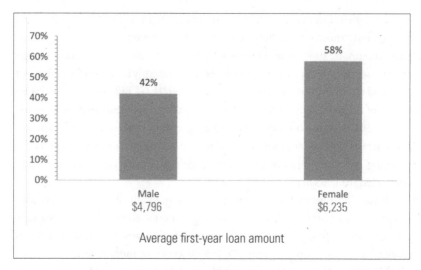

Figure 2.6. Proportion of first-year undergraduate student veterans with loan debt and the amount by gender.

When examining by race, ethnicity, and gender, differences in the proportion of first-year undergraduate veterans who received loans, coupled with the varying amounts accrued across the groups, suggest the need to further explore the factors that contribute to indebtedness among this diverse and growing student population. Our findings open lines of inquiry on the income backgrounds and benefit utilization of first-year student veterans who differ in terms of their race, ethnicity, and gender. Further research can examine the intersections between military affiliation, demographic characteristics, and the needs and experiences of servicemembers and veterans in higher education.

Thus far, discussion has focused on the income background and financial aid characteristics of first-year undergraduate student veterans. But what about other facets of the college experience, and are there differences to which the higher education community should be mindful as they relate to military service backgrounds? We offer exploratory insight on two key themes that illuminate additional lines of scholarly and practical inquiry to prompt strategic thinking toward a more inclusive understanding of our nation's servicemembers and veterans.

Connecting Service Background to the Equity Discussion

To examine differences by service background, we again used data from NPSAS (NCES, 2015) on two exploratory factors: (a) enrollment in a STEM discipline and (b) risk factors associated with non-completion. Though not all military-connected backgrounds are captured in the NPSAS dataset (i.e., dependents or ROTC/NROTC), this source does yield sufficient information to explore points of similarity on factors associated with the experiences and outcomes of military-connected individuals. To that end, we studied undergraduates who identify as members of the National Guard, reservists, active duty personnel, or veterans.

Technological innovation increasingly requires knowledge and skill in a STEM discipline as a prerequisite for readiness to succeed in today's knowledge-based economy (Carnevale, et al., 2010; Committee on STEM Education, 2013). However, research has noted a gap between occupations that increasingly require proficiency in STEM knowledge domains and the corresponding supply of graduates with sufficient skills in these areas (Rothwell, 2014). Among military-connected undergraduates, participation in STEM varies by service background. A recent report by Molina and Morse (2015) illustrated substantive differences between members of the National Guard, active duty personnel, reservists, and veterans in the proportion of individuals who enroll in an undergraduate STEM discipline while attending a postsecondary institution (see Figure 2.7). Whereas one in five undergraduate student veterans major in STEM, fewer than 1 in 10 members of the National Guard enroll in a STEM program. By comparison, 15% of active duty personnel and 16% of reservists enroll in a STEM discipline. With service responsibilities that often bolster STEM proficiency, many individuals with a military connection possess skills that are highly valuable within an increasingly knowledge-based economy.

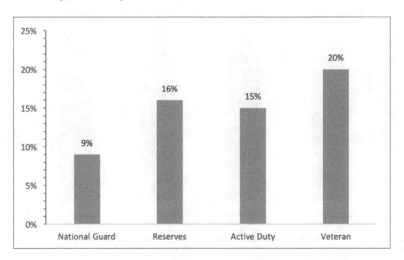

Figure 2.7. Military-connected undergraduates enrolled in STEM fields by service status.

Opportunities to anticipate and address the factors that are associated with non-completion among military-connected students also exist. Researchers have identified seven factors that influence postsecondary non-completion (Choy, 2002; Coley, 2000; Horn, Premo, & Malizio, 1995; Schmid & Abell, 2003; Skomsvold, Walton Radford, & Berkner, 2011). These factors have contributed to the development of a measure by the NCES (2015) that examines the risk of non-completion among all individuals who enroll in postsecondary education across the United States. These factors do not prescribe that any particular student will depart prior to completing higher education, nor do they encompass all factors tied to non-completion. Still, they provide a proxy measure for the challenges some students navigate in pursuit of their postsecondary credentials. Further, it is important to note that these challenges are not deficits. Rather, they present opportunities for the higher education community to reflect on whether institutional policies and support structures encompass the needs and characteristics of students on campus. The factors include delayed college enrollment, no high school diploma, part-time college enrollment, financial independence, responsibility for dependents, single-parent status, and full-time work while in college.

As these factors relate to servicemembers and veterans on campus, Figure 2.8 offers an analysis of the number of non-completion risk factors exhibited by military-connected undergraduates. As noted in the figure, only 7% of reservists and 6% of National Guard members exhibited no risk factors associated with postsecondary non-completion. By contrast, all active duty personnel and veterans exhibited at least one factor associated with non-completion.

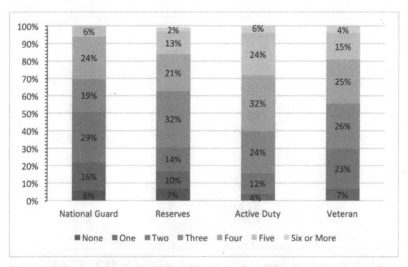

Figure 2.8. Number of non-completion risk factors for military-connected undergraduates by service status.

Remarkably, more than 6 in 10 active duty undergraduates exhibited four or more factors. With support structures that encompass the needs and characteristics of servicemembers and veterans, their strengths and aspirations can overshadow the challenges they navigate to pursue and attain a postsecondary education. Anticipating and addressing these needs offers an opportunity to support access, persistence, and attainment among military-connected students.

Implications for Policy and Practice

Our nation's military is diverse. Yet, those with a current or prior connection to the military have largely been treated as a homogenous entity on campus, namely veterans, thereby conveying a one-size-fits-all understanding of a population that possesses important differences according to their demographic characteristics and socioeconomic statuses. Such an understanding may overlook substantive differences, like those presented in this chapter, that influence postsecondary access and success. An improperly formed narrative may also lead to success expectations that, when not met, engender deficit thinking that undermines the challenges and associated needs that would support the success of this diverse population. Integral to this discussion is the recognition, of course, that inequity extends beyond the postsecondary setting and cuts across our nation's economic, social, and political structures. However, higher education professionals have long navigated challenges posed by inequity to affirm educational opportunity for many. Indeed, we can bolster our institutional strategies and policies where possible and appropriate to support the postsecondary success of servicemembers and veterans.

This chapter first and foremost serves as a primer on the intersections between military-connectedness and the broader inequities that impede postsecondary access and success. We also offer encouragement for higher education leaders, practitioners, and scholars to spark new lines of inquiry or practical considerations toward a more holistic narrative of the characteristics, experiences, and needs of the military-connected individuals on our campuses. Toward this end, we offer considerations to prompt further thought on the next steps that the higher education community might take to understand and address inequities that servicemembers and veterans may face in relation to their postsecondary aspirations and pursuits.

Theme 1: Demographic and Socioeconomic Characteristics

Factoring in demographic and socioeconomic characteristics that may influence the college experience, what opportunities are there to assess the efficacy of programs, resources, and support services as they relate to the military-connected students on your campus? Many students may identify as a veteran, but others may also or more closely identify as being on active duty, or as a member of the National Guard or reserves, to name a few important examples. Capturing information that enables practitioners to examine the intersecting identities (i.e., race, ethnicity, gender, student classification level) with military service offers insight that can, in turn, situate institutional strategies to identify equitable and inclusive approaches to support postsecondary access, persistence, and attainment among what may be a diverse, military-connected student population on your campus.

Theme 2: Understanding Affordability, Unmet Financial Need, and Student Debt

Are there opportunities to use existing institutional data sources to develop insight on affordability, unmet financial need, and student debt among military-connected students on your campus? As we noted in this chapter, not all military-connected students apply for and receive educational benefits provided by the VA or DoD, and many servicemembers and veterans accrue debt while enrolled. Though the Post-9/11 GI Bill offers substantial financial assistance for eligible recipients, those who receive this earned educational benefit may exhaust the total amount for which they are eligible prior to completion of a postsecondary education (Molina, 2015). Further, the income background, fixed living costs, and family responsibilities, coupled with the price to attend an institution, may lead to disparities among some students more than others. The institution may have data that can awaken important insight on the use of earned VA or DoD education benefits, unmet financial need, and debt among military-connected individuals and inform discussion on strategies to maximize the students' use of their earned benefits and minimize the debt they accrue while enrolled.

Theme 3: Training for Faculty, Staff, and Students

Are there opportunities to conduct training on campus that educates faculty, staff, and students about misconceptions and stereotypes of servicemembers and veterans and that promote welcoming and inclusive educational and social environments? Though differences exist between servicemembers and veterans on factors associated with their postsecondary experiences and outcomes, how the higher education community uses this information to create equitable and inclusive campus environments is of high importance. Differences are not deficits. Rather, a more inclusive narrative on our campuses can bolster a welcoming environment for servicemembers and veterans. Such a narrative can also support campus efforts to shift views and interactions that may imply deficits in the capacity for servicemembers and veterans to be successful in postsecondary settings and, instead, enlighten areas where practice can realign to affirm the strengths that military-connected students bring to campus.

Theme 4: Further Examining Access, Persistence, and Attainment

What lines of scholarly inquiry can researchers provide to further examine equity as it relates to postsecondary access, persistence, and attainment among military-connected students? Though this chapter breaks ground on the intersections between persistent inequities and the postsecondary experiences of servicemembers and veterans, our findings call on the need for more insight to closely examine the intersections and implications for policy and practice. We call upon scholars to add empirical continuity to this new line of inquiry into the experiences, needs, and outcomes of our nation's diverse military-connected individuals, and to position new insight to affirm their postsecondary access and success.

Conclusion

In this chapter, we offered a primer on the intersections between students with a connection to the military and our nation's broader effort to understand and address disparities to the postsecondary educational opportunities that persist along demographic and socioeconomic lines. We began by examining points of difference on the income and financial aid characteristics of first-year student veterans by race, ethnicity, and gender. Then, we presented differences on key factors tied to the postsecondary experience by military service. These insights awaken new lines of scholarly inquiry and practical consideration as they relate to the postsecondary experiences and outcomes of military-connected students.

As the higher education community looks toward the future of research, institutional policy, and practice for servicemembers and veterans on campus, we are presented with an opportunity to build on our commitment to their success. We can navigate our nation's longstanding struggle with inequities that linger across demographic and socioeconomic lines to illuminate more paths to opportunity for the servicemembers and veterans who enroll on our campuses. Higher education professionals can generate a more holistic narrative of the characteristics, strengths, and needs of these students, thereby using these to define and refine strategies that empower veterans and other military-connected individuals for opportunity now and throughout their lives.

References

Aud, S., Fox, M., & KewalRemani, A. (2010). *Status and trends in the education of racial and ethnic groups.* Washington, DC: National Center for Education Statistics, U.S. Department of Education. Retrieved from http://nces. ed.gov/pubs2010/2010015.pdf

Bensimon, E. M. (2005). Closing the achievement gap in higher education: An organizational learning perspective. In A. Cesar (Ed.), *Organizational learning in higher education* (Vol. 131, pp. 100–111). San Francisco, CA: Jossey-Bass.

Cahalan, M. & Perna, L. (2015). *Indicators of higher education equity in the United States* (Equity Indicator 3a: What is the maximum Pell amount relative to college costs?). Washington, DC: Pell Institute for the Study of Opportunity in Higher Education and PennAHEAD. Retrieved from http://www. pellinstitute.org/downloads/publications-Indicators_of_Higher_ Education_Equity_in_the_US_45_Year_Trend_Report.pdf

Carnevale, A., Jayasundera, T., & Gulish, A. (2015). *Good jobs are back: College graduates are first in line.* Washington, DC: Center on Education and the Workforce, Georgetown University. Retrieved from https://cew. georgetown.edu/cew-reports/goodjobsareback/

Carnevale, A., Smith, N., & Strohl, J. (2010). *Help wanted: Projections of jobs and education requirements through 2018.* Washington, DC: Center on Education and the Workforce, Georgetown University. Retrieved from https://cew. georgetown.edu/wp-content/uploads/2014/12/fullreport.pdf

Choy, S. (2002). *Nontraditional undergraduates.* Washington, DC: U.S. Department of Education. Retrieved from https://nces.ed.gov/pubs2002/2002012.pdf

Coley, R. (2000). *The American community college turns 100: A look at its students, programs, and prospects.* Princeton, NJ: Educational Testing Service. Retrieved from https://www.ets.org/Media/Research/pdf/PICCC.pdf

Committee on STEM Education. (2013). *Federal science, technology, engineering, and mathematics (STEM) 5-year strategic plan.* Washington, DC: National Science and Technology Council. Retrieved from https://www.whitehouse. gov/sites/default/files/microsites/ostp/stem_stratplan_2013.pdf

Complete College America. (2011). *Time is the enemy.* Washington, DC: Author. Retrieved from http://www.completecollege.org/docs/Time_Is_the_ Enemy.pdf

Espinosa, L., & Nellum, C. (2015, Spring). *Five things student affairs professionals can do to support diverse students in STEM* (NASPA Research and Policy Institute Issue Brief) Washington, DC: NASPA – Student Affairs Administrators in Higher Education. Retrieved from http://www.naspa.org/rpi/reports/5- things-student-affairs-professionals-can-do-to-support-diverse-STEM

Horn, L., Premo, M., & Malizio, A. (1995). *Profile of undergraduates in U.S. postsecondary education institutions: 1992–93.* Washington, DC: U.S. Department of Education. Retrieved from http://nces.ed.gov/pubs/96237.pdf

Jank, S., & Owens, L. (2012). *Inequality in the United States. Understanding inequality with data.* Stanford, CA: Center for Education Policy Analysis, Stanford University. Retrieved from https://web.stanford.edu/group/scspi/slides/Inequality_SlideDeck.pdf

Kena, G., Aud, S., Johnson, F., Xiaolei, W., Zhang, J., Rathbun, A., ... Kristapovich, P. (2014). *The condition of education 2014.* Washington, DC: U.S. Department of Education. Retrieved from http://nces.ed.gov/pubs2014/2014083.pdf

Molina, D. (2015, December 7). *#EducateVeterans on student financial aid* [Blogpost]. Retrieved from http://higheredtoday.org/2015/12/07/educateveterans-on-student-financial-aid/

Molina, D., & Morse, A. (2015). *Military-connected undergraduates: Exploring differences between National Guard, reserve, active duty, and veterans in higher education.* Washington, DC: American Council on Education & NASPA – Student Affairs Administrators in Higher Education. Retrieved from http://www.acenet.edu/news-room/Documents/Military-Connected-Undergraduates.pdf

National Center for Education Statistics (NCES). (2015). *NPSAS undergraduate codebook.* Washington, DC: U.S. Department of Education. Retrieved https://nces.ed.gov/datalab/powerstats/pdf/npsas2012ug_subject.pdf

National Center for Education Statistics (NCES). (2016). *Beginning Postsecondary Student Longitudinal Survey (04:09) (Quickstats).* Washington, DC: U.S. Department of Education.

Rodriguez, C., Kirshstein, R., Banks Amos, L., Jones, W., Espinosa, L., & Watnick, D. (2012). *Broadening participation in STEM: A call to action.* Retrieved from http://www.air.org/sites/default/files/downloads/report/Broadening_Participation_in_STEM_Feb_14_2013_0.pdf

Rothwell, J. (2014). *Still searching: Job vacancies and STEM skills.* Washington, DC: The Brookings Institution. Retrieved from http://www.brookings.edu/~/media/research/files/reports/2014/07/stem/job-vacancies-and-stem-skills.pdf

Schmid, C., & Abell, P. (2003). Demographic risk factors, study patterns, and campus involvement as related to student success among Guilford Technical Community College students. *Community College Review, 31*(1), 1–16.

Skomsvold, P., Walton Radford, A., & Berkner, L. (2011). *Six-year attainment, persistence, transfer, retention, and withdrawal rates of students who began postsecondary education in 2003–04*. Washington, DC: U.S. Department of Education. Retrieved from http://nces.ed.gov/pubs2011/2011152.pdf

Steele, J. L., Salcedo, N., & Coley, J. (2010). *Service members in school: Military veterans' experiences using the Post-9/11 GI Bill and pursuing postsecondary education* (Research Report No. 312527). Washington, DC: Rand.

U.S. Bureau of Labor Statistics. (2015, December). *Table 1.4: Occupations with the most job growth, 2014 and projected 2024 (Numbers in thousands)*. Washington, DC: Employment Projections Program, Author. Retrieved from http://www.bls.gov/emp/ep_table_104.htm

U.S. Department of Veterans Affairs. (2016). *Education and training: Post-9/11 GI Bill*. Washington, DC: Author. Retrieved from http://www.benefits.va.gov/gibill/post911_gibill.asp

Worley, R. (2015, July). *Education service update*. Presented at the annual conference of the Western Association of Veterans Education Specialists. Anaheim, California. Retrieved from http://uswaves.org/images/2015/final/education_service_update.pdf

CHAPTER 3

★★★★★★★★★★★★★★★★★★★★★★★★★★★★★★★

The Journey or the Destination: Exploring Engagement Patterns of Disabled Student Veterans

Amanda Kraus, R. Cody Nicholls, and James S. Cole

Higher education has worked in recent years to create more inclusive campus practices for student veterans, and disability is an important aspect of this community. To date, the U.S. Department of Defense (DOD, 2016) estimates more than 60,000 servicemembers have been wounded in action. Resulting disabilities include hearing and/or vision loss, mobility impairment, and amputations (Kraus & Rattray, 2012). In addition to the physical or visible manifestations of service-related injury, the current generation of veterans has given voice to invisible injuries and implications of military service. A projected 20% of those who served in Iraq and Afghanistan have posttraumatic stress disorder (Tanielian & Jaycox, 2008), and more than 350,000 servicemembers are diagnosed with a traumatic brain injury (TBI; DOD, 2016). There are also high rates of comorbidity among invisible injuries. These statistics have important implications for higher education, as an estimated 25% of student veterans have a disability (Tanielian & Jaycox, 2008), and student veterans are twice as likely as their non-veteran peers to have at least one disability (National Survey of Student Engagement, 2010).

To address the unique characteristics of student veterans, including those with disabilities, college and university professionals have developed vet-friendly campuses across the country (ACE, 2013) with services, such as dedicated spaces for student veterans to gather and seek refuge from the hectic nature of campus; Veterans Affairs (VA) work study positions; and participation in the Yellow Ribbon program to more seamlessly facilitate the approval of transfer credit. Campuses are also identifying points of contact across important student services, such as counseling and psychological services, financial aid, or disability services, who are prepared to respond to the concerns of military-connected students.

Little research, however, has been conducted to understand the impact of these programs and services on engagement. While we understand general trends and characteristics of student veterans, we do not have a clear sense of what makes them successful in higher education with respect to involvement or engagement. There is even less descriptive information available to understand the behaviors and experiences of disabled student veterans. This chapter uses findings from the 2015 National Survey on Student Engagement (NSSE) as well as individual interviews to explore the engagement patterns of disabled student veterans in their final year of university and better understand how and why these students persist to graduation.

Disability in Higher Education

To ensure that all students have an accessible and equitable experience at their college or university, disability service offices or resource centers coordinate reasonable accommodations for students with documented disabilities. In order to access accommodations, a student must affiliate with the office and discuss barriers he or she experiences on campus, in the classroom, in residence halls, at campus events, and elsewhere. A student may also need to provide medical documentation for additional context to help the staff member understand the request and the barrier the student is experiencing. Through an interactive process, disability services personnel coordinate an accommodation that will facilitate full access and participation without compromising any essential functions of the experience. Accommodations are not just limited to the classroom; rather, they are designed to to make all campus experiences accessible, including programs, events, and cocurricular learning opportunities (e.g., internships, service-learning).

The current process by which students request and subsequently access disability-related accommodations presupposes they identify as having a disability. Additionally, this process assumes access to current medical documentation. While disability is an important and real aspect of the veteran community and experience, student veterans identify ambiguously with disability (Kraus & Rattray, 2012). In a 2011 survey conducted at the University of Arizona, student veterans did not readily identify as "disabled" or even as "having a disability." While just over half of the nearly 50 respondents reported receiving VA disability benefits, only 15% of students identified as a "person with a disability." Survey respondents expressed an aversion to using terms like *disabled* or *wounded warrior*, as well as resistance to being treated as special or different from other students (Rattray, 2011). Prioritizing the team or the community, student veterans with disabilities also expressed concern that using accommodations or services might mean that another, more deserving student would not have access to them.

Unlike other disabled college students, student veterans may never have used disability-related accommodations before and, therefore, may not be aware that resources exist to mitigate disability-related barriers on campus (Burnett & Segoria, 2007). Additionally, they are less likely than traditional incoming first-year students to be guided or prompted by their parents to seek out relevant campus services. Disabled student veterans are concurrently navigating various developmental and bureaucratic processes. They are negotiating the implications of newly acquired disabilities as they learn how to be college students, all while potentially engaging with the DOD and VA as well as their university. Given the tenuous nature with which all students, including veterans, identify as disabled, it would behoove college and university personnel to operationalize new thinking on disability and inclusion that deemphasizes impairment and focuses on accessible and inclusive campus environments for all students.

Disability studies is an interdisciplinary academic discipline—much like gender studies, queer studies, or Africana studies—that critically explores disability as a social construct with far-reaching economic, political, and social implications. Research on disability explores impairment not as problematic, but as a natural part of human diversity (Donnelly, 2016). Research is framed by the social model of disability, which challenges traditional thinking about disability and defines the experience of disability as created and perpetuated by environments designed to exclude people with impairments (Shakespeare, 1997; Williams, 2001). In an environment or experience designed to be accessible and inclusive, an individual would have an impairment or physiological difference, but would not be disabled. The social model shifts the burden of accessibility away from the individual and onto the environment. As a result, the problem of accessibility is no longer the individual, but the design of an environment. With respect to college and university campuses, if all students are admitted via the same standards, then all students should be entitled to an accessible experience. Disabled students should not have to work harder to enjoy the same experiences as their non-disabled peers.

While we might philosophically understand this shift in thinking about disability and accessibility, in practice it can be challenging to move from a medical or individual model to a sociocultural approach. Universal design (UD) presents promising strategies for operationalizing a more proactive campus commitment to access by infusing flexibility and accessibility throughout all stages of the design process. UD focuses on the development of products and environments to be used by the widest range of individuals, to the greatest extent possible, without the need for adaptation of specialized modification (Connell et al., 1997). It prioritizes the following principles throughout the design process: equitable, flexible, and intuitive use; perceptible information; tolerance for error; low physical effort; and adequate size and space for approach and use. There is great opportunity to enhance and increase engagement experiences for student veterans with disabilities when we focus on designing experiences to be inclusive rather than relying on the implementation of individual accommodation to ensure access. Given the ambiguous nature by which student veterans identify as disabled, campus professionals cannot rely on them to request disability-related accommodations on campus (Burnett & Segoria, 2007); rather, we must design curricular and cocurricular experiences to be barrier-free to encourage the participation of disabled student veterans in all campus opportunities.

Overview of Study

To explore the engagement patterns of disabled student veterans, we used a mixed-methods approach (Creswell, 2014). In part one of our study, a secondary analysis of data collected at doctoral-granting and research universities from the 2015 NSSE College Student Report, an annual survey of first-year and senior college students that measures student engagement, was performed. Using stratified random sampling techniques adjusting for age and sex (representative of student veteran demographics), we delimited this analysis to four groups of college seniors: student veterans with disabilities ($n = 1,211$), student veterans with no documented disability ($n = 4,186$), students in the general population who have a documented disability ($n = 10,476$), and students in the general population who do not have a documented disability ($n = 91,029$). Using the student groups as independent variables, multivariate techniques were employed to test for mean differences. Effect sizes were checked *post hoc* and reported in terms of high, medium, or low practical significance. The analysis yielded four noteworthy findings, which are described in the next section.

In accordance with a mixed-methods protocol, these four findings were used to inform the qualitative method, in particular the creation of an interview protocol. We conducted six individual, semi-structured interviews (see Appendix) at a large public research university in the Southwestern United States, nationally recognized for its student veteran program and disability services. Interviews lasted an average of 75 minutes each. Interviewers represented both the veteran and disability communities to help interviewees feel safe. We solicited interest in the project by advertising through the campus veterans center. We required all interviewees to identify as a student veteran with a disability. Of the sample, two identified as women and four as men. The group represented all branches of service, except the U.S. Coast Guard, but had limited diversity with respect to race, ethnicity or sexual orientation. The participants ranged in age from late-20s to mid-40s and represented a variety of academic majors and were all in their senior or final year of study.

To analyze interview data, we employed a phenomenological approach. Given the interviewers' veteran and disability status, we began each interview with a "description of [our] own experiences" (Creswell, 1998, p. 147) with the ultimate goal of incorporating both the researchers' and the respondents' ideas and perspectives on the engagement of disabled student veterans on campus. Each interview was digitally recorded, with appropriate permissions, and professionally transcribed verbatim. Upon thorough analysis of each transcript, we extracted particularly meaningful statements that helped explain and justify the students' experiences on campus with respect to their disabilities, veteran status, academic interests, and engagement. We began to identify trends across the six interviews and then coded these themes per the NSSE findings.

Findings

The analysis of the 2015 NSSE dataset yielded four findings worth noting based on effect sizes, having achieved statistical significance, and at least a modest level of practical significance (see Table 3.1). Student comments related to these findings have been woven into the quantitative analysis to enhance our understanding of the educational experience for student veterans with disabilities. A fifth theme emerging from the interview data is also discussed.

Perceived Gains

The first finding was related to NSSE's Perceived Gains (PG) scale, a 10-item scale measuring the degree to which students reported having made gains in a variety of personal, practical, and general education competency areas as a result of their undergraduate education. Student veterans who indicated having at least one diagnosed disability scored statistically significantly lower than all other groups: general population students (nearly 10% lower), non-veteran students with disabilities (5% lower), and student veterans without disabilities (5% lower).

Consistent with the NSSE's findings on perceived gains, interviewees did not identify meaningful gains with respect to personal, practical, or general

Table 3.1

Student Veterans With at Least One Documented Disability Compared With Other Student Groups

	Perceived gains	Discussion with diverse others	Collaborative learning	Student–faculty interaction
Student veterans with no documented disability	5% lower	Slightly higher	8% higher	15% higher
Students in the general population who have a documented disability	5% lower	5% higher	Slightly higher but statistically equal	6% lower
Students in the general population who do not have a documented disability	10% lower	7% higher	Slightly higher but statistically equal	6% higher

education that they would attribute to their undergraduate education. Nor did they identify disability as a factor in either facilitating or hindering perceived gains. Rather, interviewees described gains made during their military service, which were then applied to their university experience.

> One of the Marine Corps leadership traits is that you seek self-improvement; you always must be improving yourself.

> The military is an institution, and there's structure with that organization and if you know how to navigate that, then you should be able to navigate other structures in other institutions.

> So when you work 10 to 12 hours a day, five to seven days a week … and just knowing what your priorities were and having to tackle that even though you want to do something else. And that was really hammered into me and then, I was the guy that had to make sure it was hammered into everyone else. Then [it] just became a part of me … I cannot unplug from the matrix … it's ingrained at this point.

> What I gained … was three lines from the Soldiers' Creed, 'I will always place the mission first. I will never accept defeat. I will never quit.' … So, I remind myself of these things I've been taught to get through graduate school.

Respondents prioritized finishing their degrees. This single-minded focus may provide some insight into their relatively lower perceived gain scores that were revealed in the survey findings.

It just comes down to sheer motivation ... I've been given this task, even though it's my own task, you know—to get this done. That's really my biggest thing.

So ... as [for] pursuing my degree and being here at the school, that's really my biggest motivator is just I knew where I was, I don't want to be there anymore.

I'm here to get my stuff done, to be assessed, and to move on.

I want something for my money. I'm going to get a master's out of it and that means increased amount of money. It means a little bit more respect at the job because I'm going to be new at the job.

My motivation is the finish line.

They expressed little interest in additional engagement on campus or with other students, with the exception of other student veterans.

One of the really interesting things that I have had the chance to volunteer for at the VET Center was the last Veterans Day [event] they had [on] the mall. I think that was a really great way to integrate the veteran community as a whole.

I wish I could attend more vet things. I wish I could be more helpful to other vets, and attend more vet events, but the problem is like they all seem to be when either I'm in class or my daughter has got softball.

[I wanted to do this interview] because the VET Center is really good to me. So ... when they need volunteers if I can, I try to.

If there's something I can be a part of, if there's something I can fit into my schedule and the VETS Center asked for people, I'd like to do that.

Discussion With Diverse Others

The second finding was related to the Discussion with Diverse Others (DO) scale, a four-item scale that measures the degree to which students reported interacting with and learning from others with different backgrounds and life experiences. Here, student veterans with disabilities scored slightly higher than student veterans, in general, but statistically significantly higher than general population students (nearly 7% higher) and non-veteran students with disabilities (5% higher). This finding suggests that student veterans may be better positioned to achieve academic success in several of today's student learning outcomes related to diversity, inclusivity, and cultural awareness. Participant interviews provided modest empirical confirmation. Interviewees acknowledged they were comfortable interacting with diverse individuals due to their experience in the military, although this was not a major theme.

> You know, sometimes, it's great. I have worked with some really good individuals, who are very diligent. They also have a goal. ... Even though they're young or they come from different experiences, they're goal-oriented and they're on it.

Their military experience helped them engage naturally and easily with group learning situations and in collaborating on projects with diverse peers.

Collaborative Learning

NSSE's Collaborative Learning (CL) scale is a four-item scale measuring the degree to which students collaborated with peers in solving problems or mastering difficult material. Use of CL allows students to "break down stereotypes, learn to work in groups, develop listening skills, learn the art of compromising and negotiating, learn interpersonal skills, ... and [be] exposed to a variety of different people" (Cabrera, Crissman, Bernal, Nora, Terenzini, & Pascarella, 2002). Student veterans with disabilities scored slightly higher than, but statistically equal to, general population students and other students with disabilities. However, student veterans with disabilities scored statistically significantly higher on CL than student veteran colleagues without disabilities (nearly 8% higher), although the effect size was small ($d = .10$).

In reflecting on meaningful, collaborative efforts with their classmates, several participants discussed their own leadership role within the group. Given the teamwork and leadership skills they developed in the military, interviewees explained that group work came easily to them. They often took a leadership role and were effective in designating appropriate roles for each student in the group.

> I find myself always taking charge right off the bat without even realizing I'm taking charge. And then, I'll have to step back and go, 'Oh, so how would you handle this situation?' And so, that part I find difficult and fun at the same time. ... Knowing that I still have that drive ... some of that ability to take initiative to do what has to get done.

> I come into group projects with a mentality of take-charge ... I'm in charge until someone else tells me that they know better than me in this, so I'm in charge.

When I came in, neither of my group members really gave it much thought. I was like, 'Cool. I already had two studies written out and you can pick from one of the two.' ... So now, I just try to have everything done for our group project before I meet who is in my group.

Student–Faculty Interaction

Finally, the Student–Faculty Interaction (SF) scale is a four-item scale that measures the degree to which students reported interacting with faculty, which can positively affect academic motivation (Trolian, Jach, Hanson, & Pascarella, 2016). In this case, student veterans with disabilities scored significantly higher than general population students (nearly 6% higher) and student veterans without disabilities (nearly 15% higher). The mean difference for SF between veteran groups had a modest effect size ($d = .17$). Findings from the subsequent interviews suggested that SF is of positive value for learning and motivation, though all groups scored statistically significantly lower in SF than the non-veteran students with disabilities group.

Participants described an easy connection with faculty who they felt valued their mature perspectives and military experience.

> Some of my instructors are about my age ... I'm actually older than one of them, which kind of throws me off a little bit, but it's very relaxed. They understand I am a student learner. ... So, they are always a little more willing to work with me.

> One very influential professor I have ... knew I was prior-service. He knew I was an athlete. He was married to an athlete. He was another Californian ... and we just got along really well. You know, I wasn't 19, I was 27, 28 years old. So, you're dealing with PhDs who are 27, 28 years old. So, you're peers. Even though they're there and you're here.

> It's just nice. It was nice to be [treated as] not a student but, you know, an adult.

Campus Climate

The majority of students in the sample indicated the campus was not designed or meant for students like them. Due to their age, trajectory to university, past professional or military experience, students felt that they were not truly a part of the campus community. These students described friends, hobbies, and activities, yet could not say that they felt deeply connected to the university.

It's—I don't feel like I belong just because of me ... I'm not like them [the traditionally aged students]. I can't enjoy all that [engagement] stuff. So, I haven't. There's part of me that says, 'Go ahead and ... get involved and try some things,' but the other part of me says, 'If you're wasting time with that, there's stuff that you could be doing that's probably more smart. You should be getting that done instead.' Johnny and Mike go to high school together. Johnny goes to the military. Mike goes to college. Johnny does six months of training and feels like he is an adult now when he gets out of training. Mike messes around for three years, gets his degree in his fourth or fifth year, and now his life starts. So you see, he had time to sort of let steam out, have fun, mature slowly. Mike had six months of training, [was] given a gun and said [go] guard this building or you're going to die. So, it's sort of different. It was a huge culture change.

Interestingly, one student voiced a pejorative view of accommodation, which hints at coddling or over-helping student veterans:

If you're a vet, you're going to have accommodation, you're going to have more club and social opportunities that are geared toward you ... I don't feel a need to [be] receiving accommodation.

This negative view of accommodation is not unusual, even for those students who have disabilities themselves. For example, Barazandeh (2005) found that "students may be criticized for not having a 'legitimate' disability" (p. 5).

Limitations

We acknowledge certain limitations in the execution of this study, specifically a relatively small interview sample by which to elucidate the NSSE findings. While NSSE data are extremely generalizable, conducting interviews at only one institution may limit the scope of our findings and implications. Another complication in authentically understanding the experiences of disabled student veterans, and also evidenced specifically in this study, is the inconsistency and ambiguity with which they identify as disabled or discuss disability-related issues. Given the size and scope of the site for these interviews, it is unlikely that our findings would contribute to a greater awareness of engagement patterns for disabled student veterans enrolled in community colleges, historically Black colleges and universities (HBCUs), or for-profit institutions.

Discussion and Implications

All respondents identified as veterans with disabilities. During their interviews, we discussed disability with them to the extent they would engage, which was relatively little. While they did disclose their diagnoses, they did not discuss disability as a significant piece of their identity or as impacting their campus experience. As a result, we can extrapolate very little about the impact of disability on their engagement or outcomes.

This lack of emphasis on disability could be potentially explained by the aforementioned reluctance veterans have in discussing disability personally, or the fact that these individuals are relatively newly disabled and still learning what disability means to them, or by the culture on this specific campus, which serves as a leader in disability services and campus access. It is possible that the campus culture promotes higher rates of inclusion and access for disabled students, lessening barriers to students' experience.

Student veterans, and especially those student veterans with disabilities, approach and experience higher education differently from their non-veteran, non-disabled peers. Student veterans come into higher education with significant work and life experience; their military service has instilled in them great practical skills with respect to leadership and communication. Disability is also an important aspect of the student veteran community, though individuals may be uncomfortable or uncertain identifying as disabled.

With respect to reported gains, disabled student veterans indicated less meaningful practical, personal, and academic outcomes when compared with nonveteran and nondisabled students. Are student veterans with disabilities somehow getting less out of college? One explanation is that many student veterans came to their disabilities relatively later in life than other college students with disabilities. The struggles of dealing with a life-changing injury(ies) of war, whether physical and/or psychological, and the associated distractions may have a dampening effect on college performance, especially during the first year of his or her transition and adjustment to college. However, student veterans likely have already developed significant personal and professional skills that prepare them to be successful college students. In order to appeal to their past experiences, faculty and staff must represent and validate these experiences. Much like translating military skills into a civilian context for the purposes of crafting a resume can help with job searching, finding ways to capitalize on the military experiences and skills that student veterans possess may help them realize greater perceived and actual gains in college. Disabled student veterans in this study described very specific goals for pursuing higher education, such as graduation and obtaining employment, while a traditionally aged, nonveteran undergraduate may not have such a clear sense of purpose. In crafting meaningful opportunities for engagement, highlighting practical outcomes that relate to career development, and also drawing upon the skills that veterans have developed is recommended.

Disabled student veterans report a high level of comfort and competence in working with others. They indicate willingness and interest in working with diverse students, collaboration, and student–faculty interaction. Incorporating intentional opportunities for collaboration in engagement opportunities would not only capitalize on some of their reported strengths but may also increase their sense of perceived gains.

In exploring the specific experiences of disabled student veterans, we must look at the accessibility of campus and engagement opportunities. Student veterans are reluctant to identify as disabled and, therefore, may not request reasonable accommodations as readily as other disabled undergraduates (DiRamio, Ackerman, & Garza Mitchell, 2008). Students with newly acquired disabilities may not understand campus processes to request accommodations or how to be considered eligible for such services. To ensure their full and meaningful participation in important learning and social experiences, campus professionals must design them with access in mind. Rather than wait for an individual student to encounter a barrier and request an accommodation, it is incumbent upon faculty and staff to employ universal design strategies that maximize access. By creating experiences such as internships, field trips, or events to be accessible, engagement opportunities are welcoming and inclusive for all, regardless of disability or other diverse characteristics.

Applying principles of universal design to the physical and learning environments of the campus might mean creating common pathways and entrances so that all students feel welcome and understand that diversity is appreciated. When designing public messaging, class content, or learning activities, UD principles ensure that information and materials are perceptible to a wide range of users. Having multiple ways to engage with content also maximizes accessibility. Ultimately, good design can ensure that disabled and nondisabled students have similar, if not identical, experiences and build a stronger sense of community and inclusion. These conditions will likely contribute to increased engagement and persistence by all students.

Conclusion

Disabled student veterans enter higher education with diverse backgrounds and unique experiences that may differentiate them from their nondisabled, nonveteran undergraduate counterparts. Through their military service, disabled student veterans acquired and developed highly relevant skills that inform their college experience. While they are less likely to report meaningful gains across personal, professional, and academic areas, they are more comfortable in relating to diverse individuals and collaborating with students and faculty. It would behoove higher education professionals to increase opportunities for collaboration in their engagement efforts and tie outcomes to practical goals. Because we cannot rely on student veterans to identify themselves as disabled or request reasonable accommodations on campus, we must design engagement experiences to be accessible without the need for an accommodation or modification. As we continue to explore the experiences of disabled student veterans with respect to engagement, we must appreciate the unique skills, experiences, and goals with which they approach higher education and work to intentionally design accessible and inclusive engagement opportunities that appeal to them.

References

American Council on Education (ACE). (2013). *Toolkit for veteran-friendly institutions*. Retrieved from https://vetfriendlytoolkit.acenet.edu

Barazandeh, G. (2005). Attitudes toward disabilities and reasonable accommodation at the university. *The Undergraduate Research Journal, 7*, 1–12.

Burnett, S., & Segoria, J. (2007). Collaboration for military transition students from combat to college: It takes a community. *Journal of Postsecondary Education and Disability, 22*(1), 53–58.

Cabrera, A. F., Crissman, J. L., Bernal, E., Nora, A., Terenzini, P. T., &. Pascarella, E. T. (2002). Collaborative learning: Its impact on college students' development and diversity. *Journal of College Student Personnel, 43*(1), 20–34.

Connell, B. R., Jones, M., Mace, R., Mueller, J., Mullick, A., Ostroff, E., … Vanderheiden, G. (1997). *The principles of universal design*. Raleigh, NC: North Carolina State University, The Center for Universal Design. Retrieved from https://www.ncsu.edu/ncsu/design/cud/about_ud/udprinciplestext.htmnorth

Creswell, J. W. (1998). *Qualitative inquiry and research design: Choosing among five traditions*. Thousand Oaks, CA: Sage.

Creswell, J. W. (2014). *A concise introduction to mixed methods research*. Thousand Oaks, CA: Sage.

DiRamio, D., Ackerman, R., & Garza Mitchell, R. L. (2008). From combat to campus: Voices of student-veterans. *NASPA Journal, 45*(1), 73–102.

Donnelly, C. E. (2016). Re-visioning negative archetypes of disability and deformity in fantasy: *Wicked, Maleficent,* and *Game of Thrones. Disability Studies Quarterly,* 36(4), doi: 10.1806/dsq.v36i4.5313.

Kraus, A., & Rattray, N. (2012). Understanding disability in the student veteran community. In F. A. Hamrick & C. B. Rumann (Eds.), *Called to serve: A handbook on student veterans and higher education* (pp. 116–137). San Francisco, CA: Jossey-Bass.

National Survey of Student Engagement. (2010). *Major differences: Examining student engagement by field of study—annual results 2010.* Bloomington, IN: Indiana University Center for Postsecondary Research.

Rattray, N. (2011). *Survey results on health and wellness among student veterans at the University of Arizona.* Retrieved from http://drc.arizona.edu/veterans-reintegration-education/sites/drc.arizona.edu.veterans-reintegration-education/files/Survey%20Results%20-%20Health%20and%20Wellness%20among%20Student%20Veterans%20at%20the%20University%20of%20Arizona%20-%202011.pdf

Shakespeare, T. (1997). The social model of disability. In L. J. Davis (Ed.), *The disability studies reader* (pp. 266–273). New York, NY: Routledge.

Tanielian, T. L., & Jaycox, L. (2008). *Invisible wounds of war: Psychological and cognitive injuries, their consequences, and services to assist recovery.* Santa Monica, CA: Rand.

Trolian, T. L., Jach, E. A., Hanson, J. M., & Pascarella, E. T. (2016). Influencing academic motivation: The effects of student–faculty interaction. *Journal of College Student Development,* 57(7), 810–826.

U.S. Department of Defense (DOD). (2016). *Total deaths KIA non-hostile pending WIA OIF.* Retrieved from http://www.defense.gov/casualty.pdf

Williams, G. (2001). Theorizing disability. In G. L. Albrecht, K. D. Seelman, & M. Bury (Eds.), *Handbook of disability studies* (pp. 123–144). Thousand Oaks, CA: Sage.

Appendix

Semi-structured Interview Protocol
1. What motivated you to attend college?
2. Tell us about your undergraduate experience. Major, opportunities, research, involvement, experiences that stand out.

Disability:
3. How do you feel that your veteran or disability status impacts your ability to work with others? With faculty? Get involved on campus?
4. Follow-up: Did accessibility, or lack thereof, impact your ability to be involved as a student?
5. Follow-up: How would you describe the climate for vets on campus? Do you feel that there were ample opportunities to make connections, get involved?
6. What does disability mean? How does disability impact your goals for higher education?

Perceived Gain:
7. How would you say that your undergraduate experience benefitted you? Personally? Professionally? Practically?
8. What were some goals you had around attending college and getting a degree? How did disability impact these goals?
9. What kinds of things did you get involved with outside of class? Extracurricular? Extra work with faculty?
10. To what do you attribute your personal, professional, practical growth?
11. How do you define what you are getting out of college?

Working Effectively With Others:
12. What kinds of experiences did you have in college that required your work with other students? Group projects? Clubs?
13. Is working with others something that interests you? Do you seek out opportunities to work with students on various things? How? Why or why not?

Acquiring Job Skills:

14. Do you feel that your military service provided you opportunities to develop skills to work effectively with others? How does this compare to your experiences in college?
15. According to NSSE, it looks like student vets are not getting as much out of college, can you tell us what you think about this?
16. What kinds of skills do you believe are critical to be successful in this area?
17. What kinds of skills have you acquired in college to prepare you for your career?
18. How did you acquire these skills?

Critical Thinking, Real-world, Complex Problem-Solving:

19. When you think about critical thinking, how do you believe your experience at UA has contributed to helping you develop critical-thinking skills or the ability to analyze critically?
20. How do you believe your peers approach critical analysis?
21. Please give some examples of experiences that encourage you to think critically and ask questions.

Interacting with Diverse Populations:

22. I imagine that in the military, you interacted with a diverse group of people. How might you speak to the value you place on working with diverse folks?
23. Please talk with us about how diverse you believe the UA campus is. Please give examples from your classes or extracurricular involvement.
24. Follow-up: Given your experience in the military, do you believe that you seek out opportunities to work with diverse people? Tell us about that.

Collaborative Learning:

25. Something that tends to be important to veterans is a commitment to team, teamwork, collaboration. How do you feel that you were able to work or learn collaboratively on campus? Please give some examples.
26. How do you believe your peers think about collaboration? Please give examples.

Student–Faculty Interaction:

27. Talk with us about your interactions with faculty.
28. Did you work with faculty outside of the classroom? Pursue any additional labs, research, etc.)
29. Follow-up: How have these relationships with faculty made an impact on your UA experience? Helped prepare you for your career?

CHAPTER 4

Mental Health and Academic Functioning of Student Servicemembers and Veterans in Higher Education: The Importance of Social Support

Adam E. Barry, Shawn D. Whiteman, and Shelley MacDermid Wadsworth

Throughout this chapter, we have chosen to use the term *military-affiliated college student* to characterize military personnel in postsecondary education—active, inactive, or retired. Too often, various catchall phrases have been used in the literature to describe students who have served or are currently serving in the armed forces, but these terms frequently exclude some part of the population. For instance, the term *student veteran* excludes those still associated with the military (e.g., reservist or National Guard) by assuming all those enrolled have completed their tenure and active role in the military. Additionally, use of the term *military undergraduate* implies active military personnel and/or veterans are not pursuing advanced degrees. The importance of using appropriate nomenclature was highlighted in a special issue of the *Journal of American College Health* dedicated to research examining the health and well-being of military-affiliated college students who served in Operation Enduring Freedom/Operation Iraqi Freedom (OEF/OIF; Barry, 2015). Moreover, systemic literature reviews examining military-affiliated students in higher education also recommended researchers and practitioners avoid using terminology that is not inclusive or fully representative (Barry, Whiteman, & MacDermid Wadsworth, 2014). While a majority of higher education professionals have done a good job over the years of respecting individualism and promoting inclusiveness when working with unique student populations, it is important we continue this trend when dealing with military-affiliated college students.

To date, it is clear that military-affiliated college students represent a distinct sub-group on college campuses, with markedly different experiences and needs than their civilian peers (Barry et al., 2014). Quantitative studies that include civilian comparison groups assert military-affiliated college students exhibit significantly lower GPAs (Durdella & Kim, 2012), increased likelihood of engaging in numerous health-risk behaviors (Widome, Laska, Gulden, Fu, & Lust, 2011), lower perceived peer social support (Whiteman, Barry, Mroczek, & MacDermid Wadsworth, 2013), different motivations for alcohol use (Whiteman & Barry, 2011), and differential links between their alcohol use/misuse and associated mental health symptoms (Barry, Whiteman, MacDermid Wadsworth, & Hitt, 2012). Qualitative investigations echo and support these findings, with military-affiliated college students consistently articulating how different they are from their civilian peers in regard to experiences, maturity levels, needs, and/or personal difficulties (Barry et al., 2014; DiRamio, Ackerman, & Mitchell, 2008; Rumann & Hamrick, 2010). Simply put, military-affiliated college students feel disconnected from their civilian counterparts (ACE, 2008).

Given that one out of every three persons deployed in support of OEF/OIF will experience either posttraumatic stress disorder (PTSD), traumatic brain injury (TBI), or a major depressive disorder or symptoms (Tanielian & Jaycox, 2008), the mental health of military-affiliated college students represents an important focal area. Generalized anxiety, experiencing depressive symptoms, and the presence of PTSD symptoms have been found to have a direct negative effect on the academic adjustment of military-affiliated college students (Schonfeld et al., 2015). Additionally, compared to their civilian peers, military-affiliated college students exhibit a higher likelihood of self-harm (Blosnich, Kopacz, McCarten, & Bossarte, 2015). Among a sample of 628 military-affiliated college students, approximately half (46%) of the sample reported thinking of suicide at some point in the past.

Establishing interpersonal relationships with other peers on campus has been highlighted by military-affiliated college students as both challenging and stressful (Olsen, Badger, & McCuddy, 2014). For instance, one of the salient themes emerging from the qualitative study conducted by DiRamio and colleagues (2008) was "connecting with peers." Thus, it is clear that social support represents an important factor impacting a military-affiliated college student's adjustment and engagement in higher education. While it is clear that military-affiliated college students may have difficulties relating to other civilian students (DiRamio et al., 2008; Livingston, Havice, Cawthon, & Fleming, 2011), they have expressed desire to interact with other military-affiliated students on campus (Strickley, 2009). To that end, we provide a brief primer on the protective effect of perceived peer support. Specifically, we summarize the extensive literature base highlighting the broad implications of receiving social support among the general population, and the limited quantitative investigations that outline the implications of receiving social support among military-affiliated college students. Finally, we present unique findings that examine the protective effects of receiving social support for military-affiliated college students, and outline implications for research, practice, and policy in higher education.

Implications of Receiving Social Support – General Population

Previous research has linked social support to improved physical health and decreased mortality rates (Berkman, Glass, Brissette, & Seeman, 2000; Brummett et al., 2001; Rutledge et al., 2004; Uchino, 2004; 2006). Additionally, social support has been linked to better mental health indicators, such that college students who receive high-quality social support are less likely to experience depression and anxiety than those who receive low-quality social support (Hefner & Eisenberg, 2009; Kawachi & Berkman, 2001). Moreover, increases in social support over time are associated with improvements in psychological well-being such as fewer symptoms of depression and greater self-esteem (Galambos, Barker, & Krahn, 2006). Social support—particularly from peers—positively impacts academic adjustment for college students and results in improved retention rates and grade point average (Dennis, Phinney, & Chuateco, 2005). Simply put, social support is a strong protective factor for the mental health and adjustment of civilian college students and military-affiliated college students alike.

Implications of Receiving Social Support – Military-Affiliated College Students

Overall, there are few examinations into the association of social support and behavioral and mental health outcomes among military-affiliated college students. That said, the available literature asserts perceived social support has a direct positive influence on academic adjustment and individual functioning (Campbell & Riggs, 2015). Moreover, as social support increases among those who served in OEF/OIF, post-traumatic stress symptomology decreases (Pietrzak, Johnson, Goldstein, Malley, & Southwick, 2009; Wilcox, 2010). In a seminal piece examining differences between civilian students and those who served in OEF/OIF, Whiteman and colleagues (2013) found military-affiliated college students reported less emotional support from university friends. While both groups experienced increases in the level of emotional support received across time, it is noteworthy that emotional support received by military-affiliated college students never reached the same level of support as their civilian counterparts. Work by Eakman, Schelly, and Henry (2016) echoes these findings, asserting that military-affiliated students report lower levels of psychosocial protective factors, such as support, compared with their matched nonmilitary-affiliated peers. This is unfortunate, as the limited work examining the implications of social support among military-affiliated college students suggests that it may be very important. In particular, military-affiliated college students who reported receiving greater social support from sources outside of the university, such as family and non-university friends, reported experiencing less frequent PTSD symptoms (Elliot, Gonzalez, & Larsen, 2011). Family social support has also been found to moderate the association between avoidant coping and symptoms of anxiety and depression (Romero, Riggs, & Ruggero, 2015). Receipt of social support from those within higher education, such as university peers, has been found to be a protective factor on academic functioning for students in general, such that individuals reporting more social support also report greater GPAs and higher educational self-efficacy. Additionally, perceived support from university peers has been highlighted as protective against psychological distress, but the protective effects are stronger for civilians when compared to military-affiliated college students (Whiteman et al., 2013). Given the paucity of investigations specifically examining social support among military-affiliated college students, this chapter makes a valuable contribution to this literature.

As noted above, receipt of social support from those outside (family and coworkers) and inside of higher education (university friends/peers) has important protective effects. Additionally, military-affiliated college students themselves have specifically highlighted the desire to receive support from other military-affiliated personnel. To date, we are unaware of any investigations that simultaneously examined the unique contribution of nonmilitary-connected (e.g., family/friends) and military-affiliated supports (military coworkers). Consequently, we examined the effects of receiving social support from family, friends, and military coworkers simultaneously to determine whether social support from other military personnel contributed to military-affiliated college students' academic functioning and mental health, above and beyond that provided from family and friends.

Methods

Participants

Data were drawn from the first wave of a brief longitudinal study of military-affiliated and civilian college students (when measures central to the research questions were collected). In this study, we focus on the social support 189 military-affiliated college students (male = 154; female = 44) provided each other. On average, military-affiliated college students were 29.41 (SD = 8.20) years old, were White and mostly non-Hispanic (95%). All branches of the military were represented in the sample, with relatively equal distribution among the Air Force (16%), Army (27%), Marines (14%), Navy (14%), and National Guard (24%); a small proportion of the sample served in the Coast Guard (1%) or the Reserves (5%). Overall, these distributions mirror that of active duty members across service branches (U.S. Department of Defense, 2008).

Procedure

Participants were recruited from both private and public institutions, with varying enrollment sizes (4,000 to 40,000 students) and classifications (e.g., two-year or four-year, residential and commuter) within one Midwestern state. Institutions had to meet the following inclusion criteria to be eligible to participate: (a) qualified to administer Veterans Affairs (VA) education benefits, per the state approving agency; (b) administrative headquarters located in the state in which this study took place; and (c) academic credits awarded at the institution were accepted for credit at other in-state institutions. In total, 24 institutions met the aforementioned criteria. Of those qualifying institutions, 16 were represented in the final sample (67% institutional response rate).

After having all procedures vetted through appropriate institutional review boards, data were collected via web-based surveys. Students from each participating institutions were contacted via a university registrar representative at their respective institutions with an electronic recruitment letter inviting participation. Because recruitment materials were channeled through institutional representatives, we could not determine how many military-affiliated college students were contacted on each campus. As a result, we were unable to calculate response and participation rates. By replying to the recruitment invitation, students indicated their interest in participating. These individuals were subsequently sent a secure link to a web-based survey that took approximately 45 to 60 minutes to complete. Responses were anonymous, with all personal information kept in a separate secured survey. Participants received an honorarium of $50 for their participation.

Measures

Demographic information. Participants provided a variety of background information, including age, sex, and racial/ethnic minority group membership. Additionally, military-affiliated college students reported their military branch, pay grade, and current status (i.e., active duty, Reserves, National Guard).

Social support. On a scale from 0 (never) to 2 (always), military-affiliated college students were asked to rate how frequently they received assistance from three different sources (i.e., family, friends, and military coworkers) across three areas of support: informational ("I can talk and get advice about things that are important to me"), instrumental ("I can call on them to spend time and energy to help take care of something I need"), and emotional ("I can get together with them to have fun or relax"). For each source, scores were summed with higher scores denoting more support. For the current study, support from family and friends was averaged into a single index, so that differences between military-affiliated peers could be compared to nonmilitary-affiliated friends and family.

Academic functioning. Several different measures indexed military-affiliated college students' academic functioning. First, academic motivation was assessed using the four-item amotivation subscale from Valllerand et al.'s (1992) Academic Motivation Scale. On a scale ranging from 1 (not at all) to 5 (exactly) participants rated their motivations towards academics. Scores were averaged across items, with higher scores representing greater amotivation (or less motivation).

Military-affiliated college students' educational self-efficacy was assessed using a modified version of the Educational Degree Behaviors Self-Efficacy Scale (Gloria, Robinson Kurpius, Hamilton, & Wilson, 1999) and the College Self-Efficacy Inventory (Solberg, O'Brien, Villareal, Kennel & Davis, 1993). Specifically, on a scale from 1 (not at all) to 7 (extremely), military-affiliated college students rated their confidence with 28 statements about their performance in college (e.g., "How confident are you that you could write course papers?"). Scores were averaged across the 28 items, with higher scores indicative of greater self-efficacy (Cronbach's $\alpha = .86$).

Military-affiliated college students' college-related stress was indexed using Schafer's (1992) 29-item College Stress Scale. On a scale ranging from 1 (not at all stressful) to 5 (highly stressful) participants rated their degree of stress with their college experience (e.g., "worrying about grades" and "too little time"). Scores were averaged across the 29 items with higher scores denoting greater stress (Cronbach's $\alpha = .89$).

Finally, military-affiliated college students reported their perceptions of the supportiveness of their university environment using Gloria and Robinson Kurpius's (1996) 14-item University Environment Scale (UES). On a 7-point Likert scale ranging from 1 (not at all) to 7 (a great deal), participants rated items such as: "University staff have been warm and friendly," "I do not feel valued as a student on campus," and "The university seems to value minority students."

Negatively worded items were reverse coded, and scores were summed across the items with higher scores indicating a more supportive environment (Cronbach's $\alpha = .84$).

Mental health. Military-affiliated college students' mental health was indexed using two scales. First, participants rated their depressive symptoms using the 20-item CES-D (Radloff, 1977). On the CES-D, participants rated the frequency they felt certain emotions during the past week, such as "I felt that everything I did was an effort," "I felt lonely," "I talked less than usual," and "I could not get 'going.'" Scores were averaged across the items with higher scores denoting more depressive symptoms (Cronbach's $\alpha = .93$). Second, participants' psychological and somatic symptoms were indexed using the 18-item Brief Symptom Index (BSI; Derogatis, 2001). On a 5-point Likert scale ranging from 0 (not at all) to 4 (extremely), participants were asked to report the frequency with which they were distressed or bothered by different psychological (e.g., "nervousness of shakiness inside" and "feeling of worthlessness") and somatic symptoms (e.g., "pains in heart or chest" and "faintness or dizziness") in the past seven days. Scores were summed across the 18 items with higher scores indicating more psychosomatic problems (Cronbach's $\alpha = .90$).

Results

To address our goals, we performed a series of hierarchical multiple regressions. In each model, we controlled for age (centered at its mean) and gender (effect-coded such that males = -1 and females = 1). Effects for social support from family/friends and military coworkers were tested simultaneously to determine whether social support from military coworkers contributed to military-affiliated college students' academic functioning and mental health above and beyond that provided from family and friends.

With respect to academic functioning, models consistently revealed that social support from other military members was positively related to educational self-efficacy and perception of the university environment as supportive and negatively related to academic amotivation and perceived college-related stress (see Table 4.1). Interestingly, social support from family and friends was unrelated to each of these outcomes. For mental health, a different pattern emerged. Specifically, social support from family and friends was negatively linked to both psychosomatic and depressive symptoms. Yet, social support from other military members was not associated with either mental health outcome (see Table 4.2).

Table 4.1

Summary of Hierarchical Multiple Regression Analyses for Variables Predicting Military-Affiliated College Students' Academic Functioning

Variable	Academic amotivation			Educational self-efficacy			College stress			University environment		
	B	SE	β	B	SE	β	B	SE	β	B	SE	β
Intercept	2.01***	.24		156.14***	5.47		2.48***	.14		4.54***	.22	
Age	-.02†	.01	-.14	.32	.22	.11	-.01	.01	-.06	.02	.01	.13
Gender	-.13	.09	-.11	4.32*	2.02	.16	.14**	.05	.20	.05	.08	.05
Social support from family and friends	-.03	.03	-.07	.42	.66	.05	.00	.02	.01	.05	.03	.15
Social support from military	-.10*	.04	-.20	3.49***	.94	.31	-.05*	.02	-.19	.09*	.04	.21
R^2	.09			.15			.07			.11		
F	4.09**			6.95***			3.09*			4.75**		

†$p < .10$. *$p < .05$. **$p < .01$. ***$p < .001$.

Table 4.2
Summary of Hierarchical Multiple Regression Analyses for Variables Predicting Military-Affiliated College Students' Mental Health

Variable	Psychosomatic symptoms			Depressive symptoms		
	B	SE	β	B	SE	β
Intercept	1.88***	.24		21.14***	2.33	
Age	-.01	.01	-.09	-.16†	.10	-.13
Gender	.02	.05	.02	.58	.85	.05
Social support from family and friends	-.04*	.02	-.22	-.88**	.28	-.27
Social support from military	-.03	.02	-.12	-.53	.39	-.12
R^2	.08			.12		
F	3.83**			5.06***		

†$p < .10$. *$p < .05$. **$p < .01$. ***$p < .001$.

Discussion

Our findings highlight the important protective role that social support may play in the mental health of military-affiliated college students. Thus, it is important that universities and colleges recognize the powerful positive relationship between social support from other military-connected personnel and academic factors that could negatively impact the academic experience and persistence of military-affiliated college students. In particular, our findings highlight the positive relationship between social support and educational self-efficacy; perceptions of the university environment as supportive; and the negative relationship between social support, academic motivation, and perceived college-related stress. Given that military-affiliated college students face unique challenges when adjusting to student life (Bonar & Domenici, 2011; DiRamio et al., 2008; Livingston et al., 2011) and exhibit frequent and severe psychological symptoms (Rudd, Goulding, & Bryan, 2011), working to increase the social support they receive represents an important priority area in order to ensure satisfactory progress to graduation for this population.

The results of this study suggest that social support from fellow military-affiliated college students is not simply something that is desired or valued, but that appears to be significantly related to factors associated with academic success. This finding provides evidence supporting the value of efforts implemented by universities to foster such support, including peer mentoring programs, creation of veteran service officer positions and veteran success centers, and special orientation or class sessions for military-affiliated college students. Our findings also suggest, however, that these efforts may do more to promote academic success than prevent mental health problems. Others have noted the powerful positive impact of social support among returning servicemembers, and recommended that community-based approaches and interventions that seek to enhance social support be implemented (Carlson, Stromwell & Lietz, 2013). We echo these recommendations and call on college health professionals and decision makers in higher education to establish policies and practices that can increase opportunities for military-affiliated college students to interact with, and support, one another.

It is worth noting that interactions between military-affiliated college students and other members of the college community (i.e., civilian students and faculty) have not always been highlighted as positive. Specifically, multiple qualitative studies feature conflicts between military-affiliated college students and faculty members (DiRamio et al., 2008; Elliot et al., 2011), with one participant even calling for professors to attend a mandatory informational session focusing on the sensitivity of military-affiliated college students to "certain subjects, visuals, and other stimuli" (Elliot et al., 2011, p. 288). In a commentary advocating for military-affiliated college students, one university professor asserted "we in higher education share responsibility for these veterans on our campus, and as they return to civilian life, we should be part of the cohesive social support system that assists in the transition" (Thompson, 2011, p. 4). Thus, while it is possible that programs and strategies can be enacted to bring military-affiliated college students together in order to maximize received social support, it is important that other potential sources of support, such as university faculty and staff, not be overlooked. For example, to create a more positive social climate VET NET Ally, a four-hour training seminar, was developed to educate faculty and staff on pre- and post-military culture, personal identity issues, and available campus services to aid military-affiliated college students (Thomas, 2010). Ness, Middleton, and Hildebrandt (2015) have noted that PTSD symptoms and avoidance motivations among military-affiliated college students is attenuated when they perceive warm, positive relations with others on campus. Peer mentoring has been recommended as a strategy to foster the perception of positive relations to others (Ness et al., 2015).

While the findings herein clearly outline the protective effect of social support for military-affiliated college students, it is important to note that we did not examine differences across some important demographic factors, such as race/ethnicity or sexual orientation. These omissions are noteworthy given military-affiliated college students who identify as lesbian, gay, bisexual, or questioning may be more likely than their heterosexual military-affiliated student peers to report experiencing high levels of mental health symptoms, such as feeling helpless, feeling very lonely, seriously considering suicide, and experiencing anxiety and depression (Pelts & Albright, 2015). Additionally, Native American military-affiliated college students report increased rates of suicidal ideation, suicidal planning, and suicide attempts (Bryan, Theriault, & Bryan, 2015). Thus, continued and more nuanced examinations of social support among military-affiliated college students are warranted.

Conclusion

Based on the extant literature and the findings of this study, social support from family, friends, and other military-connected peers appears to be related differently to academic outcomes and mental health, with the latter more strongly related to support from family and friends. The emotional connections with family and friends may provide an atmosphere that promotes successful coping by military-affiliated college students and increases the likelihood that they will display resilience. The importance of family, friends, and fellow military-affiliated college students for different outcomes suggests that efforts to increase social support focus on all possible sources, rather than assuming that military peers constitute the most important group. Adopting strategies that leverage multiple sources of support and integrating these sources into a unified, multifaceted framework are likely to have the greatest impact on the health and well-being of military-affiliated college students. Recognizing the interdependence of psychosocial, psychological, and physical health, Spelman, Hunt, Seal, and Burgo-Black (2012) have similarly called for VA medical providers to adopt interdisciplinary approaches to care. DiRamio and colleagues (2008) have also called for holistic interventions that seek to minimize the stress, isolation, and associated difficulties that accompany transitions from military to student life. Based on the current published literature, anchoring such approaches to an overall goal of increasing social support may be a worthwhile endeavor. Moreover, we recommend the development of programs and interventions that leverage not only military-affiliated college students' need for more social support but also their desire to receive that support from other military-affiliated college students.

In developing strategies and programs to enhance social support on campus, it is important to consider: (a) returning military-affiliated college students exhibit low (47%) mental health service usage from VA, civilian, or military facilities (Bonar, Bohnert, Walters, Ganoczy, & Valenstein, 2015); (b) there are a wide range of intrapersonal, interpersonal and organizational barriers for military-affiliated college students to seeking health care (Misra-Hebert et al., 2015); and (c) military-affiliated college students are not comfortable seeking out social support on the college campus (Livingston et al., 2011; Olsen et al., 2014). Thus, practitioners and providers should not adopt a "build it and they will come" mentality. In other words, simply offering counseling services for military-affiliated college students, or developing a "Veteran Resource Center" does not ensure military-affiliated college students will use these services or that such resources will enhance social support. Rather, we recommend purposefully incorporating military-affiliated college students into the formative planning stages of program or policy development. In particular, military-affiliated college students would be vital assets to program developers by giving insights into areas including, but not limited to: (a) where would military-affiliated students like to meet together? (b) what activities would military-affiliated students like to do together? (c) would military-affiliated college students prefer connecting with those of the same sex? (d) how could family members of military-affiliated college students be integrated into activities with other military-affiliated students? Insights into questions such as these would greatly aid college health practitioners and decision makers in the development of strategies, policies, and programs designed to increase opportunities for military-affiliated college students to receive, and provide, social support.

References

American Council on Education. (2008). *Serving those who serve: Higher education and America's veterans: November issue brief.* Washington, DC: Author. Retrieved from http://www.acenet.edu/Content/NavigationMenu/ProgramsServices/MilitaryPrograms/serving/Veterans_Issue_Brief_1108.pdf

Barry, A. E. (2015). Student service members/veterans participating in higher education: What we know to date. *Journal of American College Health, 63*(7), 415–417.

Barry, A. E., Whiteman, S., & MacDermid Wadsworth, S. (2014). Student service members/veterans in higher education: A systematic review. *Journal of Student Affairs Research & Practice, 51*(1), 31–42.

Barry, A. E., Whiteman, S., MacDermid Wadsworth, S., & Hitt, S. (2012). The alcohol use and associated problems of student service members/veterans in higher education. *Drugs: Education, Prevention & Policy, 19*(5), 415–425.

Berkman, L. F., Glass, T., Brissette, I., & Seeman, T. E. (2000). From social integration to health: Durkheim in the new millennium. *Social Science & Medicine, 51*, 843–857.

Blosnich, J. R., Kopacz, M. S., McCarten, J., & Bossarte, R. M. (2015). Mental health and self-directed violence among student service members/veterans in postsecondary education. *Journal of American College Health, 63*(7), 418–426.

Bonar, E. E., Bohnert, K. M., Walters, H. M., Ganoczy, D., & Valenstein, M. (2015). Student and nonstudent national guard service members/veterans and their use of services for mental health symptoms. *Journal of American College Health, 63*(7), 437–446.

Bonar, T. C., & Domenici, P. L. (2011). Counseling and connecting with military undergraduates: The intersection of the military service and university life. *Journal of College Student Psychotherapy, 25*, 204–219.

Brummett, B. H., Barefoot, J. C., Siegler, I. C., Clapp-Channing, N. E., Lytle, B. L., Bosworth, H. B., & Mark, D. B. (2001). Characteristics of socially isolated patients with coronary artery disease who are at elevated risk for mortality. *Psychosomatic Medicine, 63*, 267–272.

Bryan, A. O., Theriault, J. L., & Bryan, C. J. (2015). Self-forgiveness, posttraumatic stress, and suicide attempts among military personnel and veterans. *Traumatology, 21*(1), 40–46.

Campbell, R., & Riggs, S. A. (2015). The role of psychological symptomatology and social support in the academic adjustment of previously deployed student veterans. *Journal of American College Health, 63*(7), 473–481.

Carlson, B.E., Stromwell, L.K., & Lietz, C.A. (2013). Mental health issues in recently returning women veterans: Implications for practice. *Social Work, 58*(2), 105–114.

Dennis, J. M., Phinney, J. S., & Chuateco, L. I. (2005). The role of motivation, parental support, and peer support in the academic success of ethnic minority first-generation college students. *Journal of College Student Development, 46*, 223–236.

Derogatis, L. R. (2001). *BSI 18, Brief Symptom Inventory 18: Administration, scoring and procedures manual*. Minneapolis, MN: NCS Pearson.

DiRamio, D., Ackerman, R., & Mitchell, R. L. (2008). From combat to campus: Voice of student-veterans. *NASPA Journal, 45*(1), 73–102.

Durdella, N., & Kim, Y. K. (2012). Understanding patterns of college outcomes among student veterans. *Journal of Studies in Education, 2*(2), 109–129.

Eakman, A. M., Schelly, C., & Henry, K. L. (2016). Protective and vulnerability factors contributing to resilience in post-9/11 veterans with service-related injuries in postsecondary education. *American Journal of Occupational Therapy, 70*(1), 1–10. doi:10.5014/ajot.2016.016519

Elliott, M., Gonzalez, C., & Larsen, B. (2011). U.S. military veterans transition to college: Combat, PTSD, and alienation on campus. *Journal of Student Affairs Research and Practice, 48*, 279–296.

Galambos, N. L., Barker, E. T., & Krahn, H. J. (2006). Depression, self-esteem, and anger in emerging adulthood: Seven-year trajectories. *Developmental Psychology, 42*, 350–365.

Gloria, A. M., & Robinson Kurpius, S. E. R. (1996). The validation of the Cultural Congruity Scale and the University Environment Scale with Chicano/a students. *Hispanic Journal of Behavioral Sciences, 18*(4), 533–549.

Gloria, A. M., Robinson Kurpius, S. E., Hamilton, K. D., & Wilson, M. S. (1999). African American students' persistence at a predominantly White university: Influences of social support, university comfort, and self-beliefs. *Journal of College Student Development, 40*, 257–268.

Hefner, J., & Eisenberg, D. (2009). Social support and mental health among college students. *American Journal of Orthopsychiatry, 79*, 491–499.

Kawachi, I., & Berkman, L. F. (2001). Social ties and mental health. *Journal of Urban Health: Bulletin of the New York Academy of Medicine, 78,* 458–467.

Livingston, W. G., Havice, P. A., Cawthon, T. W., & Fleming, D. S. (2011). Coming home: Student veterans' articulation of college re-enrollment. *Journal of Student Affairs Research and Practice, 48,* 315–331.

Misra-Hebert, A. D., Santurri, L.., DeChant, R., Watts, B., Rothberg, M., Sehgal, A. R., & Aron, D. C. (2015). Understanding the health needs and barriers to seeking health care of veteran students in the community. *Southern Medical Journal, 108*(8), 488–493.

Ness, B. M., Middleton, M. J., & Hildebrandt, M. J. (2015). Examining the effects of self-reported posttraumatic stress disorder symptoms and positive relations with others on self-regulated learning for student service members/veterans. *Journal of American College Health, 693*(7), 448–458.

Olsen, T., Badger, K., & McCuddy, M. D. (2014, October – December). Understanding the student veterans' college experience: An exploratory study. *The U.S. Army Medical Department Journal,* 101–108.

Pelts, M. D., & Albright, D. L. (2015). An exploratory study of student service members/veterans' mental health characteristics by sexual orientation. *Journal of American College Health, 63*(7), 508–512.

Pietrzak, R. H., Johnson, D. C., Goldstein, M. B., Malley, J. C., & Southwick, S. M. (2009). Psychological resilience and postdeployment social support protect against traumatic stress and depressive symptoms in soldiers returning from Operations Enduring Freedom and Iraqi Freedom. *Depression and Anxiety, 26*(8), 745–751.

Radloff, L. S. (1977). The CES-D Scale: A self-report depression scale for research in the general population. *Applied Psychological Measurement, 1,* 385–401.

Romero, D. H., Riggs, S. A., & Ruggero, C. (2015). Coping, family social support, and psychological symptoms among student veterans. *Journal of Counseling Psychology, 62*(2), 242–252.

Rudd, M. D., Goulding, J., & Bryan, C.J. (2011). Student veterans: A national survey exploring psychological symptoms and suicide risk. *Professional Psychology: Research and Practice, 42*(5), 354–360.

Rumann, C. B., & Hamrick, F. A. (2010). Student veterans in transition: Re-enrolling after war zone deployments. *The Journal of Higher Education, 81*(4), 431–458.

Rutledge, T., Reis, S. E., Olson, M., Owens, J., Kelsey, S. F., Pepine, C. J., ... Matthews, K. A. (2004). Social networks are associated with lower mortality rates among women with suspected coronary disease: The National Heart, Lung, and Blood Institute-sponsored Women's Ischemia Syndrome Evaluation study. *Psychosomatic Medicine, 66,* 882–888.

Schafer, W. (1992). *Stress management for wellness* (2nd ed.). Fort Worth, TX: Harcourt, Brace, Jovanovich.

Schonfeld, L., Braue, L. A., Stire, S., Gum, A. M., Cross, B. L., & Brown, L. M. (2015). Behavioral health and adjustment to college life for student service members/veterans. *Journal of American College Health, 63*(7), 428–436.

Spelman, J. F., Hunt, S. C., Seal, K. H., & Burgo-Black, A. L. (2012). Post deployment care for returning combat veterans. *Journal of General Internal Medicine, 27*(9), 1200–1209.

Solberg, V. S., O'Brien, K., Villareal, P., Kennel, R., & Davis, B. (1993). Self-efficacy and Hispanic college students: Validation of the College Self-Efficacy Instrument. *Hispanic Journal of Behavioral Science, 15,* 80–95. doi: 10.1177/07399863930151004

Strickley, V. L. (2009). *Veterans on campus* [White Paper]. Little Falls, NJ: PaperClip Communications.

Tanielian, T., & Jaycox, L. H. (Eds.). (2008). *Invisible wounds of war: Psychological and cognitive injuries, their consequences, and services to assist recovery.* Santa Monica, CA: RAND, Center for Military Health Policy Research.

Thomas, M.W. (2010). *A safe zone for veterans: Developing the VET NET Ally program to increase faculty and staff awareness and sensitivity to the needs of military veterans in higher education.* (Unpublished doctoral dissertation). California State University, Long Beach, CA.

Thompson, J. (2011). Our student soldiers: Lessons from the north and left. *Journal of College & Character, 12*(3), 1–5.

Uchino, B. N. (2004). *Social support and physical health: Understanding the health consequences of relationships.* New Haven, CT: Yale University Press.

Uchino, B. N. (2006). Social support and health: A review of physiological process potentially underlying links to disease outcomes. *Journal of Behavioral Medicine, 29,* 377–387.

U.S. Department of Defense. (2008). *Demographics 2008: Profile of the military community.* Available from http://download.militaryonesource.mil/12038/MOS/Reports/2008%20Demographics.pdf

Vallerand, R. J., Pelletier, L. G., Blais, M. R., Briere, N. M., Senecal, C., & Vallieres, E. F. (1992). The Academic Motivation Scale: A measure of intrinsic, extrinsic, and amotivation in education. *Education and Psychological Measurement, 52,* 1003–1017. doi: 10.1177/0013164492052004025

Whiteman, S. D., & Barry, A. E. (2011). A comparative analysis of student service members/veteran and civilian student drinking motives. *Journal of Student Affairs Research and Practice, 48*(3), 297–313.

Whiteman, S. D., Barry, A. E., Mroczek, D. K., & MacDermid Wadsworth, S. (2013). The development and implications of peer emotional support for student service members/veterans and civilian college students. *Journal of Counseling Psychology, 60*(2), 265–278.

Widome, R., Laska, M. N., Gulden, A., Fu, S. S., & Lust, K. (2011). Health risk behaviors of Afghanistan and Iraq war veterans attending college. *American Journal of Health Promotion, 26*(2), 101–108.

Wilcox, S. (2010). Social relationships and PTSD symptomatology in combat veterans. *Psychological Trauma: Theory, Research, Practice, and Policy, 2*(3), 175–182.

SECTION TWO
★★
STUDENT VETERANS IN THE 21ST CENTURY:
PROGRAMS AND ACADEMIC OUTCOMES

CHAPTER 5

Serving Those Who Served: Promising Institutional Practices and America's Military Veterans

Dani Molina and Tanya Ang

Since the passage of the Post-9/11 GI Bill in 2008, Americans and higher education institutions have invested in college access and success for military-connected individuals. For example, more than $53 billion has been spent through the Post-9/11 GI Bill to help educate over 1.4 million servicemembers, veterans, and their families (Worley, 2015). In higher education, a 2012 survey from the American Council on Education (ACE) and its association partners found that roughly 62% of institutions provide programs and services designed to support the higher education success of military-connected individuals (McBain, Kim, Cook, & Snead, 2012).

Nonetheless, little is known about the return on investment for the success of student veterans. For instance, how many veterans who entered college as a result of the Post-9/11 GI Bill completed their education? What factors helped facilitate or impede their progress? What can we learn from veterans who did not complete a four-year college education? Among colleges and universities, what practices had a direct impact on student veterans' likelihood of completing their college education? What percentage of veterans continued into graduate or professional school? These questions have not been answered by descriptive or empirical research to date. ACE's work, however, shows that taking a collaborative community and campus approach will best support the postsecondary aspirations of U.S. servicemembers. Here, the authors highlight strategies and best practices emerging from ACE-sponsored national and campus-based initiatives.

A History of Serving Those Who Served

ACE has a historic commitment to helping our nation's colleges and universities support servicemembers and veterans. First created in 1918, 14 higher education associations formed the Emergency Council on Education to ensure the United States had a ready supply of technically trained military personnel in

World War I. In July 1918, it adopted the name American Council on Education and invited higher education institutions to join the council (Zook, 1950). In 1942, ACE spearheaded the development of military programs for those who left college to serve in World War II. Two years later, ACE advocated for passage of the Servicemen's Readjustment Act (also known as the GI Bill) to provide education benefits to veterans of the war (ACE, 2016). Since passage of the GI Bill, ACE's Military Programs has provided a collaborative link between the U.S. Department of Defense (DOD) and higher education institutions through the review of military training and occupations for the award of equivalent college credits for servicemembers and veterans.

Now, with the drawdown of servicemembers from the wars in Iraq and Afghanistan, it is expected that more than five million post-9/11 servicemembers will leave the military by the year 2020 (U.S. Government Accountability Office, 2013). In order to prepare for the millions of servicemembers who were anticipated to transition out, ACE advocated for passage of the Post-9/11 GI Bill in 2008, which expanded postsecondary education benefits to servicemembers, veterans, and their families. At the same time, ACE held a presidential summit in 2008—Serving Those Who Serve: Higher Education and America's Veterans (ACE, 2008)—attended by more than 200 college and university presidents, senior military leaders, student veterans, campus professionals, and other key stakeholders who engaged in open dialogue about the barriers veterans face accessing and succeeding in higher education. Through the early support of organizations like the Walmart Foundation, Kresge Foundation, and Lumina Foundation, ACE created a multi-year, comprehensive agenda—the Serving Those Who Serve Initiative—to support higher education in building capacity to enroll servicemembers and veterans (ACE, 2008).

In 2008, ACE partnered with the Walmart Foundation to explore existing programs and services that support veterans in higher education, promote innovative lessons and ideas, and disseminate promising practices and research to institutions of higher learning (ACE, 2016). Through this partnership, ACE provided 20 colleges and universities across the country Success for Veterans Award Grants of $100,000 aimed at helping those institutions expand their support services for military-connected students (i.e., active duty, reserve, National Guard, veteran, and dependent; ACE, 2016).

ACE partnered with the Kresge Foundation to sponsor the Veterans Success Jam in 2010, an unprecedented national conversation about supporting veterans' higher education access and success (ACE, 2016). The three-day event brought together more than 3,000 key stakeholders, including representatives from campuses, student veterans, government agencies, and nonprofit organizations, to discuss key issues and practices, and generated new ideas and promising practices to build and enhance support for military-connected students (ACE, 2016).

Findings from the Veterans Success Jam and Success for Veterans Award Grants led to the development of the Toolkit for Veteran Friendly Institutions (www.vetfriendlytoolkit.org), a free online resource that enhances collaboration among higher education professionals and provides resources and information on programs and services aimed at supporting servicemembers, veterans, and their families in higher education (ACE, 2016). Currently, more than 2,000 registered users participate in this collaborative environment and share tools to help institutions build or enhance programs that best meet the needs of their military-connected students. The Toolkit contains real-life examples of successful veteran policies and programs while highlighting promising practices, community resources, and success stories.

Lessons Learned

Like the Toolkit for Veteran Friendly Institutions, the Serving Those Who Serve initiative (ACE, 2009, 2010, 2011, 2016) also generated a number of promising practices. Taken together, these practices provide a useful framework for developing support initiatives and include the following:

Gaining leadership support. Resources on campuses are often scarce, leading to a number of student groups vying for support to ensure the success of their individual programs. Consequently, it is important to garner the support of an individual at the administrative level who can advocate on behalf of military-connected students. Top-down support, whether from the President/ Chancellor's Office, Provost's Office, or Vice President for Student Affairs, can help to increase the success of the programs and services implemented on the campus to support military-connected students. Leadership commitment many times translates into operational policies and procedures that can sometimes take longer without top-level backing. It also reinforces the institution's commitment to the success of military-connected students.

Taking a collaborative approach to support. One of the most important factors related to military-connected student success is the need to develop collaborative community and campus partnerships. For many years, colleges and universities have developed partnerships to respond to institutional, regional, and national challenges. Institutions can use these partnerships to implement integrated and comprehensive programs and services for military members, veterans, and their dependents. Community and campus approaches that address issues, such as housing, health care, career development, financial aid, and educational benefits, help military-connected students stay in college and meet their degree completion goals. If a college or university is interested in making a big impact with few resources, establishing a veterans task force of high-level administrators and representatives from the various campus offices can go a long way. The task force can meet on a regular basis and include representatives from financial aid, the registrar's office, admissions, outreach, educational opportunity programs, the veterans certification office, housing, disability support services, academic affairs, institutional leadership, the veterans services office, and student veterans.

Engaging your military-connected students. Another important practice is to involve military-connected students in the process of creating or enhancing existing programs and services. Providing opportunities for students to be a part of the process helps an institution ensure it is meeting student needs while also communicating its commitment to military-connected students. Holding roundtable discussions, e-mailing student surveys, and including student representatives on task forces and committees are examples of ways institutions have been able to provide a sounding board for their military-connected students. Student veterans can serve as the pulse of the veteran experience in higher education, describing what works and what does not from their perspective. Moreover, campus staff can encourage military-connected students to organize and create student veteran organizations dedicated to sharing information and learning about issues that may affect others who share this status.

Enhancing communication with the military and veteran community. Too often, colleges and universities offer programs and services of which faculty, staff, and students are unaware. Prospective and current military-connected students should be informed of campus and community resources. This can be accomplished by creating a user-friendly webpage for the veterans program, detailing the institutions' policies on issues such as credit transfer and financial aid, as well as highlighting upcoming events and activities. By linking to this site from the institution's homepage, military-connected students are able to easily access this information. Other ways institutions have found success in communicating with military-connected students are through social media, such as Facebook, Twitter, and LinkedIn, or word-of-mouth from other military-connected students. Some colleges and universities have found success through e-mail; however, most institutions have found there are other, more effective ways to communicate with their military-connected students. The best way to know the most effective forms of communication is by talking with students to find out what works for them.

Establishing a single point of contact. Military-connected students benefit from having knowledgeable campus staff they can trust and who will share information and help them navigate higher education. Ideally, this single point of contact will have deep understanding of the military culture, transition issues military-connected students face, the institution's admissions and application processes, financial aid policies, and campus support services focused on retaining the student veteran until graduation. This person would also have a strong working relationship with other offices in order to provide a warm handoff no matter where the military-connected student goes.

Creating a veteran-specific orientation/workshop. Some institutions have found great success in holding veteran-specific orientations, which offer an opportunity for incoming servicemembers and veterans to learn about services and programs available to support their time in college. Moreover, these early workshops help foster a climate of inclusion and give veterans the opportunity to meet with other military-connected students who may have similar questions about the transition and onboarding process. Campus professionals should follow up with veterans shortly after campus orientation and remind them of support services that may have been overlooked.

Providing faculty and staff training. Conducting faculty and staff training on military culture and veteran education benefits is one of the best ways to reduce the stigma and misunderstanding surrounding military-connected students. A number of training opportunities exist, including Operation College Promise, Kognito, VET NET Ally, and Military Ally, all of which are information technology vendors providing support for student veterans. Most of these vendors offer training opportunities specific to regions across the country. Moreover, local Vet Centers and VA Medical Hospitals can be leveraged to raise awareness of veteran-specific mental and physical issues, such as posttraumatic stress (PTS) and traumatic brain injuries (TBI), and the importance of VA health care. These trainings help educate faculty and staff about barriers to college success and relevant campus services.

Collecting data on military-connected students and college outcomes. It is impossible to serve military-connected students if we do not know who they are and what their needs are. As a result, it is recommended that institutions of higher learning collect basic military and veteran status information from students through admissions, financial aid, and registrar's intake forms/surveys, including graduate and professional school programs. Once contact information is collected, administrators can reach out to their military-connected students and share information that will help those students address challenges they may encounter during their academic career. Moreover, having military and veteran status identifying information can help administrators answer questions about their academic performance and factors related to their college retention when merged with other institutional research data, such as demographics, grades, and financial aid information.

Critical Areas for Support

In addition to these more general practices, several critical areas require special attention from higher education when serving military-connected students. These include pre-enrollment advising, financial aid, academic support, and degree aspirations beyond the bachelor's. Each is discussed in greater detail in the sections that follow.

Pre-Enrollment Advising

Given the amount of time, effort, sacrifice, and money students devote to the pursuit of postsecondary education, it is imperative that they have the necessary information to choose an institution and degree program that will provide the largest return on their investment. Many servicemembers and veterans are first-generation college students who do not have access to the same types of services available to high school students going through the college admissions process. Other military-connected individuals have been out of school for a long period of time and do not feel adequately prepared for the academic rigors of a college education. Additionally, many are not aware of the resources and support systems needed as they choose and apply to institutions of higher learning. There are many factors prospective students need to consider when choosing a college or university, but students often do not have access to this basic higher education information, such as what it means to be an accredited institution, the types of degree programs available (i.e., associate, bachelor's, master's, certifications, and licensures), and the differences among private, public, for-profit, or not-for-profit institutions.

Providing the necessary guidance and information and setting prospective military-connected students up for success early helps them make informed decisions about when and where to use their finite GI Bill benefits to meet their education and career goals. Therefore, it is critical to have frequent planning discussions prior to enrollment, so that entering students have a clear outline of coursework needed to complete their program of study, especially if that includes transferring to other institutions that will enhance their career prospects.

Between April 2007 and December 2014, ACE had the opportunity to provide pre-enrollment advising and support to more than 800 severely injured servicemembers through its Severely Injured Military Veterans: Fulfilling Their Dreams (SIMV) program. During their recovery at Walter Reed National Military Medical Center in Bethesda, Maryland, servicemembers were introduced to an academic advisor who assisted them with developing individual educational plans based on their academic and career goals (DiRamio & Spires, 2009). The counselor also arranged the necessary support to prepare for pre-enrollment placement tests, locate institutions best suited to their goals, and prepare and submit admissions applications to institutions of their choice.

Through this work, ACE was able to help a significant number of servicemembers and veterans attain a goal many had never thought possible. Many not only finished their bachelor's degrees but went on to pursue graduate degrees. Based on the success of this work, ACE began to document and look to find emerging promising practices that could be replicated by others throughout the country to reach a larger number of servicemembers and veterans to help them navigate the complex and often cumbersome process of choosing, applying, and getting accepted to an institution of higher learning.

Service to School helps veterans gain admission into undergraduate and graduate programs at the nation's top colleges and universities and to maximize their finite GI Bill education benefits. More than 200 ambassadors made up of former and current student veterans assist and mentor veterans through the admissions and application process. Institutions of higher learning, especially community colleges, can share this valuable information with veterans who are interested in receiving a college education from one of the nation's top tier institutions, an important endeavor given that too few enlisted military veterans earn an education from selective institutions (Service to School, 2016).

To further explore and illuminate the importance of admissions and academic advising, ACE spearheaded the Service Member and Veteran Academic Advising Summit in June 2014. The ultimate goal of the two-day summit was to develop strategies for providing support to servicemembers and veterans through the college application and pre-enrollment process (ACE, 2015). Approximately 100 participants from higher education institutions, federal agencies, military and veteran service organizations, the U.S. Armed Forces, employers, and student veterans discussed existing and emerging issues related to the college application, admissions, and the pre-enrollment advising process for servicemembers and veterans. Five themes emerged from the meeting, and several recommendations for action were created to enhance the likelihood servicemembers and veterans will enroll in colleges and universities that will meet their academic and career goals (ACE, 2015). These themes included the need for

- individual, flexible, and relationship-centered support services;

- stakeholder organizations to advocate for servicemembers and veterans, but also for servicemembers and veterans to be empowered to advocate for themselves;

- communication among military branches, federal agencies, higher education institutions, and employers to maintain efficient processes and facilitate collaboration toward common goals;

- full-spectrum navigation from military recruitment to civilian employment, particularly in the application of continued assistance after degree completion to promote meaningful employment; and

- building capacity, knowledge, and awareness across stakeholder groups regarding the concerns central to servicemembers' and veterans' college education.

Financial Aid

Too few veterans will enter higher education after military service. Even fewer will go on to earn a bachelor's or advanced degree (i.e., master's or doctoral degree). The Student Veterans of America (SVA) found that roughly half (52%) of GI Bill users earned a postsecondary credential between 2002 and 2010 (Cate, 2014). Educational attainment varied from earning a certificate to doctorate and everything in between (i.e., associate and bachelor's degrees). However, little empirical research to date shows how veterans approach and think about higher education, or their perceptions on the need to receive a college education. Chapter 1 in this volume provides some insight into motivations for pursuing postsecondary education among military-connected individuals.

Recent research from ACE and NASPA shows that, although earning money for college is a prime reason for joining the military, a large share of veterans (41%) do not receive VA education benefits—a factor that may lead many veterans to drop out or not enroll in higher education (Molina & Morse, 2015). Additionally, the report showed that more than 30% of veterans received loans, even though the GI Bill was designed to cover a large part, if not all, of the costs associated with going to college. Remarkably, the report also showed that 52% of veterans received grant aid, indicating that veterans continue to have unmet financial need even after including VA education benefits (Molina & Morse, 2015). See Chapter 2 for a more detailed discussion of these issues.

Although some veterans may have not met the 36-month time on active duty requirement to receive 100% of the Post-9/11 GI Bill, more research is needed to examine whether time-in-service or other circumstances are related to need for additional financial support (Molina, 2015). Research shows that college affordability plays an important role in the enrollment, persistence, and completion, particularly for low-income and racial/ethnic minorities. Therefore, we need to better understand how financial aid and veteran education benefits interact to promote or inhibit college access and success (Molina, 2015).

Another important scenario to consider is whether veterans are making efficient use of their education benefits. Researchers from RAND Corporation noted that several DoD and VA education benefits are available to veterans in tandem, which could lead veterans to deplete their finite benefits without earning a college education (Buryk, Trail, Gonzalez, Miller, & Friedman, 2015). On one hand, veterans who use their GI Bill benefits and federal student aid simultaneously are likely to deplete education benefits more quickly. On the other hand, veterans who strategically use one benefit before the other may be more likely to persist given that there is additional financial support for completing a baccalaureate degree.

As the number of post-9/11 veterans entering college increases, higher education professionals can support their access and success by ensuring that military-connected individuals understand education benefit eligibility and availability. Military-connected students have several options for financial support at the federal, state, campus, and private levels. However, it is imperative that they are educated on financial aid options and how to apply.

Academic Support

A number of organizations exist to support the enrollment and progression of military-connected individuals in higher education. For instance, Veterans Upward Bound is designed to help servicemembers develop their academic skills through tutoring and remedial work in critical subjects, such as writing, English, and mathematics, as well as support in completing the college and financial aid applications. This federally funded program through the U.S. Department of Education can help higher education institutions with limited understanding of military-connected culture, academic tutoring, and counseling resources to support veterans who may need support tailored to their needs (U.S. Department of Education, 2016).

Another organization, the Warrior Scholar Project, provides enlisted veterans free one- and two-week academic boot camps hosted at the nation's top colleges and universities during the summer. The program helps veterans build their academic self-confidence, prepares them to be leaders in college, and teaches them how to think critically in higher education. Higher education institutions, particularly community colleges, can connect their student veterans to the Warrior–Scholar Project so that they receive free academic support needed to succeed in the university setting (Warrior–Scholar Project, 2016).

The Next Step: Graduate and Professional School

Researchers have documented the importance of earning a college education. According to Georgetown University's Center on Education and the Workforce (Carnevale, Rose, & Cheah, 2011), a college degree continues to be key in providing economic opportunity, positively influencing an individual's potential earnings as more education is earned. Moreover, the report demonstrates that "all graduate degree holders can expect lifetime earnings at least double that of those with only a high school diploma" (Carnevale et al., 2011, p. 4). The authors also found that individuals with doctoral and professional degrees had the highest median lifetime earnings compared with others with less education.

Given the increasing reliance on four-year and advanced degrees for social and economic mobility, academic advisors and other campus professionals should encourage veterans to pursue an education beyond a bachelor's degree. According to the U.S. Department of Veterans Affairs, between 2000 and 2009, "a higher percentage of veterans than non-veterans had completed some college, but not a degree" (U.S. Department of Veterans Affairs, 2011, p. 4). Among the post-9/11 generation of veterans, only 27% had earned a bachelor's or advanced degree (i.e., master's, doctoral, or professional; U.S. Department of Veterans Affairs, 2015). These findings demonstrate that, although veterans have additional financial support relative to their nonveteran counterparts, there remain barriers to earning a four-year or advanced education. Therefore, campus and community professionals should cultivate a narrative around increasing the college participation and progression rates of veterans, particularly for veterans who aspire to earn less than a bachelor's degree.

Conclusion

ACE has had a long history helping those who served in the military to access and succeed in higher education. With the expectation of more than five million post-9/11 servicemembers transitioning out of the military by 2020, colleges and universities must take steps to ensure the appropriate support systems are in place to serve this growing, yet often misunderstood, student population. This chapter offered a number of promising practices centered on supporting military-connected individuals to enter and complete college. Institutions of higher learning can learn about effective practices and institutional policies from other colleges and universities through the Toolkit for Veteran Friendly Institutions. Some of the most important findings from ACE's more than eight-year effort include the need for pre-enrollment advising and education about available financial aid. Too few veterans enter higher education and even fewer will eventually earn a four-year education. Educating individuals with prior or current military service about the need for a college education, and a graduate education in particular, will help meet our national attainment goals and will ensure that our post-9/11 generation of military-connected individuals have prosperous and rewarding futures.

References

American Council on Education (ACE). (2008). *Serving those who serve: Higher education and America's veterans* (Issue Brief). Washington, DC: Author.

American Council on Education (ACE). (2009). *Serving those who serve: Making your institution veteran-friendly.* Washington, DC: Author.

American Council on Education (ACE). (2010). *Veterans success jam: Ensuring success for returning veterans.* Washington, DC: Author.

American Council on Education (ACE). (2011). *Promising practices and veterans' education: Outcomes and recommendations from success for veterans award grants.* Washington, DC: Author.

American Council on Education (ACE). (2015). *ACE's 2015 service member and veteran academic advising summit report.* Washington, DC: Author.

American Council on Education (ACE). (2016). *Center for Education Attainment and Innovation: Who we are, who we serve* [Brochure]. Washington, DC: Author.

Buryk, P., Trail, T. E., Gonzalez, G. C., Miller, L. L., & Friedman, E. M. (2015). *Federal educational assistance programs available to service members: Program features and recommendations for improved delivery.* Santa Monica, CA: RAND Corporation. Retrieved from http://www.rand.org/pubs/research_reports/RR664.html

Carnevale, A. P., Rose, S. J., & Cheah, B. (2011). *The college payoff: Education, occupations, and lifetime earnings.* Retrieved from http://cew.georgetown. edu/collegepayoffhttps://cew.georgetown.edu/report/the-college-payoff/

Cate, C. A. (2014). *Million records project: Research from Student Veterans of America.* Washington, DC: Student Veterans of America. Retrieved from http://studentveterans.org/images/Reingold_Materials/mrp/download-materials/mrp_Full_report.pdf.

DiRamio, D., & Spires, M. (2009). Partnering to assist disabled veterans in transition. In D. DiRamio & R. Ackerman (Eds.), *Creating a veteran-friendly campus: Strategies for transition and success* (New Directions for Student Services No. 126, pp. 81–88). Hoboken, NJ: Wiley.

McBain, L., Kim, Y. M., Cook, B. J., & Snead, K. M. (2012). *From soldier to student II: Assessing campus programs for service members and veterans.* Washington, DC: American Council on Education.

Molina, D. (2015, December 7). *#EducateVeterans on student financial aid* [Blog post]. Retrieved from http://higheredtoday.org/2015/12/07/educateveterans-on-student-financial-aid/

Molina, D., & Morse, A. (2015). *Military-connected undergraduates: Exploring differences between National Guard, reserve, active duty, and veterans in higher education.* Washington, DC: American Council on Education & NASPA – Student Affairs Administrators in Higher Education.

Service to School. (2016). *Service to School.* Retrieved from http://service2school. org/

U.S. Department of Education. (2016). *Veterans Upward Bound.* Retrieved from http://www2.ed.gov/programs/triovub/index.html

U.S. Department of Veterans Affairs. (2011). *Educational attainment of veterans: 2000 to 2009.* Retrieved from http://www.va.gov/vetdata/docs/SpecialReports/education_FINAL.pdf

U.S. Department of Veterans Affairs. (2015). *Profile of post-9/11 veterans: 2013.* Retrieved from http://www.va.gov/vetdata/docs/SpecialReports/Post_911_Veterans_Profile_2013.pdf

U.S. Government Accountability Office. (2013). *VA education benefits: Student characteristics and outcomes vary across schools.* Washington, DC: Author.

Warrior–Scholar Project. (2016). *The Warrior–Scholar Project.* Retrieved from http://warrior-scholar.org/

Worley, R. M., II. (2015). *Education service update.* Presented at annual conference of the Western Association of Veterans Education Specialists (WAVES). Anaheim, CA: WAVES. Retrieved from http://uswaves.org/images/2015/final/Education_Service_Update.pdf

Zook, G. F. (1950). The American Council on Education. *The Phi Delta Kappan, 31*(7), 312–318.

CHAPTER 6

Navigating Toward Academic Success: Peer Support for Student Veterans

Michelle Kees, Brittany Risk, Chrysta Meadowbrooke, Jane L. Spinner, and Marcia Valenstein

Student veterans have been an important presence on college campuses since the passage of the 1944 Montgomery GI Bill in support of World War II veterans. The Post-9/11 Veterans Education Assistance Program, or Post-9/11 GI Bill, took effect in 2009, and more than one million people benefited during its first four years (U.S. Department of Veterans Affairs, 2013). An estimated five million people will be classified as post-9/11 veterans by 2020, significantly increasing the potential use of these benefits (U.S. Government Accountability Office, 2013). Peer-support programs offer an innovative and effective approach for helping student veterans and the academic institutions they attend make the best use of the large-scale investment in veteran education. This chapter describes Peer Advisors for Veteran Education (PAVE), a nationwide peer program designed to help student veterans achieve personal and academic success.

Student Veterans Face Many Challenges

Veterans in general may experience a number of common challenges when transitioning to life outside the military, such as adjusting to a civilian lifestyle, managing economic changes, navigating interpersonal relationships, and establishing a new self-identity (Institute of Medicine, 2013; Sayer, Carlson, & Frazier, 2014; Werber et al., 2010). For some veterans, accommodating to physical injuries or disabilities is also a reality (CDC, NIH, DoD, and VA Leadership Panel, 2013; Taylor, Morin, Gonzalez, Motel, & Patten, 2011). Additionally, mental health issues can be a concern, with heightened rates of alcohol misuse, depression, anxiety, and posttraumatic stress disorder (PTSD) seen in many veteran populations (Barry, Whiteman, MacDermid Wadsworth, & Hitt, 2012; Calhoun, Elter, Jones, Kudler, & Straits-Tröster, 2008; Thomas et al., 2010;

Tanielian & Jaycox, 2008; Rudd, Goulding, & Bryan, 2011; Valenstein et al., 2015). Moving into a student role as a veteran or servicemember can compound these issues and generate additional stress.

Student veterans often have to manage stressors not typically faced by traditional college students, including the needs to refresh their academic skills after time away from schooling, negotiate the differences between military and academic cultures, navigate complex requirements to claim GI Bill benefits, and tend to interpersonal relationships that may have already experienced some disruption (Barry, Whiteman, & MacDermid Wadsworth, 2014; DiRamio, Ackerman, & Mitchell, 2008; Durdella & Kim, 2012; Griffin & Gilbert, 2015; Rumann & Hamrick, 2010). Student veterans in a RAND study ($n = 220$; Steele, Salcedo, & Coley, 2010) identified the following as moderate or major problems while in college: financially supporting self and family (66% of the sample); balancing coursework and other responsibilities (56%); and finding like-minded peers or staff (42%). While certainly not all veterans struggle during college, there is clear evidence supporting a need for services to help these students achieve their academic and career goals.

Academic Institutions Also Need Support

Academic institutions face their own challenges in supporting the large number of post-9/11 veterans enrolling in college. Institutions are increasingly recognizing the unique needs of student veterans, but funding and implementing programs to support veterans has been difficult (Callahan & Jarrat, 2014; Hitt et al., 2015; Vacchi, 2012). For example, the National Center for Education Statistics surveyed 1,520 higher education institutions and found that 96% of the institutions actively enroll military servicemembers and veterans (Queen & Lewis, 2014). However, the majority of these institutions did not yet have a comprehensive infrastructure in place to support student veterans' well-being and academic success. Few of the institutions had customized student services for this population in the areas of academic advising (27%), career planning (24%), academic support/tutoring (17%), or help with finding non-work-study jobs (19%). Only 22% of the institutions surveyed offered mental health counseling designed to meet the special needs of servicemembers and veterans.

The RAND study on promoting student veteran well-being identified several key action points for academic institutions, including the availability of dedicated resources for veteran services coordinators, consistent opportunities for sharing veteran-focused campus information with student veterans, and encouraging the creation of student veteran communities (Steele et al., 2010). A report published by the American Council on Education recommended improving assistance to veterans with the psychosocial aspects of transitioning into college and also offering professional development training to staff and faculty to increase their knowledge and sensitivity about student veterans' experiences (McBain, Kim, Cook, & Snead, 2012). The needs of student veterans and educational institutions combine to create an imperative to develop sustainable programs that will help increase these students' well-being on campuses and better position them for academic and employment success.

The Power of Peers

Support services can be beneficial for helping student veterans adjust to college and achieve their academic goals (Lang & Powers, 2011). However, many student veterans are reluctant to seek help because of perceived military norms (e.g., strength, self-reliance, stoicism) and concerns about stigma (Alfred, Hammer, & Good, 2014; Blais & Renshaw, 2013; Bonar, Bohnert, Walters, Ganoczy, & Valenstein, 2015; Dickstein, Vogt, Handa, & Litz, 2010; DiRamio, Jarvis, Iverson, Seher, & Anderson, 2015; Livingston, Havice, Cawthon, & Fleming, 2011). Peer-to-peer programs have been identified as an approach to overcoming these barriers (Nelson, Abraham, Walters, Pfeiffer, & Valenstein, 2014; Zinzow, Britt, McFadden, Burnette, & Gillispie, 2012). For student veterans, peer programs are a natural fit. Military service is unlike any other human experience. No one knows more about the issues facing a student veteran—in combat or on campus—than another student veteran. Peer programs capitalize on the central tenet of *nemo resideo* ("leave no one behind") and the importance of the buddy system, which are woven throughout the military ethos, beginning in the early days of basic training and carrying through battle. Building on recommendations from the RAND study (Steele et al., 2010), peer programs also create a natural opportunity for community among student veterans. Likewise, peers are a key component on college campuses and are often tapped to help incoming students adjust to college life (Shook & Keup, 2012; Swenson, Nordstrom, & Hiester, 2008).

Veteran peers who have "been there" can offer a unique perspective in normalizing the student veteran experience (Cornish, Thys, Vogel, & Wade, 2014). Student veterans who have been on campus for a year or two are likely to have important insights into what might make the transition to college easier for incoming student veterans. Within the context of the buddy system, they are often willing to share this knowledge with new student veterans to make their early experiences more positive and successful. Peer programs can also foster a sense of connectedness and belonging for student veterans, two factors that are important to academic success (Hausmann, Schofield, & Woods, 2007; Hoffman, Richmond, Morrow, & Salomone, 2003; Whiteman, Barry, Mroczek, & MacDermid Wadsworth, 2013) but that have been found lacking in student veterans (DiRamio et al., 2008; Durdella & Kim, 2012).

Peers likely also have an advantage when it comes to building rapport with student veterans. Common ground, combined with good communication skills that convey respect and build trust, can open the door for ongoing dialogue and relationship building (Mead, Hilton, & Curtis, 2001; Davidson, Bellamy, Guy, & Miller, 2012). Peers may be particularly effective in recognizing and overcoming stigma, assuring student veterans that asking for help is not a sign of weakness (Solomon, 2004). Peers can thus be a credible source of support for student veterans, connecting around a shared experience and facilitating connections to needed resources. A well-designed peer program could offer a strategic solution for academic institutions seeking to better support their student veteran population.

A Promising Approach: Peer Advisors for Veteran Education

Peer Advisors for Veteran Education (PAVE) provides a promising approach for supporting student veterans as they transition from military to academia and ultimately to successful employment. PAVE was developed at the University of Michigan in 2012 in partnership with Student Veterans of America (SVA) specifically to meet the needs of student veterans on college campuses. Its design was informed by an existing peer program for servicemembers and veterans, Buddy-to-Buddy (Greden et al., 2010; Dalack et al., 2010), which is recognized as a best practice peer model for military populations by the Defense Centers of Excellence for Psychological Health and Traumatic Brain Injury (Money et al., 2011). Leaders in higher education and mental health, the Veterans Health Administration, the military, student veteran stakeholders, and SVA came together to design PAVE.

PAVE is a peer-to-peer program that connects incoming student veterans with successful student veterans already on campus. Through peer support, PAVE builds on the camaraderie that veterans experience in the military to create a sense of community and facilitate access to resources that contribute to academic and personal success. The goals of PAVE are to help student veterans navigate college life; increase feelings of connectedness to campus; identify mental health concerns or other challenges (e.g., educational, social, financial) that may affect functioning or academic success; and link student veterans to appropriate on- and/or off-campus resources as needed.

The following subsections describe the roles and activities of team members implementing PAVE at campuses nationwide and outline the main elements of the program.

The PAVE Model

PAVE uses a tiered model of training and implementation in which the National and Campus Teams work together to help meet the needs of student veterans (Figure 6.1). The National Team provides training, support, coaching, and technical assistance to the Campus Teams. The Campus Teams, which include a representative from campus administration, the Veteran Services Coordinator, and a Team Leader, then recruit and support Peer Advisors as they reach out to and engage with student veterans on campus.

National Team. The National Team is housed at M-SPAN (Military Support Programs and Networks) at the University of Michigan Depression Center and Department of Psychiatry. Members of the National Team support all aspects of implementation and tailor the PAVE program for campuses across the country. The National Team establishes and maintains contact with student affairs offices, advises Veteran Services Coordinators, facilitates joint conference calls and webinars with PAVE Campus Teams, produces monthly newsletters with program tips, and provides technical and logistical support to Campus Teams as they implement PAVE. As subject matter experts on military and veteran populations, peer support, outreach/recruitment, and mental health, the National Team also creates training materials, facilitates training for each campus, and oversees the collection of data for program evaluation. In addition, through an established partnership, SVA provides support for PAVE at the national and local chapter levels.

Campus Team. The Campus Team at each participating school consists of campus administration and trained student veterans. Campus administration includes leaders such as the dean of students, key faculty members, or student services administrators invested in student veterans. These members of the Campus Team act as University Champions for PAVE, securing vital support at the institutional level so that staff and students can perform the ongoing activities of the program. The Veteran Services Coordinator (VSC), or similar representative from the student veteran office, is integral to the Campus Team and to implementing PAVE. The VSC provides on-campus oversight of the PAVE program, drawing on training, materials, and tailored support from the National Team to ensure the program's success and sustainability. Several VSC PAVE responsibilities incorporate volunteer management activities: recruiting

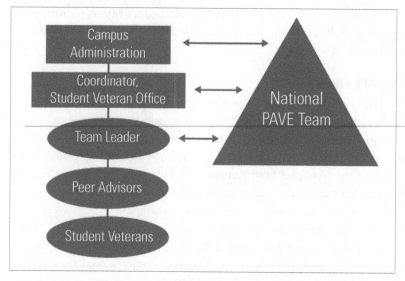

Figure 6.1. The PAVE model of tiered roles for training and implementation.

and supervising Team Leaders; facilitating recruitment and training of Peer Advisors; and providing motivation, encouragement, and support to all student volunteers. VSCs interact with the National Team to report on program activities, identify successes and challenges, and help generate best practices. Through their work, VSCs may also identify gaps in services and resources on campus.

The Team Leader is also a critical member of the Campus Team and serves as the student veteran manager of the PAVE program. Team Leaders serve as ambassadors for the program; recruit, train, and oversee Peer Advisors; and engage student veterans who would benefit from the program. Like VSCs, Team Leaders' activities include encouraging and supporting the Peer Advisors. Team Leaders also identify resources on and off campus that student veterans might need and develop referral procedures for these services. On a regular basis, Team Leaders review interaction logs completed by Peer Advisors as they engage with students, and report to VSCs and the National Team about program activities.

Each Campus Team includes a cadre of Peer Advisors. Peer Advisors are experienced and trained student veterans who serve as peers to incoming student veterans. Working directly on the frontline of the PAVE program, Peer Advisors establish rapport and relationships with student veterans through outreach and check-ins, documenting their work in an online reporting system. Depending on the campus size and needs, Peer Advisors may be assigned one to five incoming student veterans, sometimes matched on characteristics such as the military branch in which they served or their academic major. Peer Advisors are trained to provide information on the easy needs first (e.g., parking, places to eat, social gatherings), which begins to build the credibility and trust essential to helping with more difficult challenges that may emerge later.

Student Veterans. At the heart of PAVE are the student veterans associated with the school—all student veterans, not just those who might be struggling. PAVE creates the structure and space so that every student veteran can access a community of support to help maximize their success on campus.

PAVE Activity. The PAVE program focuses on three pillars of activity:

- **Outreach:** Launching successful strategies for connecting to student veterans on campus, sharing awareness about the PAVE program, and engaging student veterans in peer support;

- **Support:** Providing peer support according to the needs of each participating student veteran; and

- **Linkage to resources:** Identifying commonly requested services and programs, establishing relationships with staff in each of these programs, determining pathways for making referrals and warm hand-offs to key services, and referring student veterans to solid, reliable resources.

Campus Teams carry out these activities to enable the core of the work: the contacts and relationships between Peer Advisors and student veterans. Through one-on-one outreach, Peer Advisors personally connect with other students, offer support, and link student veterans with appropriate on- and off-campus resources that can help them successfully navigate campus life.

Program Elements

The National and Campus Teams work together closely to establish and sustain PAVE on individual campuses. The main elements of PAVE include training, implementation support, online tools, and program evaluation (Figure 6.2).

Training. Using a train-the-trainer model to support program sustainability, the National Team conducts in-person training with the Campus Teams, including University Champions, VSCs, and Team Leaders. The VSCs and Team Leaders then train the Peer Advisors at their schools. The training curriculum incorporates a series of modules focused on the three pillars of PAVE (Outreach, Support, and Linkage to Resources), with a mixture of didactic, interactive, media-based, and vignette teaching approaches, giving participants a chance to

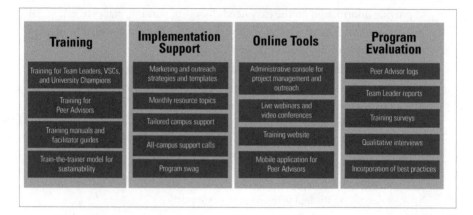

Training	Implementation Support	Online Tools	Program Evaluation
Training for Team Leaders, VSCs, and University Champions	Marketing and outreach strategies and templates	Administrative console for project management and outreach	Peer Advisor logs
Training for Peer Advisors	Monthly resource topics	Live webinars and video conferences	Team Leader reports
Training manuals and facilitator guides	Tailored campus support	Training website	Training surveys
Train-the-trainer model for sustainability	All-campus support calls	Mobile application for Peer Advisors	Qualitative interviews
	Program swag		Incorporation of best practices

Figure 6.2. Elements of the PAVE program. (VSCs = Veteran Services Coordinators)

practice new skills. Training modules include an overview of the PAVE model; delineation of roles, responsibilities, and boundaries; best practice outreach and engagement strategies; key communication skills helpful for engaging and supporting peers; and approaches to building a network of on- and off-campus resources. The training culminates in a tailored work plan for implementing PAVE developed by each Campus Team. Participants also receive a compendium of written and electronic materials to support campus implementation and sustainability.

Multiple interactive exercises included in training give Team Leaders and Peer Advisors practice in the skills they will use when connecting with student veterans. For example, Campus Teams learn about *warm hand-offs*—referring student veterans directly to a specific, identified person whenever possible, rather than just handing out a phone number. Calling ahead to make sure the student veteran is expected goes a long way toward making the veteran feel taken care of, building trust and credibility. Checking on how things went with both the veteran and the referral resource, as appropriate, further builds relationships and paves the way for future referrals. Providing training opportunities to practice handling specific situations like these helps generate discussion among the Campus Team members about different approaches and increases confidence in their ability to apply new skills and knowledge.

Training also provides information about the signs and symptoms of common mental health problems that can occur in veterans transitioning from the military to academia and includes addressing stigma as an important issue to overcome in order for someone to be willing to ask for help. For example, one training activity focuses on how stigma impacts help-seeking behavior—for help of any kind, not just mental health—and the strategies that can be used to reduce stigma and barriers to care for student veterans. Though it is rare for Team Leaders and Peer Advisors to encounter a student veteran who is suicidal or exhibiting dangerous behavior, the training contains information to prepare them to recognize the potential need for professional intervention, and to contact people who can take over in such emergency situations (e.g., 911, the National Suicide Hotline, campus-specific emergency protocols and resources).

Peers in helping roles need to receive support too, so training materials encourage Team Leaders and Peer Advisors to stay strong by managing stress, getting enough sleep, eating right, exercising, and having their own support systems, including regular debriefing with others in PAVE or with a counselor. In addition, VSC training includes suggestions for volunteer management and how to help Team Leaders and Peer Advisors find the right balance to maintain their own health and academic success.

Implementation support. The National Team provides implementation support to Campus Teams in a variety of ways. Marketing the program on campus and reaching out to student veterans who could benefit from PAVE is a primary ongoing activity. Outreach requires some trial and error to establish which strategies work best for each campus. The National Team provides tailored support to Campus Teams about multiple approaches, such as using social media, newsletters, and events to tell student veterans about PAVE and stay connected with them. Examples of successful events held on PAVE campuses include new student veteran breakfasts, speaker presentations, résumé workshops, military family days, and service days for veteran causes. The National Team provides templates that Campus Teams can adapt for their communications with student veterans (e.g., initial contact and follow-up e-mails, newsletters, event posters). Items such as T-shirts and mugs displaying the PAVE logo help raise PAVE's visibility on campus, while also conveying appreciation to student volunteers for their efforts.

Another aspect of tailored support occurs as the National Team helps VSCs develop succession plans for the Team Leader and Peer Advisor positions, since student volunteers are often juniors or seniors who cycle out of their PAVE roles when they graduate. VSCs also receive assistance in determining selection criteria to use when recruiting Team Leaders and Peer Advisors, such as their own successful adjustment to campus, commitment to the program, leadership and communication skills, and capacity to take on additional responsibilities.

Monthly resource topics for review and discussion reinforce and add further depth to the initial training received by Campus Teams. All-campus support calls offer an opportunity for Campus Teams to talk with the National Team about challenging situations, share ideas, learn about resources, and receive support from each other.

Online tools. The National Team hosts a secure, interactive platform for project management and outreach. This software platform helps VSCs and Team Leaders facilitate PAVE. The site enables each Campus Team to both get an overview of Peer Advisor activities at their school and drill down into specific interactions logged by Peer Advisors. Team Leaders, VSCs, and the National Team can review the logs, provide feedback when necessary, and keep track of Peer Advisors' follow-up plans after each peer interaction. Regularly updated logs also establish a record of successes and potential areas for improvement.

As part of an expansion of the program in 2016, the National Team oversaw the creation of new technological components to support large-scale implementation of PAVE. This includes an administrative console for VSCs and Team Leaders to track and connect with student veterans, a campus-tailored mobile application to provide Peer Advisors with easy access to resources and to track their work with student veterans, and a web-based training program for Peer Advisors. Online tools facilitate other means of sharing information as well. The online platform is a storehouse for useful ideas, information, resources, and sample interactions that Peer Advisors and other team members can revisit as they work on PAVE. The National Team also provides support and information to the Campus Teams through live webinars and video conferences.

Program evaluation. PAVE employs multiple methods to obtain data and feedback that help document program use and guide improvements over time. Peer Advisor logs contain such information as dates and types of contacts (e.g., e-mail, phone, in person); reason for contact (e.g., introduction to PAVE, event reminders, informal socializing, requests for assistance); and any identified areas of concern (e.g., academic, financial, VA benefits, housing, mental health). The logs also indicate referrals made to specific resources (e.g., campus veterans office, academic advising, tutoring, financial aid, counseling, VA services). Peer Advisors may include descriptions of interactions that provide rich insight into the challenges and successes of student veterans on campus. Keeping updated logs helps the Campus and National Teams better advocate for student veteran needs, enhance available resources, and develop new avenues of programming.

Through Team Leader reports, the VSC and the National Team learn about program progress as well as any concerns that need attention. This helps the National Team provide support to the Campus Team and can also generate ideas for changes that might benefit the PAVE program locally or nationally.

Surveys of Campus Team members before and after training focus on changes in knowledge and attitudes (e.g., about student veteran culture, strategies for outreach and engagement, available resources, mental health concerns, effects of stigma), degree of confidence and competence in applying newly learned concepts to implement PAVE, and satisfaction with training sessions and materials. Qualitative interviews with VSCs, Team Leaders, and Peer Advisors several months after PAVE training provide an avenue for deeper reflection on the PAVE implementation process, including experiences with the materials and tools, programmatic and technical support, perceived degree of success in implementing PAVE, and barriers to implementation.

Information gathered through these means not only facilitates program evaluation but also leads to development of best practices. The National Team incorporates these ideas in the PAVE program design and rolls them out for Campus Teams to implement.

The Impact of PAVE

Implementation of PAVE has occurred across several phases since 2012, with ample training and support time built in to establish the program at each campus. Between August 2013 and July 2016, PAVE was operational at 13 campuses across the country, with the bulk of activity occurring during the traditional fall and spring semesters. Within that period, the National Team provided training to 17 VSCs and University Champions (two trainings) and 262 Team Leaders and Peer Advisors (56 trainings). The response to trainings was very positive, with nearly all participants stating they were satisfied or very satisfied with their training sessions. Attendees noted the positive atmosphere, small groups, and knowledgeable trainers as favorite elements of the training.

Making a Difference in the Lives of Student Veterans

Peer Advisors use an online logging system to track their activity with student veterans through the PAVE program. A review of logging records across a three-year period (from August 2013 to August 2016) showed that PAVE reached 2,143 student veterans, with more than 3,900 logs. A log might include a single contact or a series of contacts over time, with contacts including e-mail, text, telephone call, one-on-one meeting, or group activity. As a caveat, ensuring consistent logging of student veteran contacts has been a challenge for some Campus Teams, and these numbers likely represent an underestimation of program reach.

The logging records reflect the ongoing one-on-one contacts and group events that sustain PAVE's community of support for all student veterans, not just those who might be struggling. Yet many student veterans do struggle, and PAVE can be particularly helpful for them. Peer Advisor logs indicate the following top three concerns identified during interactions with student veterans:

- education (e.g., studying, tutoring, registering for classes, questions about specific majors);

- benefits/claims (e.g., eligibility, enrollment, claims processing for VA health care, questions about GI Bill); and

- mental health (e.g., depression, anxiety, posttraumatic stress, anger, suicidal ideation, substance use, sleep disruption or nightmares).

The vignettes below from Peer Advisor logs illustrate some of the ways PAVE Campus Teams have helped student veterans by connecting them with other student veterans and, when needed, with resources to address their concerns. Note that while a particular issue sometimes takes center stage, stressors can become interwoven during a student veteran's tenure in college, requiring sustained interpersonal support and referral to a range of services to help student veterans succeed.

Welcoming into the community. A Peer Advisor reached out to a student veteran to welcome her to campus and introduce himself as a Peer Advisor with PAVE. He offered to provide a campus tour before classes started, and the student veteran agreed to meet. The Peer Advisor showed the student veteran the buildings where her fall classes would be held and the locations of other campus resources, including the veteran services office. He also invited her to the upcoming student veteran welcome dinner and the next student veterans club meeting. The student veteran expressed her appreciation to the Peer Advisor for reaching out, providing the tour, and helping her connect with other student veterans, especially since she was new to the state and did not know anyone nearby.

Helping with educational issues. A student veteran began coming to the veteran lounge on campus to study. His assigned Peer Advisor made a connection with him there over the course of several encounters. Eventually the student shared that he had a long history of untreated anxiety, which made studying difficult, and he had failed a mid-term. The Peer Advisor referred the student to the local VA for help with anxiety, and the student began treatment. The Peer Advisor also wanted to refer the student to the campus tutoring center but learned that the center was at capacity and unable to assist at that time. The Peer Advisor talked with the Team Leader, who found other veteran volunteers who could help tutor the student. The Peer Advisor and Team Leader provided ongoing support to the student veteran, helping him make progress and stay connected during this challenging time.

Helping with benefits questions. In the veteran lounge on campus, a student veteran overheard a Peer Advisor talking about Chapter 31 benefits with another individual and asked what they were. The Peer Advisor explained and discussed the differences between Chapter 31 (Vocational Rehabilitation and Employment, or VR&E) and Chapter 33 (Post-9/11 GI Bill). After the conversation, the Peer Advisor researched the VA website for further information about VR&E benefits, e-mailed the links to the student veteran, and connected him via e-mail with the vocational rehabilitation counselor serving their university. The student veteran pursued VR&E benefits and expressed gratitude for the referral to the counselor. The Peer Advisor and student veteran now regularly see each other on campus to touch base and socialize.

Helping with mental health concerns. A Peer Advisor noticed toward the end of a semester that his interactions with one of his assigned student veterans had become very brief, with the student veteran quickly stating he was doing great and not giving details. At the start of the next semester, the Peer Advisor invited the student veteran to lunch. When they met, the student veteran shared that during the end of the previous semester, he had fallen into a depressed state, and his grades declined rapidly. He had rarely attended classes during that month and would need to retake them. He also stated that over break he spent several days at home, isolated and withdrawn. The Peer Advisor talked more with the student veteran and asked if he would be interested in on-campus counseling. The student veteran said yes, and the two walked to the counseling center to make an appointment. The student veteran seemed confident that the counseling would help and was very thankful that someone was willing to take him there.

Voices of the Campus Teams

Through a series of semi-structured qualitative interviews, Campus Team members were asked to share their perspectives of PAVE and the impact of PAVE at their campus. Peer Advisors and Team Leaders have also shared how they personally benefited from the program by becoming part of a community and giving back to others.

> A veteran comes to our office and meets someone who has been in the military or who is currently serving in the military, and it's that instant bond, instant camaraderie. It's an understanding that "I've been there" and "You've been there" and we're going to work together to help you get through this. —Veteran Services Coordinator

> I'm the first in my family to go to college so it was definitely a foreign experience to me, and I tried to latch on to other military members in the community as quickly as possible just because I knew that the academics would be tough, so I wanted something familiar when I got here at the university. —Peer Advisor

> One of the best parts about PAVE this semester was being able to help out student veterans like me who were going through the same things I had when I first started school here. —Team Leader

> I feel that it is the positive reinforcement, moral support, and the encouragement that [make] the difference, and that is why PAVE is successful, and will continue to be successful in positively changing veteran and veteran dependents' lives in the future. —Team Leader

Members of the Campus Teams tend to feel a strong personal commitment to PAVE and its goals, which can then benefit both themselves and the overall program through their actions.

Implementation Challenges

The National and Campus Teams have met with several challenges while implementing PAVE. Initially identifying student veterans who might benefit from the program posed difficulties as student veterans may be hesitant to self-identify a need for assistance or peer support. This may be due to a combination of such issues as stigma around asking for help, lack of understanding of the program's purpose, and the need for improved and sustainable outreach activities. Some Peer Advisors feel discouraged when they do not experience the level of enthusiasm and engagement they anticipated from incoming student veterans. Furthermore, Peer Advisors and Team Leaders are students themselves, juggling their own studies and other life responsibilities while participating in PAVE. They sometimes have trouble finding the time and motivation to follow through with documenting their work in the online reporting system. As expected, successful Peer Advisors eventually graduate and leave the campus and program, but some Team Leaders and Peer Advisors cycled out of the program more quickly than foreseen during PAVE's early days. Commitments to the program may end early due to academic, family, or personal issues. Finally, the PAVE model originally called for Team Leaders and Peer Advisors to train their successors, but often the student team members were unavailable or unable to fulfill this function.

Determining how to manage these challenges led to many program improvements over time. For example, the National Team introduced an opt-out policy such that each incoming student veteran is matched with a Peer Advisor at every campus. This helps relieve the misconception that only troubled student veterans benefit from connecting with Peer Advisors. The National Team has worked extensively with the Campus Teams to develop additional outreach strategies that bring greater program awareness and engage hard-to-reach student veterans. The National Team also helps Campus Teams by holding support calls to address their outreach experiences, emphasizing the potential benefits that stem from reaching out even if no immediate help is requested and even when the direct results might never be known. Reframing experiences in this way has helped Peer Advisors stay engaged and motivated to continue with the program. Another successful change was to give VSCs responsibility for program oversight and to provide support and training to help them in this role. VSCs now recruit Team Leaders and Peer Advisors and manage their ongoing training under the train-the-trainer model. The National Team also helps VSCs address issues with log submissions and with adjustments to student team member roles when needed so that program responsibilities do not impact the Peer Advisors' own chances to succeed academically.

Factors for Program Success

Given PAVE's strong focus on helping people, the Campus Team naturally plays a major role in the program's success. Involving leadership at all levels of the university is key. When there is buy-in "up and down, down and up" the chain— campus administration, VSC, Team Leader, and Peer Advisors committed to student veterans' success—the program can thrive, drawing on reliable availability of resources and enthusiastic student participation.

In particular, VSCs who are energetic and engaged make a difference. VSCs know their school and their students, positioning them well for program implementation and selection of reliable, empathetic Team Leaders and Peer Advisors. The process of tailoring PAVE to a school's unique characteristics benefits from the VSC's experiences and ability to involve campus administration and student veteran leadership. VSCs also provide necessary year-to-year stability and guidance. Students contribute greatly to the program but have inherent constraints on their time and energy, given the goal of graduating and moving on to their careers. VSCs help choose and prepare successive groups of students who will make their own contributions over time.

Teamwork is another factor for success with PAVE, as in the military. On Campus Teams, the VSCs, Team Leaders, and Peer Advisors share the workload according to their roles, so that student veterans can engage in a community of support, but none of the program activities rest too heavily on the shoulders of any one person. Also, PAVE helps enhance the level of teamwork across campus as it works in concert with other campus programs, leveraging their strengths and raising awareness among student veterans about those resources. An active Student Veterans of America (SVA) chapter on campus can make a significant difference in the program's successful outreach, as can a veterans lounge or other central congregating place.

Following the PAVE model developed by the National Team also supports local success. The model incorporates the collective knowledge gained through experiences at multiple campuses, yet has the flexibility to enable tailoring at each campus to best meet the needs of their student veterans and ensure sustainability. Using the National Team's framework of best practices and support also leaves Campus Teams freer to focus on their individual student veterans' needs rather than spending the extensive time needed to create a peer program from scratch.

Expansion of PAVE

In spring 2016, PAVE partnered with SVA to launch a competitive application process to recruit 30 additional partner campuses (Figure 6.3). In August 2016, we held a National Training Conference that brought together Campus Teams from the original and new PAVE schools, training 79 VSCs and University Champions as well as 49 Team Leaders and Peer Advisors in the PAVE model and best practices. Attendees then returned to their campuses to carry out tailored work plans for connecting with and providing support to student veterans. As mentioned earlier, the program expansion included development of a new online platform that integrates an administrative console, a tracking system

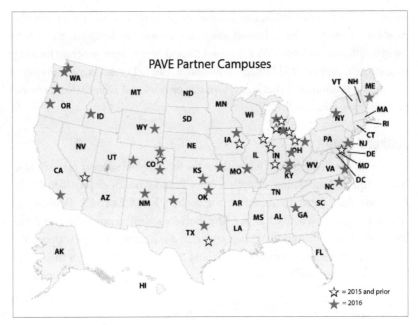

Figure 6.3. PAVE's partner campuses.

to facilitate Peer Advisors' work, and a web-based training program. As part of training in the PAVE model, Team Leaders and Peer Advisors completed a series of online training modules that describe the PAVE program in depth and cover essential topics, such as outreach strategies, how to best support student veterans, effective approaches for connecting to resources, red flags of suicide and mental health concerns, how to combat stigma, and self-care. In fall 2016, 388 Team Leaders and Peer Advisors completed the online training program. During that same time period, Campus Teams reported via the new online platform that they reached 2,929 student veterans through the PAVE program. In our next steps, diverse funding streams are sought to support continued national expansion of the PAVE program to other campuses.

Conclusion

Many student veterans will encounter short-term issues during their time on campus, while many others face more serious concerns. Despite these challenges, student veterans tend to perform well in college. The Million Records Project, a large-scale analysis of postsecondary academic outcomes in student veterans, found that although veterans may take longer to complete their degrees than traditional students, they ultimately have comparable graduation rates (Cate, 2014). Student veterans benefit from services dedicated to supporting them and their particular needs, which may not be addressed adequately by services designed primarily to assist traditional students. PAVE, a well-designed peer-to-peer program focusing on outreach, support, and linkage to resources, can help student veterans join a like-minded community that helps them stay on track and achieve their personal and academic goals.

Authors' Note

PAVE would not be possible without the funding and support of the Bristol-Myers Squibb Foundation. Supplementary funding has been provided by the Welcome Back Veterans initiative, the Robert R. McCormick Foundation, Major League Baseball Charities, the Bob Woodruff Foundation, and the Wounded Warrior Project. We are grateful to our funders for their support. We also thank Student Veterans of America and our PAVE campuses for their ideas, participation, and feedback. Most of all, we express our gratitude to the men and women who serve our country and their families. To learn more about the PAVE program, please visit www.PAVEOnCampus.org.

References

Alfred, G. C., Hammer, J. H., & Good, G. E. (2014). Male student veterans: Hardiness, psychological well-being, and masculine norms. *Psychology of Men & Masculinity, 15*(1), 95–99.

Barry, A. E., Whiteman, S. D., & MacDermid Wadsworth, S. (2014). Student service members/veterans in higher education: A systematic review. *Journal of Student Affairs Research and Practice, 51*(1), 30–42.

Barry, A. E., Whiteman, S. D., MacDermid Wadsworth, S., & Hitt, S. (2012). The alcohol use and associated mental health problems of student service members/veterans in higher education. *Drugs: Education, Prevention & Policy, 19*(5), 415–425.

Blais, R. K., & Renshaw, K. D. (2013). Stigma and demographic correlates of help-seeking intentions in returning service members. *Journal of Traumatic Stress, 26*(1), 77–85.

Bonar, E. E., Bohnert, K. M., Walters, H. M., Ganoczy, D., & Valenstein, M. (2015). Student and nonstudent National Guard service members/veterans and their use of services for mental health symptoms. *Journal of American College Health, 63*(7), 437–446.

Calhoun, P. S., Elter, J. R., Jones, E. R., Kudler, H., & Straits-Tröster, K. (2008). Hazardous alcohol use and receipt of risk-reduction counseling among US veterans of the wars in Iraq and Afghanistan. *Journal of Clinical Psychiatry*, 69(11), 1686–1693.

Callahan, R., & Jarrat, D. (2014). Helping student service members and veterans succeed. *Change: The Magazine of Higher Learning, 46*(2), 36–41.

Cate, C. A. (2014). *Million Records Project: Research from Student Veterans of America.* Washington, DC: Student Veterans of America. Retrieved from http://studentveterans.org/images/Reingold_Materials/mrp/download-materials/mrp_Full_report.pdf

CDC, NIH, DoD, and VA Leadership Panel. (2013, June). *Report to Congress on traumatic brain injury in the United States: Understanding the public health problem among current and former military personnel.* Washington, DC: Centers for Disease Control and Prevention (CDC), the National Institutes of Health (NIH), the Department of Defense (DoD), and the Department of Veterans Affairs (VA). Retrieved from http://www.cdc.gov/traumaticbraininjury/pdf/report_to_congress_on_traumatic_brain_injury_2013-a.pdf

Cornish, M. A., Thys, A., Vogel, D. L., & Wade, N. G. (2014). Post-deployment difficulties and help seeking barriers among military veterans: Insights and intervention strategies. *Professional Psychology: Research and Practice, 45*(6), 405–409.

Dalack, G. W., Blow, A. J., Valenstein, M., Gorman, L., Spinner, J., Marcus, S., ... Lagrou, R. (2010). Working together to meet the needs of Army National Guard soldiers: An academic-military partnership. *Psychiatric Services, 61*(11), 1069–1071.

Davidson, L., Bellamy, C., Guy, K., & Miller, R. (2012). Peer support among persons with severe mental illnesses: A review of evidence and experience. *World Psychiatry, 11*(2), 123–128.

Dickstein, B. D., Vogt, D. S., Handa, S., & Litz, B. T. (2010). Targeting self-stigma in returning military personnel and veterans: A review of intervention strategies. *Military Psychology, 22*(2), 224–236.

DiRamio, D., Ackerman, R., & Mitchell, R. L. (2008). From combat to campus: Voices of student-veterans. *Journal of Student Affairs Research and Practice, 45*(1), 73–102.

DiRamio, D., Jarvis, K., Iverson, S., Seher, C., & Anderson, R. (2015). Out from the shadows: Female student veterans and help-seeking. *College Student Journal, 49*(1), 49–68.

Durdella, N., & Kim, Y. K. (2012). Understanding patterns of college outcomes among student veterans. *Journal of Studies in Education, 2*(2), 109–129.

Greden, J. F., Valenstein, M., Spinner, J., Blow, A., Gorman, L. A., Dalack, G. W., ... Kees, M. (2010). Buddy-to-Buddy, a citizen soldier peer support program to counteract stigma, PTSD, depression, and suicide. *Annals of the New York Academy of Sciences, 1208*, 90–97.

Griffin, K. A., & Gilbert, C. K. (2015). Better transitions for troops: An application of Schlossberg's transition framework to analyses of barriers and institutional support structures for student veterans. *The Journal of Higher Education, 86*(1), 71–97.

Hausmann, L. M., Schofield, J., & Woods, R. (2007). Sense of belonging as a predictor of intentions to persist among African American and white first-year college students. *Research in Higher Education, 48*(7), 803–839.

Hitt, S., Sternberg, M., MacDermid Wadsworth, S., Vaughan, J., Carlson, R., Dansie, E., & Mohrbacher, M. (2015). The higher education landscape for US student service members and veterans in Indiana. *Higher Education, 70*(3), 1–16.

Hoffman, M., Richmond, J., Morrow, J., & Salomone, K. (2003). Investigating "sense of belonging" in first-year college students. *Journal of College Student Retention, 4*(3), 227–256.

Institute of Medicine. (2013, March). *Returning home from Iraq and Afghanistan: Assessment of readjustment needs of veterans, service members, and their families.* Washington, DC: The National Academies Press. Retrieved from http://www.nationalacademies.org/hmd/Reports/2013/Returning-Home-from-Iraq-and-Afghanistan.aspx

Lang, W. A., & Powers, J. T. (2011, November). *Completing the mission: A pilot study of veteran students' progress toward degree attainment in the post 9/11 era.* Chicago, IL: Pat Tillman Foundation.

Livingston, W. G., Havice, P. A., Cawthon, T. W., & Fleming, D. S. (2011). Coming home: Student veterans' articulation of college re-enrollment. *Journal of Student Affairs Research and Practice, 48*(3), 315–331.

McBain, L., Kim, Y. M., Cook, B. J., & Snead, K. M. (2012). *From soldier to student II: Assessing campus programs for veterans and service members.* Washington, DC: American Council on Education. Retrieved from http://www.acenet.edu/news-room/Documents/From-Soldier-to-Student-II-Assessing-Campus-Programs.pdf

Mead, S., Hilton, D., & Curtis, L. (2001). Peer support: A theoretical perspective. *Psychiatric Rehabilitation Journal, 25*(2), 134–141.

Money, N., Moore, M., Brown, D., Kasper, K., Roeder, J., Bartone, P., & Bates, M. (2011). *Best practices identified for peer support programs* [White paper]. Washington, DC: Defense Centers of Excellence for Psychological Health and Traumatic Brain Injury. Retrieved from http://www.dcoe.mil/content/Navigation/Documents/Best_Practices_Identified_for_Peer_Support_Programs_Jan_2011.pdf

Nelson, C. B., Abraham, K. M., Walters, H., Pfeiffer, P. N., & Valenstein, M. (2014). Integration of peer support and computer-based CBT for veterans with depression. *Computers in Human Behavior, 31,* 57–64.

Queen, B., & Lewis, L. (2014). *Services and support programs for military service members and veterans at postsecondary institutions, 2012–13* (NCES 2014–017). Washington, DC: National Center for Education Statistics, U.S. Department of Education. Retrieved from https://nces.ed.gov/pubsearch/pubsinfo.asp?pubid=2014017

Rudd, M. D., Goulding, J., & Bryan, C. J. (2011). Student veterans: A national survey exploring psychological symptoms and suicide risk. *Professional Psychology: Research and Practice, 42*(5), 354–360.

Rumann, C. B., & Hamrick, F. A. (2010). Student veterans in transition: Re-enrolling after war zone deployments. *The Journal of Higher Education, 81*(4), 431–458.

Sayer, N. A., Carlson, K. F., & Frazier, P. A. (2014). Reintegration challenges in U.S. service members and veterans following combat deployment. *Social Issues and Policy Review, 8*(1), 33–73.

Shook, J. L., & Keup, J. R. (2012). The benefits of peer leader programs: An overview from the literature. In J. R. Keup (Ed.), *Peer leadership in higher education* (New Directions for Higher Education No. 157, pp. 5–16). San Francisco, CA: Wiley.

Solomon, P. (2004). Peer support/peer provided services: Underlying processes, benefits, and critical ingredients. *Psychiatric Rehabilitation Journal, 27*(4), 392–401.

Steele, J. L., Salcedo, N., & Coley, J. (2010). *Service members in school: Military veterans' experiences using the Post-9/11 GI Bill and pursuing postsecondary education.* Santa Monica, CA: RAND Corporation. Retrieved from http://www.rand.org/content/dam/rand/pubs/monographs/2011/RAND_MG1083.pdf

Swenson, L. M., Nordstrom, A., & Hiester, M. (2008). The role of peer relationships in adjustment to college. *Journal of College Student Development, 49*(6), 551–567.

Tanielian, T., & Jaycox, L. H. (Eds.) (2008). *Invisible wounds of war: Psychological and cognitive injuries, their consequences, and services to assist recovery.* Santa Monica, CA: RAND Corporation. Retrieved from http://www.rand.org/content/dam/rand/pubs/monographs/2008/RAND_MG720.pdf

Taylor, P., Morin, R., Gonzalez, A., Motel, S., & Patten, E. (2011). *For many injured veterans, a lifetime of consequences.* Washington, DC: Pew Research Center. Retrieved from http://www.pewsocialtrends.org/files/2011/11/Wounded-Warriors.pdf

Thomas, J. L., Wilk, J. E., Riviere, L. A., McGurk, D., Castro, C. A., & Hoge, C. W. (2010). Prevalence of mental health problems and functional impairment among active component and National Guard soldiers 3 and 12 months following combat in Iraq. *Archives of General Psychiatry, 67*(6), 614–623.

U.S. Department of Veterans Affairs. (2013, November). *One million now benefit from Post-9/11 GI Bill* [Press release]. Washington, DC: Office of Public and Intergovernmental Affairs, Author. Retrieved from http://www.va.gov/opa/pressrel/pressrelease.cfm?id=2490

U.S. Government Accountability Office. (2013, July). *VA education benefits: Student characteristics and outcomes vary across schools* (Publication No. GAO-13-567). Retrieved from http://www.gao.gov/assets/660/656204.pdf

Vacchi, D. T. (2012). Considering student veterans on the twenty-first-century college campus. *About Campus, 17*(2), 15–21.

Valenstein, M., Clive, R., Pfeiffer, P., Ganoczy, D., Walters, H., West, B., ... Lepkowski, J. (2015, July). *Veteran college students' mental health: A nationally representative study.* Poster presented at the 30th VA Health Services Research and Development Service (HSR&D) and Quality Enhancement Research Initiative (QUERI) National Meeting, Philadelphia, PA.

Werber, L., Schaefer, A. G., Osilla, K. C., Wilke, E., Wong, A., Breslau, J., & Kitchens, K. E. (2010). *Support for the 21st-century reserve force: Insights to facilitate successful reintegration for citizen warriors and their families.* Santa Monica, CA: RAND Corporation. Retrieved from http://www.rand.org/content/dam/rand/pubs/research_reports/RR200/RR206/RAND_RR206.pdf

Whiteman, S. D., Barry, A. E., Mroczek, D. K., & MacDermid Wadsworth, S. (2013). The development and implications of peer emotional support for student service members/veterans and civilian college students. *Journal of Counseling Psychology, 60*(2), 265–278.

Zinzow, H. M., Britt, T. W., McFadden, A. C., Burnette, C. M., & Gillispie, S. (2012). Connecting active duty and returning veterans to mental health treatment: Interventions and treatment adaptations that may reduce barriers to care. *Clinical Psychology Review, 32*(8), 741–753.

CHAPTER 7

★★★★★★★★★★★★★★★★★★★★★★★★★★★★★★★★★★

Completing the Mission II: A Study of Veteran Students' Progress Toward Degree Attainment in the Post-9/11 Era

Wendy A. Lang and Tom O'Donnell

On June 30, 2008, the U.S. Congress passed legislation that changed the landscape for a generation of college students who have military experience in the post-9/11 era. The Veterans Educational Assistance Act, or what is now commonly referred to as the Post-9/11 GI Bill, distinguished itself as the most generous educational entitlement for the military since the Servicemen's Readjustment Act of 1944 or GI Bill. As anticipated, the influx of these learners to college campuses has surged in the eight years since its enactment, resulting in nearly two million military-affiliated students, including active duty, reservists, Guard, and veterans, attending higher education institutions across the nation. The result is an unprecedented opportunity for military learners to attain a postsecondary degree and benefit from the increased earning potential and expanded career paths that higher education offers. According to data compiled by a U.S. Department of Veterans Affairs (n.d.) initiative known as VITAL (Veterans Integration to Academic Leadership), 62% of those using this benefit are the first in their family to pursue a college degree. This alone assures that the Post-9/11 GI Bill will be a generational game changer for many who take advantage of its offerings.

The generosity of this program, however, tells only part of the story. Veterans separating from military service were faced with a struggling economy when the program was unveiled in 2008. Unemployment among those separating increased in part due to an influx of former servicemembers who were now new job seekers. As the years passed, drawdowns that generated involuntary separations exacerbated the swell of former military flooding the job market, with the impact being felt the hardest by the youngest among them. The 2014 unemployment rate for the youngest veterans (i.e., under the age of 25) was 21% compared with a 6% unemployment rate for all veterans during the same period

(U.S. Bureau of Labor Statistics, 2014). This reality lead to many veterans using higher education as a reintegration alternative, much like their predecessors of the World War II era.

Colleges and universities across the nation began to witness the increasing presence of military students and struggled with how to appropriately adapt to their varied needs. Most are taking steps to support these students as they transition from military service to college enrollment (McBain, Kim, Cook, & Snead, 2012). At the same time, the significant price tag associated with this entitlement, which is estimated at more than $65 billion to date, has driven an increased emphasis on evaluating outcomes of the recipients. To enhance accountability, President Barack Obama signed Executive Order 13607 initiating the "Principles of Excellence," which is designed to ensure that student veterans, servicemembers, and their families have information, support, and protections while using federal educational benefits (U.S. Department of Defense, 2012).

Operation College Promise (OCP), now part of Thomas Edison State University, was founded by the New Jersey Association of State Colleges and Universities in 2007 to respond to the anticipated needs of these nontraditional students. The founding member institutions included Kean University, Montclair State University, New Jersey City University, The College of New Jersey, Ramapo College, Rowan University, Stockton University, Thomas Edison State University, and William Paterson University. With its beginnings as a web-based resource, the program was built with a holistic approach to serving military-affiliated students in the post-9/11 era. Early research among the founding institutions was conducted to assess common challenges that transitioning military may face and deploy strategies to respond to those challenges. Most of these campuses had evolved in the 1940s as a result of the enrollment growth fueled by the original GI Bill, but few had current programs directed specifically for a military student community. The majority relied on a certifying official who processed the paperwork for military education benefits along with other responsibilities. The challenge was to help campuses design a framework of support for these students on budgets that were decisively austere.

As schools began to see greater numbers of veterans enroll, many opted to expand their commitment by creating a position to respond directly to the needs of the military student. The individuals assuming this role often had little or no military affiliation or connection, creating a potential disconnect between campus staff and the military-connected students they served (Lang & Powers, 2011).

To counteract this potential divide, OCP developed a professional development training, the Certificate for Veterans Service Providers (CVSP). The CVSP educates service providers on military culture while preparing them to construct a campus blueprint that will enrich the experience of their military population as they move to, through, and beyond higher education. The program was initially tailored to New Jersey institutions that, with the exception of Thomas Edison State University, had a very small military enrollment. With the growing need for training, the CVSP program has been offered throughout the country, including Texas, California, Oklahoma, Rhode Island, Georgia, Maryland, and New Jersey. Approximately 700 professionals from 40 states have been certified, representing more than 100,000 military-affiliated students.

The Study

In the fall of 2011, OCP teamed up with the Pat Tillman Foundation (PTF) to begin a process of assessing student veterans' progress toward degree attainment. The initial research targeted institutions that had either attended OCP's training or were partners with the PTF. A small but diverse group of four-year institutions participated in the pilot study, analyzing the progress rate of students at institutions with robust campus support services. Since many in this new student population were in the early stages of pursuing their degrees, the researchers determined that evaluating graduation rates was, at the time, premature. Instead, an alternate formula for reviewing student progress—the Graduation Probability Indices (GPI)—was established with the input of campus leadership. The components of the GPI reflected commonly measured data points that were in place for a traditional student body: grade point average (GPA), percentage of credits earned versus pursued, and retention rates.

The 2013 study, which is the focus of this chapter, expanded the review of the three primary indices to include a separate assessment of the commonality of on-campus programs and services among the participating campuses. The review assessed the presence of components included in the basic framework developed by OCP as the *Framework for Veterans' Success* (Lang & Powers, 2011). Student responses were collected in a separate survey to provide additional feedback on the services they used and found most effective.

Conducted in the summer of 2013, the GPI research project was initiated to build on a mechanism for ongoing evaluation of student veterans' progress toward degree attainment. This assessment is not intended to be universally conclusive; rather, it is illustrative of a sample population of veteran students attending schools with robust support services.

Method

The research sample includes 741 students on 23 campuses across the nation (see Appendix for a list of participating institutions). Initial data collection requests to the institutions, the Student Identifier List (SIL), asked for up to 40 undergraduate students who met the following criteria: lower-division status (i.e., first-year students and sophomores), enrolled full time (defined as taking 12 credit hours or more), degree seeking, and using Post-9/11 GI Bill benefits. Spouses or dependents using transferred benefits and active-duty military personnel were excluded.

The first two qualifications were modified to accommodate institutions that did not have the requisite number of lower-division students. In these cases, many of the students were transfer students, and the institutional definition of their class status varied. About 45% of the sample was identified as first-year or sophomore (the largest percentage having enough credits to be classified as sophomores). The remaining students were tracked in a similar fashion and compared to the traditional student six-year graduation rate.

When the SIL was received, specific instructions on GPI data collection points were provided. Similar to the 2011 pilot, the primary components of the GPI were students' GPA, credits earned compared with those received (the success rate), and retention from fall semester to spring semester (the persistence rate). The success rate was modified to analyze the percentage of credits earned against those pursued to give a better indication of progress toward degree attainment. The previous report evaluated the percentage of students earning all credits pursued, which limited the ability to accurately evaluate the number of credits earned toward the degree. While use of on-campus services was removed from the GPI in this report, the methodology did include an evaluation of the presence of support services to assess the commonality and prominence of support services found on the participating campuses. The collection of these data is timely as we assess the effectiveness of the Post-9/11 GI Bill and the success and progress of students using it.

Participants

For the 2011–2012 school year, data on 741 student veterans were selected at random across 23 campuses. Of these students, 146 were females; making up 20% of the veteran population. Females comprise 14.6% of active duty, 19.5% of reserves, and 15.5% of National Guard members (U.S. Department of Veterans Affairs, 2013). At two schools in the sample, women made up more than half of the veteran population. Most incoming military-affiliated students in this study entered school with sufficient credits (28 on average) to be designated as having sophomore class status. Few veterans begin college with no prior academic or experiential credit. The most popular majors among the sample were engineering, business, psychology, criminal justice, biology, and history.

Grade Point Averages (GPA)

The correlation of high GPA (defined as 3.0 or greater), retention, and progress toward degree is an obvious one. A study conducted at DePaul University (2011) found that, among a general student body, students with a GPA of 3.0 or above had the highest retention rate at 85.6%. As GPAs decrease, the potential for retention also decreases. The DePaul study found, for example, that students with GPAs of 3.0 or better had the highest graduation rate, at 77.4%, while those with less than a 2.0 were least likely to earn a degree, at 13.3%. Similarly, a 2007 study by Baylor University on first-term retention rates demonstrated a stronger positive connection: 85.6% of students with greater than a 3.0 GPA went on to earn their degrees. GPA as a predictor for persistence has a similar positive correlation as an indicator of success for military-affiliated students. Students surveyed in the first year of this study averaged a 2.98 GPA (with a mode of 4.0), slightly lower than the 3.04 reported by Lang and Powers (2011), yet still indicative of a promising path toward persistence and ultimately, degree attainment. Mean GPAs for the participating schools in the current study are shown in Figure 7.1; many student veterans had average GPAs above 3.0.

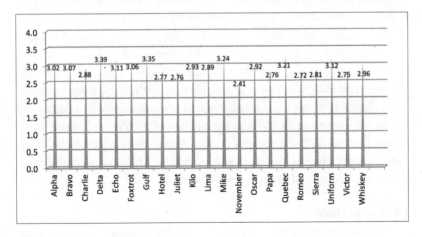

Figure 7.1. Mean GPA for sample institutions. Due to the nature of the student veteran data, school names have been anonymized to ensure privacy.

Success Rate

Given that a majority of college undergraduate programs require between 120 and 130 credit hours for degree completion, students need to attempt and successfully complete approximately 15 credits each term to graduate in less than five years. Colleges and universities must assess whether military-connected students appear to be on track to timely degree completion as compared with other students on campus.

A National Student Clearinghouse study reported "a dramatic increase in the U.S. college completion rate when nontraditional student pathways are included, driving the completion rate from 42 percent to 54 percent. In addition, the results show that over 75 percent of full-time students completed college within six years, which is higher than what has been reported in previous studies" (Cate, 2014b, p. 12). Data demonstrate that the inclusion of veterans among nontraditional students continues to raise the success rate data of the general population.

Another aspect of success for veteran students is the expectation versus the reality of the time needed to graduate. According to *The American Freshman: National Norms Fall 2012* report from the Cooperative Institutional Research Program, "the vast majority (84.3%) of incoming first-year students believe that they will graduate from college in four years. This will likely only come true for approximately half of them" (Pryor et al., 2012, p. 5). Using the GPI definition of success, or percentage of credits earned versus those pursued, veterans have met, or exceeded, the success rate of their traditional peers. In our initial report (Lang & Powers, 2011), the number of students earning all credits pursued averaged 71% for fall 2010–spring 2011. The fall 2011–spring 2012 cohort indicates a 90.5% success rate. These students averaged 24.5 credits per year, with an average transfer credit of 28 credit hours. This would indicate that these students, should they continue to progress in the same trajectory, will be eligible for a degree well within the five-year mark and with the addition of transfer credits, potentially within four years. These successes come despite the burden of also being nontraditional students who are more likely to have additional time constraints due to employment and family responsibilities.

Persistence Rate

A major area of concern in higher education is persistence. Senior administration, researchers, and policy makers continue to grapple with effective techniques for reducing the number of dropouts or stop outs. Veteran service providers are particularly aware of this objective in light of several factors. First, a discouraged military student who leaves college will be unlikely to return. Second, the Post-9/11 GI Bill places a time limit on education benefits, making efficiency in pursuing a degree imperative.

Our study indicates that the persistence rate among participants averaged 97%, slightly higher than the 94% reported in 2011 (Lang & Powers, 2011) and significantly higher than the 65.7% average first- to second-year persistence rate for traditional students reported by ACT (2008). When disaggregated (see Figure 7.2), all but one school (Victor) had persistence rates well above the rate for traditional students. Several factors may contribute to this high rate of persistence and its continuing increase. These include an improved awareness of the needs of military students and a determined effort to implement the policies to meet those needs.

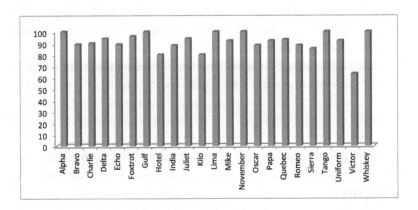

Figure 7.2. Persistence rates for sample institutions, Fall 2011 – Spring 2012.

Programs and Services

Academic research projects increasingly study the special needs of veterans and how best to accommodate them as nontraditional students (Ackerman & DiRamio, 2009; Hamrick & Rumann, 2012). An internal study at the University of South Florida (USF) was designed to "identify barriers that veterans face when they leave the military to attend college" and encourage a data-driven approach "to developing programs and services that will aid the reintegration process for veterans attending USF" (Institute for Veterans and Military Families, 2016, p. 10). Other studies, some characterized as action research using case study methods often conducted by the veterans services staff at their own institutions, include one on behavioral health screening (Schonfeld et al., 2015) and another on "the evolving needs of student veterans at Radford University" (RU Student Veterans Organization, 2012, p. 3).

According to the American Council on Education's From Soldier to Student II report (McBain et al., 2012), all types of institutions report that the most confounding challenges they see facing their military and veteran students are financial aid (likely based on delays in the receipt of VA education benefits), retention/degree completion, and social acculturation to campus life (McBain et al., 2012). Thus, a top priority must be matching the appropriate level of support required to the programs and services student veterans need to meet their goals.

Most prevalent support services on campus. In the years since the passage of the Post-9/11 GI Bill, research has identified a variety of services as effective in supporting a military student's transition from soldier to student. However, each campus is unique, and administrators should be cognizant of crafting support mechanisms that reflect their demographics while taking into account input from military-affiliated students.

Some initiatives have become commonplace among institutions. One of these is the presence of a veterans office with a coordinator to facilitate academic issues, such as registration and advising, as well as manage events and identify on-campus and community resources. A transitioning military student may not find the enrollment process intuitive, and having one central point of contact reduces the bureaucratic obfuscation and bridges the gap between the structured design of the military and the more amorphous campus environment. Supporting the establishment of a student-operated veterans club or association has proven to be beneficial to both veterans and the entire student body, as these groups foster activities on campus that can lessen the military-civilian divide.

Yellow Ribbon/in-service state tuition programs, evaluation and receipt of credit for military training, student veteran websites/portals, and career counseling also prove to be assets in attracting military students and facilitating their progress toward degree completion. Once reserved for a small group of institutions, more and more campuses are focusing on flexibility in their review and assessment of military transfer credit. Similarly, a growing number of institutions and states made higher education more affordable by instituting Yellow Ribbon, a federal program that encourages private colleges and universities to split the cost of their more expensive tuition with the VA. The Veterans Access, Choice and Accountability Act (Choice Act), which requires preferred tuition rates for qualified veterans and their dependents regardless of residency, is also changing the landscape of college affordability (Fulton &

Sponsler, 2015). Initiatives on the rise on these campuses including having on-site counselors trained in posttraumatic stress disorder and traumatic brain injury, separate student veteran orientations, and special veteran ceremonies.

Veterans' Survey of Support Services. OCP conducted an online survey to gauge the opinions of veterans on the effectiveness of some of the more popular support services. The results very much mirrored the programs and services discussed above, which supports the notion that campuses are attaining the input of the military population and responding appropriately to the needs of this population. Among respondents, the vast majority acknowledge the availability a veterans' office/coordinator on campus as a great benefit. This also suggests a positive correlation between providing a veterans office/coordinator on campus and higher retention rates among the veteran population.

The second most popular service on campus is the formation of a student veterans organization (SVO) along with a veterans center. One of the objectives of the SVO is to make the general student body aware of veteran presence and to contribute to an enhanced college experience for the entire campus. This is frequently accomplished through participation in activities such as fundraising events and collaborating with other student organizations and community service projects. The SVO creates a sense of community among veterans during their critical transition from active duty to college life. It is worth noting, according to this survey, that the most beneficial campus service was a veterans center on campus, especially one with a specific office or lounge where students could meet, work together, and share experiences and challenges while learning about military student benefits and programs.

Additional services that veterans indicated they would like included:

- priority registration for classes to allow for the timely processing of military education benefits,

- greater collaboration between student veterans organizations and the administration,

- employment opportunities geared toward graduating veterans,

- additional veteran-specific training for better communication and interaction with off- and on-campus communities,

- an annual veterans Meet and Greet with department heads, and

- separate orientation for new student veterans.

Room for improvement. There at least three areas on which the higher education community should focus to improve its service to student veterans.

These include transition support, increased faculty and staff training, and policies governing reenrollment processes. For example, only 37% of postsecondary institutions with services for military students and veterans provide initiatives specifically for transition assistance. According to the From Soldier to Student II survey (McBain et al., 2012), social acculturation for military and veteran students was identified by 55% of institutions as a priority, demonstrating at least an awareness of the issue even if services have not yet been sufficiently developed. The campus environment is often incongruous to a military student compared to what he or she became accustomed to during his or her service. Separate orientation opportunities are one way of offering this direct assistance.

Providing professional development for faculty and staff on the transitional needs of military students was also a priority for institutions responding to the From Soldier to Student II survey, but fewer than half provided training opportunities for faculty and staff (McBain et al., 2012). Finally, only 28% of institutions with programs and services for military personnel have developed an expedited re-enrollment process to help students restart their academic efforts (McBain et al., 2012, p. 48). Any initiative that simplifies the process of continuing higher education following a deployment will facilitate degree attainment.

Suggestions for Additional Research

Research can be improved by increasing the number of institutions in a sample and, in turn, sharing data and findings. Therefore, recruiting additional schools for OCP or for other groups that aspire, like OCP, to support student veterans in their collegiate pursuits is of paramount importance. Moreover, institutional diversity should be a goal through:

- recruiting colleges and universities from across the country;

- incorporating different educational sectors (public/private, four-year, community colleges, and vocational-technical schools);

- including institutions that are highly selective in their admissions policies and those schools that have open access for students; and

- involving a mixed group based on tuition and cost of attendance.

While continuing to track student veteran progress toward earning an educational credential, several of the authors in this book are exploring how data analysis methods can be improved to yield quality findings that better inform the veterans education community. OCP has plans to continue collecting data from our consortium of schools and to design data collection methods that are standardized and streamlined. Additionally, on a national scale, policy makers and social science researchers can ask new questions based on high-quality prior research.

Case Study: Stockton University

Stockton University (SU), a public university of the arts, sciences, and professional studies in Galloway, New Jersey, has a history of supporting military students since its founding in 1969. This tradition was enriched in 2008, when a new program was established to meet the anticipated needs of post-9/11 veterans and servicemembers. Since that time, the program has expanded exponentially with a strong emphasis on developing and cultivating strong campus and community partners.

Stockton is illustrative of how unwavering top-down support leads to strong veterans support programs. After attending an American Council on Education (ACE) retreat in 2008, SU's president issued a directive to reinvigorate the veterans program in anticipation of an influx of military-connected students. There was buy-in from the campus community to improve in the area of veterans affairs and today, after several years of commitment to the SU mission to support veterans, the program has matured into one of the most active and comprehensive in the nation.

In 2008, SU was grappling with identifying an appropriate blueprint for designing the best support services for military students. Concurrently, a state educational agency, the New Jersey Association of State Colleges and Universities (NJASCU), founded Operation College Promise, a program being developed to support institutions of higher education in crafting their veterans programs. OCP became a champion in the research, coordination, and dissemination of best practices for veterans affairs programs in the state and was essential to statewide efforts to develop a framework of support for student veterans attending New Jersey colleges and universities. In 2010, the framework of support created by the state was expanded nationally and continues to promote efforts at colleges and universities across the United States.

Several challenges emerged at SU, one being that military-connected students often commuted to campus and had less opportunity (and time) for interaction with their peers than traditional residential students. For military students, connecting with other veterans can play a vital role in managing the challenges of and assimilation to a campus culture. The campus SVO often serves as a mechanism to bridge this gap. SU, as its first priority, sought to designate a space where ongoing communication among veterans would be fostered. In

January 2009, a new lounge was completed, making SU the first in the state to house a designated space for military students. While initially only a very austere space, a bond was created and communication began to organically flow among the veterans on campus. One veteran noted, "Stockton's SVO and the veterans affairs staff helped me acclimate from military to collegiate life. Their support, advocacy and inclusion made me feel that I wasn't making this transition alone. I couldn't have done it without them."

Implementing an orientation specifically for military students has also proved beneficial for incoming students who were unfamiliar with the university environment. This daylong event provides an opportunity for these students to meet their peers and key administrative personnel. The program is not mandatory but is well attended by most new students.

Another problem that students identified in the survey was a lack of understanding of military culture among staff, which created misunderstandings between civilian staff and the new military population being served. Recognizing the need to bridge this informational gap, SU made training of campus service providers a priority and instituted a variety of interdepartmental initiatives to facilitate communication, coordination, and an overall climate of veteran-friendly practices. In 2010, Stockton sponsored OCP's inaugural Certificate for Veterans Service Providers (CVSP) program to facilitate a broader knowledge base. A faculty mentoring team and advisory board were established to support ongoing efforts and coordinate campus and community partners. One of the veterans commented,

> The veterans affairs program at Stockton University allowed me to net-work within the community and identify resources that were available to me. The strong social connections I developed as a member of the student veterans organization allowed me to navigate the challenges of higher education.

Higher education resources are often very limited, which restricts new funding for even the worthiest of programs. For relatively small schools like Stockton, it was critical to identify external resources that could augment campus resources. Programs including Combat Papers, The Telling Project, and The Warrior Champion program were just a few that helped to bring the military–civilian communities together and nurture better understanding of some of the challenges of reintegration. The Warrior Champion program, for example, portrays an inspiring story of how wounded warriors used athletic goals during reintegration and is a mandatory part of Welcome Week activities for all new students.

There are specific needs that some student veterans may have beyond academia. The number of those with PTSD and related service conditions continues to rise and may affect military students' ability to maximize their higher education objectives. Stockton now has a full-time counselor to work exclusively with our veterans to address PTSD and other stress-related issues. Other actions, like increasing the size of the veterans lounge to address ADA compliance issues and creating veterans-only parking areas, have been implemented to facilitate success for students who may struggle.

Results

There have been several studies on the success of student veterans on campus and their progress toward degree compared with their traditional peers (Cate, 2014a; Lang & Powers, 2011). SU has been tracking these data for several years in an effort to gauge the impact of programming and demonstrate the potential of military students. As reported in the large OCP Completing the Mission reports, SU's student veteran population is flourishing. In academic year 2014–2015, 643 veterans enrolled, and 137 seniors graduated (representing a 97.6% graduation rate for that senior group). There was a 96% annual retention rate for 2009 to 2015 among military-connected students, who held an average GPA of 3.27.

Strong graduation and retention rates and above-average GPA, as well as the positive feedback from new student veterans, suggests the value of a comprehensive support framework, which is designed to recognize the unique needs of military students. One student summed up the impact of a strong and supportive campus environment with the following:

> As a veteran, I entered Stockton worried and unsure of myself. After receiving the support from staff, faculty, and other veterans, my potential has reached new heights and has no bonds to hold me back. Stockton allowed me to find my passion with social work and chipped away a stone exterior to help make me a new man.

Conclusion

While the descriptive reporting in this study is not intended to imply causation or directly support empirical claims of positive intervention effects, follow-up research using qualitative methods is recommended for identifying constructive and creative ideas for support services. For example, while it is clear that our participating institutions demonstrated strong commitments to their student veteran populations, how much that commitment resulted in better persistence rates, GPAs, and GPI scores should be further studied.

This study's findings did support the strategy of having a central point of contact for student veterans. This was an important strategy for and was indicative of campus efforts to provide a one-stop solution for registration, financial aid, academic and social counseling, as well as connecting with the student veterans organization and peers with military experience. Several other illuminating findings seemed to dispel common misperceptions held by some about student veterans. Analysis of GPAs, persistence rates, and academic success measures suggested that most participants are on track for timely degree attainment. They are taking sufficient credits to graduate within four years, and most appear to be focused and productive. When compared with the general student population, the veteran academic success metrics of persistence and retention either equaled or exceeded.

Several institutions in the study put a priority on providing adequate support for student veterans in addition to centralized service and staff. For example, several veterans affairs professionals reported establishing their own internal data collection and then offering data in order to support external researchers, whose findings helped identify strategies and resources. Another observational finding was the value of steadfast and committed support from top administrators, including presidents and provosts. Stockton University is one example of vital top-down support.

This study further illustrated that veterans programs and services can be financially practical yet still responsive to what research recommends as empirically effective. Often, veteran-specific considerations mirror the academic and social needs of students in either the general population or other nontraditional populations. Therefore, consideration should be given to the efficacy of expanding existing campus supports that are used by non-veteran students. In general, this study demonstrated that college students with military experience are not all alike nor should they be stereotyped. Some students will thrive with minimal support, while others may face challenges during their transitions to the classroom. For these students, it is most often ancillary factors (i.e., finances, housing, mental health) that impede educational progress.

There exists an urgency surrounding these issues. The effectiveness of the Post-9/11 GI Bill and the progress of veterans pursuing a college degree is a topic that continues to interest federal and state lawmakers, governmental agencies, and those interested in veterans issues. This is not surprising since this generous military educational benefits program has cost taxpayers more than $65 billion to date. In fact, the U.S. Congress will likely continue to further the debate the efficacy of the program while seeking avenues to reduce the burgeoning cost.

References

Ackerman, R., & DiRamio, D. (Eds.). (2009). *Creating a veteran-friendly campus: Strategies for transition and success* (New Directions for Student Services No. 126). San Francisco, CA: Wiley.

ACT. (2008). *National collegiate retention and persistence to degree rates.* Retrieved October 11, 2013 from: http://www.act.org/research/policymakers/pdf/retain_2008.pdf

Baylor University. (2007). Analysis of Undergraduate First Year GPA. *Office of Institutional Research & Testing, Vol. 07–08, No. 44.*

Cate, C. A. (2014a). *An examination of student veteran completion rates over service eras: An in-depth analysis of the 2010 National Survey of Veterans.* Washington, DC: Student Veterans of America. Retrieved from http://bit.ly/1VI4la1

Cate, C. A. (2014b). *Million Records Project: Research from Student Veterans of America.* Washington, DC: Student Veterans of America. Retrieved from http://studentveterans.org/aboutus/research/million-records-project

DePaul University. (2011). *First-year retention and sixth-year graduation among first-time, full-time freshmen.* Retrieved August 2013 from: http://oipr.depaul.edu/retention/gradrates.asp

Fulton, M., & Sponsler, B. (2015). *In-state tuition policies under the Veterans Access, Choice and Accountability Act.* Retrieved June 2017 from www.ecs.org/clearinghouse/01/17/42/11742.pdf

Hamrick, F. A., & Rumann, C. B. (Eds.). (2012). *Called to serve: A handbook on student veterans in higher education.* San Francisco: Jossey-Bass.

Institute for Veterans and Military Families. (2016). *Advancing veteran success in higher education.* Syracuse, NY: Author.

Lang, W., & Powers, J. T. (2011, November). *Completing the mission: A pilot study of veteran students' progress toward degree attainment in the post-9/11 era.* Retrieved from: http://www.tesu.edu/military/ocp/documents/completing_mission_i-Nov2011.pdf

McBain, L., Kim, Y., Cook, B., & Snead, K. (2012). *From soldier to student II: Assessing campus programs for veterans and service members.* Retrieved August 2013 from: http://www.acenet.edu/news-room/Pages/From-Soldier-to-Student-II.aspx

Pryor, J. H., Eagan, K., Blake, L. P., Hurtado, S., Berdan, J., & Case, M. H. (2012). *The American freshman: National norms fall 2012.* Retrieved from: http://www.heri.ucla.edu/monographs/TheAmericanFreshman2012.pdf

Radford University's Student Veterans Organization. (2012). RU veteran research showcase. *Radford University's Sound Off Newsletter, 2*(2), p. 3

Schonfeld, L., Braue, L. A., Stire, S., Gum, A. M., Cross, B. L., & Brown, L. M. (2015). Behavioral health and adjustment to college life for student service members/veterans. *Journal of American College Health, 63*(7), 428–436.

U.S. Bureau of Labor Statistics. (2014). *Employment and unemployment among all veterans, Gulf-War era veterans, and nonveterans.* Retrieved June 2017 from https://www.bls.gov/opub/ted_20141110.htm

U.S. Department of Defense. (2012). *Executive Order 13607 and the Principles of Excellence.* Retrieved June 2017 from https://www.dodmou.com

U.S. Department of Veterans Affairs. (2013). *Vet success on campus.* Retrieved from http://vetsuccess.gov/vetsuccess_on_campus

U.S. Department of Veterans Affairs. (n.d.). *Who are today's student veterans?* Retrieved from the VA Campus Toolkit website, https://www.mentalhealth.va.gov/studentveteran/studentvets.asp

Appendix

Enrollment and Tuition Costs for Participating Institutions, 2011–2012 Academic Year

Institution	Total veteran enrollment	Total student enrollment	Tuition (in–state/out)
Arizona State University	1,816	58,404	$9,720/$22,319
Baldwin Wallace University	102	3,509	$26,396/$29,396
Coastal Carolina	397	8,517	$9,760/$21,560
Colorado State University	1,348	22,500	$7,952/$23,652
Eastern Kentucky University	1,217	13,902	$6,960/$19,056
George Mason University	2,172	20,782	$9,266/$26,744
George Washington University	722	10,406	$44,148/$44,148
Georgetown University	419	7,590	$41,393/$41,393
Mississippi State University	2,111	16,312	$5,805/$14,670
Missouri State University	650	17,187	$6,598/$12,418
Montclair State University	232	14,590	$10,646/$19,394
Purdue University	517	31,988	$9,478/$27,646
Texas A&M University	560	39,867	$8,421/$23,811
University of Alabama	453	26,234	$8,600/$21,900
University of Arizona	994	30,665	$10,035/$25,494
University of Denver	259	5,453	$37,833/$37,833
University of Maryland	603	37,631	$8,655/$26,026
University of Michigan – Flint	250	6,959	$8,712/$17,014
University of Minnesota	n/a	34,812	$13,022/$18,022
University of New Mexico	n/a	22,643	$5,809/$19,919
University of South Florida	1,750	47,000	$32,364/$32,364
University of Wisconsin – Milwaukee	1,006	24,270	$8,675/$18,404
University of Wyoming	n/a	10,163	$4,125/$12,855

Source: College Navigator (National Center for Education Statistics).

CHAPTER 8

★★★★★★★★★★★★★★★★★★★★★★★★★★★★★★★★

Academic Outcomes and the Million Records Project

Chris Andrew Cate

Finding population-level data on student veterans' postsecondary academic outcomes has been a longstanding quest for researchers in higher education. Many may presume that it should be readily available or connected with all the other academic outcome data that are collected and reported annually, but when someone begins to look for these data it quickly becomes clear that they are not easy to find. Difficulties in accurately identifying student veterans and tracking their academic enrollment time line, which usually includes more than one institution, makes data gathering and analysis problematic. Additionally, lack of consensus resulting in ill-defined academic outcomes and a lack of fresh data for timely analysis of current students' performance, exacerbate the already troublesome nature of academic outcomes analysis for student veterans.

What is most often readily available are reports written several decades after the student veterans have left college. Such reports focus largely on the economic impact of the GI Bill, though other outcomes may be included. While useful in a historical context, these reports have little applicability for those needing to know the status and progress of the current generation of student veterans.

Having access to more timely data about student outcomes would be useful for several groups in higher education. Researchers and practitioners can evaluate the effect of programs and services designed to help student veterans transition to college. Colleges and universities will be able to compare their academic outcomes to a national metric and take needed actions. Veterans service organizations and the U.S. Department of Veterans Affairs would have information to counter unsubstantiated claims of poor academic outcomes for student veterans. As one researcher noted, "in the absence of quality data, thin media reports speculated vets graduated at a spectacularly low rate" (U.S. Department of Veterans Affairs, 2013, p. 1). Policy makers, stakeholders, and the public can use these results to make informed opinions about student veterans' academic progress and success as well as the GI Bill's return on investment.

The need for these data combined with its utility for several groups resulted in the creation of the Million Records Project (MRP). The MRP was developed to begin exploring the postsecondary academic outcomes of the current generation of student veterans. Results of this effort have helped expand the field's knowledge of both student veterans' academic success and the population as a whole.

This chapter begins with a review of research on postsecondary academic outcomes from the first generation of student veterans from World War II with a focus on the methodologies of each report. The chapter also examines and reviews current federal data frames that collect information on student veterans, military-connected students, and/or postsecondary outcomes. Next, the chapter summarizes results from the MRP and shares some new in-depth analysis. The chapter closes with a description of the next phase of MRP, the National Veteran Education Success Tracker (NVEST) Project.

Past Research

The first two versions of the GI Bill, after World War II and the Korean War, have been extensively researched and reported on mostly due to the large amount of time that has passed since the legislation was enacted, resulting in decades of effects to be observed, recorded, and released (Altschuler & Blumin, 2009; Humes, 2006; Olsen, 1974). In most cases, academic outcomes are used for context in explaining the GI Bill's economic effects. In the 10 years following the end of World War II, 15.7 million veterans returned to civilian life, and by the time the World War II GI Bill ended, approximately eight million veterans —over half of eligible World War II veterans—used the GI Bill to finish high school, earn a vocational certificate, or go to college (Altschuler & Blumin, 2009; Humes, 2006). The GI Bill funded the educations of 22,000 dentists, 67,000 doctors, 91,000 scientists, 238,000 teachers, 240,000 accountants, and 450,000 engineers, as well as three Supreme Court justices, three presidents, a dozen senators, 14 Nobel Prize winners, and two dozen Pulitzer Prize winners (Humes, 2006; Olsen, 1974).

The Korean War sent millions of new men and women into combat less than five years after the end of World War II. Similar to its predecessor, the response to the Korean GI Bill was enthusiastic. Within five years of the Korean War GI Bill's passage, two million out of approximately 5.3 million eligible Korean War veterans drew educational benefits (Committee on Veterans Affairs, 1972). Stanley (2003) analyzed the impact of the Korean War GI Bill on the education levels of the Korean War veterans, finding the law increased the time in postsecondary programs by an academic term and the likelihood of gradation by 5 to 6 percentage points. However, Stanley also found differences in these results based on the veterans' preservice socioeconomic status.

In the decades following, the GI Bill would have a significant effect on the education levels of veterans, military servicemembers, and the larger population. From World War II to the Vietnam War, the percentage of veterans without a high school diploma was cut by more than half, from 54.6% to 20.2%, respectively. In addition, the percentage of veterans between the ages of 25 and 29 with four or more years of college nearly tripled between the World War II and Vietnam War eras, from 11% to 31.7%, respectively (Educational Testing Service, 1973).

On March 3, 1966, President Lyndon B. Johnson signed the Veterans Readjustment Benefits Act of 1966, commonly referred to as the Cold War GI Bill. The previous GI Bills were established as compensation for veterans for their wartime service; however, the Cold War GI Bill extended benefits to veterans serving in times of both war and peace. Similar to their predecessors, research suggests Vietnam War veterans benefited both academically and economically from the GI Bill. A VA report in 1976 found Vietnam-era student veterans using the GI Bill had high rates of completion and degree attainment (U.S. Veterans Administration, 1976). Of the veterans surveyed for the report, approximately two thirds of full-time student veterans completed their postsecondary programs. The report notes that at the time of its publication, several part-time student veterans were still enrolled and persisting in their postsecondary programs, suggesting that the overall completion rate for this GI Bill cohort would be higher.

The end of the military draft in 1973 did not end the GI Bill, but it does appear to have ended the research focusing on the postsecondary academic outcomes of student veterans and military-connected students. Little research can be found on this subject after the Vietnam era. Several things could attribute to the lack of research or reporting, such as the shift in focus to outcomes of other federal financial aid programs under the Higher Education Act of 1965.

When compared to its predecessors, little research exists on the postsecondary academic outcomes of veterans using the Veterans Educational Assistance Program (VEAP) and Montgomery GI Bill (MGIB) though national surveys still provide some insight to these outcomes. The 2010 National Survey of Veterans (2010 NSV; U.S. Department of Veterans Affairs, 2010), conducted by Westat for the VA, examined and elicited feedback from beneficiaries of VA programs and services, including education benefits. In the 2010 NSV's section regarding education benefits, the survey asked veterans about degree or program completion. According to the results, 63% of survey respondents reported that they completed the postsecondary educational or vocational program for which they used their VA educational benefits (Department of Veterans Affairs, 2010).

Further in-depth analysis of the 2010 NSV by service era found that the 45-year period between the end of the Korean War and September 11, 2001, shows a stable postsecondary completion rate between 66% and 68% (Cate, 2014a). This provides some evidence that student veterans who used the VEAP and MGIB had completed at similar rates as their predecessors.

While the studies described here provide reliable and valid results on student veteran academic outcomes and the effect the GI Bill has had on the nation, they provided little actionable data for policymakers, stakeholders, and the public to assess and evaluate the GI Bill with respect to currently enrolled students. In sum, they did little to inform colleges and universities on whether and how well they were meeting the needs of student veterans and helping them succeed at their campuses.

Federal Databases

The natural places to look for data on student veteran and military-connected postsecondary academic outcomes is within the three executive branch departments that are associated with the military, veterans, and higher education: the Department of Defense, Department of Veterans Affairs, and Department of Education. Each of these departments contains a piece of information on student veterans and military-connected students, but none have comprehensive data on student veterans' postsecondary academic outcomes.

The Department of Defense (DOD) maintains data on individuals currently serving in the military and veterans who have served in the past. It can also provide information regarding military training, job and duties while in the service, and times of deployment that may interrupt postsecondary enrollment.

Regardless of branch or duty status, servicemembers receive training in a variety of areas and instruction on the latest technology to do their jobs. Most active duty servicemembers also have the option to pursue postsecondary degrees and certificates, while guardspersons and reservists may attend colleges and universities full time when not on active duty. The DOD Tuition Assistance (TA) Program is available to all active-duty servicemembers, including active-duty reservists, regardless of rank. TA tracks servicemember enrollment and course completion as long as the servicemember is using TA funds to pay for the course. If servicemembers exclusively use other funding (e.g., out-of-pocket, state funds, Title IV assistance) to pay their tuition and fees, then the DOD will not have a record of the course nor whether the servicemember completed it. In addition, the DOD does not follow the servicemember once they have fully separated from the military.

The Department of Veterans Affairs (VA), in contrast, is able to identify nearly every student veteran enrolled in a postsecondary course of study through veteran education benefits usage. The Veterans Benefits Administration's (VBA) primary responsibility and duty has been the proper and timely disbursement of benefits (e.g., medical, education, home) on behalf of veterans. Under the Post-9/11 GI Bill, this entails that tuition payments are made to the correct school or program for the veteran in time to ensure no disruption in enrollment occurs. Other benefits, such as Basic Allowance for Housing (BAH) and textbook stipends, are also made to the student veteran. To accomplish this task, VA collects information related to the amount and destination of the benefit, such as the student veteran's institution, enrollment intensity (part-time or full-time), and the amount of the disbursement.

With the enactment of the Post-9/11 GI Bill, the VA has established a new system in its certification process to obtain additional data points on student veteran academic progress and outcomes. However, these limited data points do not translate into an accurate measure of student veteran postsecondary academic outcomes. The VA is only authorized to track outcomes of veterans while using the Post-9/11 GI Bill. If a student veteran takes 37 months to complete their program and earn a degree, they would be classified as dropping out, because the Post-9/11 GI Bill only covers 36 months. The same is true for student veterans using other sources of financial aid (e.g., scholarships, grants, Title IV financial aid) during their academic career, potentially creating missing data and affecting our understanding of academic outcomes. Without secondary sources for comparison, it is extremely difficult to measure how situations like the ones described here influence the results. Therefore, while the VA can both identify student veterans and track their academic progress and outcomes, the restrictions on the data they are authorized to collect limits the completeness of reported outcomes.

The Department of Education (ED), through a variety of surveys and data-reporting systems, has collected postsecondary students' academic progress and completion rates for more than 50 years. The National Center for Education Statistics (NCES), which tracks postsecondary student academic outcomes, maintains several databases, such as the Integrated Postsecondary Education Data System (IPEDS), that contain data on postsecondary students as reported by institutions of higher education and financial aid records. However, properly identifying student veterans and military-connected students is difficult for many colleges and universities. Veterans and military servicemembers are considered a protected class under federal law, meaning institutions cannot require veterans or servicemembers to identify themselves. Because revealing veteran or military status is voluntary, many of the NCES databases do not identify and track all students who meet this definition.

IPEDS, the database most frequently used to report postsecondary student academic outcomes, is a collection of interrelated annual surveys sent to every college, university, technical, and vocational institution that participates in federal student financial aid programs. These schools are required to report data on enrollments, program completions, graduation rates, and institutional data. Because these data are collected at the institutional level, it is difficult to track individual students transferring from one school to another. This method of data collection also makes it difficult to track students who have breaks in their enrollment. Highly mobile student populations, those whose enrollment has been interrupted by military service or who may have attended several schools as they work toward their degrees, such as military students and veterans, are not likely to be included in the IPEDS data frames.

As described above, the three executive branch departments have historically collected data separately on student veterans and military-connected students. They shared relatively little data between them on student veterans and military-connected students, due to a lack of authorization and infrastructure to share such information. That is until President Barack Obama's Executive Order 13607 (2012), which among other items directed the three government departments to produce "a comprehensive strategy for developing service member and veteran student outcome measures that are comparable, to the maximum extent practicable, across Federal military and veterans educational benefit programs, including, but not limited to, the Post-9/11 GI Bill and the Tuition Assistance Program" (p. 25863).

Connecting or merging data frames addresses weakness in one or all the data frames by filling gaps or missing data, making the new data frame greater than the sum of its parts. The executive order created a mechanism for sharing data among the three departments and authority to do so, thus attempting to expand our knowledge of student veterans and military-connected students and answer long sought-after questions. However, many of the weaknesses described earlier in the departments' data collection and management system create difficulties for clean data sharing and creating stronger data frames. For example, while the VA knows a large portion of the student veteran population and the institutions they attend through Veteran Education Benefits usage, much of the ED data is at the institutional level and focuses on traditional college students. Merging these data frames does little to add value to discussions on student veteran or military-connected students. The VA is provided with institutional data on traditional students, which generally does not apply to student veterans or military-connected students, and ED receives data on financial aid programs for nontraditional students (VA Education Benefits) that do not fall under ED's purview.

Executive Order 13607 had the best of intentions in authorizing the three departments to share information and collaborate to the best of their ability to increase our understanding and reporting of student veteran and military-connected students' academic progress and outcomes. In practice, however, there has been minimal increase in our understanding and reporting regarding student veterans and military-connected students' academic outcomes, due to problems with matching or combining the individual departments' data.

Million Records Project

The need for empirical data on student veteran postsecondary academic outcomes to help inform policy makers, stakeholders, and the public led to the development of the Million Records Project (MRP). The MRP, a public–private partnership between the VA, the National Student Clearinghouse, and Student Veterans of America (SVA), was designed to address many of the weaknesses found in previously established national databases and surveys. The Clearinghouse collects student enrollment and degree data at the individual level directly from participating postsecondary institutions that use their services. This means that student veterans' academic progress and outcomes could be tracked regardless of transfer status (as long as they transferred to a school within the Clearinghouse's network) or interruptions in enrollment. By using the Clearinghouse's database, MRP created a more accurate data frame for student veteran postsecondary academic completion records. Using VA Education Benefits data ensured that each individual in MRP was a veteran, solving the need to properly identifying student veterans.

The MRP combined a national sample of one million student veterans who first used their GI Bill benefits between 2002 and 2010 with Clearinghouse completion data. Three separate GI Bill groups comprised the sample, 398,895 veterans made up the MGIB only and the Post-9/11 GI Bill groups, while 101,105 were in a combined MGIB-9/11 GI Bill group. The combined group represented those student veterans who were eligible for both benefits and exercised their option of switching from the MGIB to the Post-9/11 GI Bill. The result was a data frame containing postsecondary academic outcomes of student veterans in the post-9/11 era. For the first time in the GI Bill's history, near real-time data on the completion rate and other academic outcomes for the current generation of student veterans was available and providing actionable data for policymakers, stakeholders, and the public.

Full, detailed results of the MRP can be found in its public report (Cate, 2014b). A brief summary of the highlights from the project is provided with a couple of in-depth results that were not in the initial report. A majority (51.7%) of student veterans in this sample earned a postsecondary degree or certificate. The project found that 57.8% of student veterans who exclusively used the MGIB completed a postsecondary degree (vocational certificate or higher) and 59.7% of those who used the MGIB and the Post-9/11 GI Bill completed a postsecondary degree. Results for the Post-9/11 GI Bill-only group were not available due to the recent enactment of the program, and the sample did not have enough time to complete any postsecondary degrees at the time the records were matched.

An interesting result from the MRP was the time-to-completion for student veterans in the sample. The standard reporting practices used for time-to-completion of postsecondary degrees defined by ED is a cut-off point of four years (200% time) for associate degrees and six years (150% time) for bachelor's degrees. The MRP found that of the sample who earned an associate degree, only 52.6% of them earned it within four years. Similar results were found for student veterans completing a bachelor's degree: Only 59.4% did so within six years. These findings compare favorably with time-to-degree statistics for the general population of students, which are alarmingly low. One study reported only 37.3% of students at two-year schools graduate with an associate degree in four years (Knapp, Kelly-Reid, & Ginder, 2010). It is likely that student veterans who had longer times-to-completion were not continuously enrolled, and many factors—both personal and military-related—may have contributed to their longer academic careers. These results serve as further proof that student veterans are nontraditional students, and caution should be exercised when attempting to apply traditional student metrics, such as time-to-completion, to this population.

Of those who completed, approximately 9 out of 10 (89.7%) initially earned degrees at the associate level or higher. However, many student veterans did not stop their education after their initial degree and went on to earn higher degrees. The 31.3% of the sample who initially earned a vocational certificate went on to earn an associate degree or higher. The same trend was found with the 35.8% of the sample who initially earned an associate degree and the 20.8% who initially earned a bachelor's degree. Both groups eventually earned degrees at higher levels.

The vast majority of student veterans are enrolling in public institutions (79.2%), with a smaller percentage enrolling fairly evenly in private, nonprofit (10.7%), and proprietary schools (10.1%). Following a similar distribution, the large majority of student veterans who graduate do so from public schools (71.7%), with the remaining population graduating in much smaller but fairly even percentages from private, nonprofit (15.5%), and proprietary (12.9%) schools.

The migration of student veterans from one postsecondary sector to another was the first in-depth analysis conducted after the initial MRP report was released. The analysis compared the sector where the student veteran started to the one where they earned their initial degree (see Table 8.1). Unfortunately, institutional type (two-year versus four-year) was not available for initial enrollment, so there is no way to determine whether a student veteran transferred from a two-year college to a four-year university without earning an associate degree. Results showed that the largest percentage of migration occurred with student veterans who initially enrolled in private, not-for-profit schools; only two thirds (66.49%) of those student veterans reported remaining in that sector from initial enrollment to initial degree completion. In most cases, students migrated from the private, not-for-profit schools to public schools. The sector that retained the most student veterans from initial enrollment to first degree completed was the public sector (84.61%), and the migration was evenly distributed between the other two sectors.

Table 8.1
Student Veteran Sector Migration From Initial Enrollment to First Degree Earned (N = 412,136)

	Sector first degree earned		
Sector started	Public	Private	Proprietary
Public (n = 324,525)	84.61%	8.05%	7.34%
Private (n = 54,580)	28.00%	66.49%	5.51%
Proprietary (n = 33,031)	13.47%	3.87%	82.66%

Another in-depth analysis examined the ages of the sample when they first earned their degrees. These results shed light onto the heterogeneity of the student veteran population and provide a new perspective on student veterans (see Table 8.2). While a clear majority (61.78%) of the sample earned their degrees

Table 8.2

First Degree Completion by Age Group (*N* = 411,907)

Age group	First degree completion
24 and under	16.9%
25 – 29	37.5%
30 – 34	24.3%
35 – 39	11.2%
40 – 44	5.6%
45 – 49	3.0%
50 and over	1.6%

between 25 and 34 years of age, there is a sizable minority (21.32%) who were 35 or older when they first earned their degrees. These older student veterans are more likely career servicemembers who enroll in college after their retirement and separation from the military. They return to school with the same goal as their younger counterparts, preparing for a career in the civilian workforce. One third the size of the younger veteran cohort, older student veterans represent a segment of this heterogeneous population who are often overlooked by the media and institutions that focus on programs, services, and policies for younger students.

The MRP was the first step in addressing several of the weaknesses inherent in the national level databases and surveys that track postsecondary academic outcomes. It produced a more accurate estimate of post-9/11 student veteran academic outcomes than existing data frames and was the first project in the 70-plus year history of the GI Bill to capture and report the postsecondary academic outcomes of a large segment of the current era of student veterans. For the number of answers MRP produced, it also generated several questions, mostly around the academic progress and paths of student veterans. Do student veterans experience interruptions in their enrollment? When do they withdraw from school? How often do they transfer before earning their first degree? Each of these questions suggests an area for more detailed study that will be a focus of the next phase of research, the National Veteran Education Success Tracker (NVEST) Project. NVEST will include reports on student veterans' persistence, transfer, and attrition rates. While the MRP included both the MGIB and the Post-9/11 GI Bill, the sample for NVEST will be narrowed to only include student veterans who used the Post-9/11 GI Bill. Using a process similar to MRP, NVEST will provide an early measure of academic performance and outcomes for students using Post-9/11 GI Bill education benefits.

Conclusion

The lack of data on current student veterans' postsecondary academic outcomes creates disadvantages to all connected to student veterans. Without this information making data-driven decisions, evaluating programs and research, and advocating for veterans is more difficult. The vacuum created by missing data allows for assumptions to be turned into facts and for misinformation to become truth that ultimately harms the student veteran. Waiting for decades after the student veterans have left college to conduct research on their academic outcomes is no longer practical.

The Million Records Project and its successor, NVEST, are first steps in obtaining population level data on current era student veterans. The results from these projects can begin to answer many of the questions stakeholders, policy makers, and the public have about student veterans, their academic outcomes, and the investment being made in them through the Post-9/11 GI Bill. These projects answer several key questions about student veterans' postsecondary academic outcomes, but they do not answer all the questions. More research is needed to explore and expand our knowledge about student veterans and the factors that influence their postsecondary academic progress and outcomes.

References

Altschuler, G., & Blumin, S. (2009). *The GI Bill: The new deal for veterans.* New York, NY: Oxford University Press.

Cate, C. A. (2014a). *An examination of student veteran completion rates over service eras: An in-depth analysis of the 2010 National Survey of Veterans.* Retrieved from http://bit.ly/1VI4la1

Cate, C. A. (2014b). *Million Records Project: Research from Student Veterans of America.* Washington, DC: Student Veterans of America.

Committee on Veterans Affairs. (1972). *The three GI bills.* Washington, DC: U.S. Government Printing Office.

Educational Testing Service. (1973). *Final report on education assistance to veterans: A comparative study of three GI bills.* Ann Arbor, MI: University of Michigan Library.

Exec. Order No. 13607. (2012). *77 C.F.R. 25861.* Retrieved from https://www.gpo.gov/fdsys/pkg/FR-2012-05-02/pdf/2012-10715.pdf

Humes, E. (2006). *Over here: How the GI bill transformed the American dream.* San Diego, CA: Harcourt.

Knapp, L. G., Kelly-Reid, J. E., & Ginder, S.A. (2010). *Enrollment in Postsecondary Institutions, Fall 2008; Graduation Rates, 2002 & 2005 Cohorts; and Financial Statistics, Fiscal Year 2008 (NCES 2010–152)*. Washington, DC: National Center for Education Statistics, U.S. Department of Education. Retrieved from http://nces.ed.gov/pubsearch

Olsen, K. W. (1974). *The GI bill, the veterans, and the colleges*. Lexington, KY: The University of Kentucky Press.

Stanley, M. (2003). College education and the midcentury GI bills. *The Quarterly Journal of Economics, 118*(2), 671–708.

U.S. Department of Veterans Affairs. (2010). *National Survey of Veterans: Active duty service members, demobilized National Guard and reserve members, family members, and surviving spouses*. Washington, DC: Author.

U.S. Department of Veterans Affairs. (2013, March 4). SVA develops a clearer picture of veteran graduation rates [Weblog post]. Retrieved from http://www.blogs.va.gov/VAntage/8876/sva-develops-a-clearer-picture-of-veteran-graduation-rates/

U.S. Veterans Administration. (1976). *Completion rates for education and training under the Vietnam era GI Bill: A study*. Ann Arbor, MI: University of Michigan Library.

CHAPTER 9

★★★

Where Do They Fit? Applying the Conceptual Model of Nontraditional Undergraduate Student Attrition to Student Veterans

Ryan L. Van Dusen

Student veterans are attending college at the highest rate since the inception of the Servicemen's Readjustment Act of 1944 (GI Bill). At the high-water mark in 1947, 49% of all people admitted to college were veterans (U.S. Department of Veterans Affairs, 2016). While veteran enrollment today is not at the same high percentage of overall college enrollment, it is estimated that since the enactment of the Post-9/11 GI Bill, more than 900,000 veterans have enrolled in postsecondary education (Lighthall, 2012). Additionally, an estimated two million veterans are eligible to receive this educational benefit (Cook & Kim, 2009; Strawn, Draper, & Rothenberg, 2009).

It has been difficult to determine the level of retention and graduation rates for student veterans. During the late 20th and early 21st centuries, the government and the public have expressed increasing concern about college completion, with some states incorporating completion rates as a primary consideration for higher education funding. There are multiple studies and publications addressing the overall retention and graduation rates of college students. However, little research has been published on the retention and graduation rates of student veterans.

Historically, the Department of Veterans Affairs has not tracked retention or graduation rates of veterans enrolled using the GI Bill. In recent years, there have been attempts to do so. In a study of one million veterans from colleges and universities across the United States, Cate (2014) estimated that 51.7% of veterans enrolled in degree programs are earning baccalaureate degrees. However, student veterans take an average of 6.3 years to complete their degrees, which is past the six-year measure used by the U.S. Department of Education (Cate, 2014). Comparing these findings to data collected by National Center for Education Statistics (NCES) suggests a gap between degree completion of student veterans and traditional college students. For example, the six-year graduation rate for first-time college students is 59% (NCES, 2015). However, student veterans appear to be outperforming their nonveteran, nontraditional peers who have a graduation rate of 33.7% (New, 2014).

This chapter will examine and identify some of the factors influencing the retention of student veterans. In previous research, Van Dusen (2011) applied the six variables of Cabrera, Nora, and Casteneda's (1993) Integrated Model of Student Retention to student veterans at three universities. This study failed to identify significant impact of these variables on student retention. A second study was conducted to apply another model for student retention to determine whether this model explains the retention of student veterans. This chapter will focus on the variables identified by Bean and Metzner (1985) that influence institutional satisfaction and persistence.

Literature Review

As student veteran enrollment has increased, attention to this population in the higher education literature has also increased. This section includes a summary of recently published research, especially that reflecting on the satisfaction and retention of student veterans.

Griffin and Gilbert (2015) examined the transition of student veterans using Schlossberg's Transition Theory (Anderson, Goodman, & Schlossberg, 2012; Goodman, Schlossberg, & Anderson, 2006; Schlossberg, Waters, & Goodman, 1995) and identified several themes related to personnel and services, institutional structures, and social and cultural support. In particular, veterans offices, campus leaders, faculty, and staff need to be educated on the needs of student veterans (Griffin & Gilbert, 2015, p. 81). Further, institutions should be encouraged to create institutional structures to track student veterans during their enrollment and systems that enable veterans to apply previous credit and military programs to degree programs and efficiently process educational benefits (Griffin & Gilbert, 2015, p. 84). Finally, institutions should provide opportunities for veterans to connect with peers and campus personnel. When these conditions existed, student veterans expressed a better transitional experience.

Durdella and Kim (2012) examined the patterns of outcomes for student veterans, concluding they report lower GPAs and lower levels of sense of belonging than their traditional student peers:

> Despite spending more time studying, collaboratively working with peers, and interacting with faculty, that student veterans spend more time working and enter a research university as transfer students may intervene with the positive effects of

stronger academic engagement. Consequently, in spite of having higher levels of investment in academic activities, student veteran investment may not be as meaningful as nonveteran students. (p. 122)

Furthermore, student veterans are often "balancing work and family commitments that compete with the demands of being a college student" and are more likely to "interpret their college experiences through a military cultural lens" (Durdella & Kim, 2012, p. 123). Therefore, the student experience can be perceived much differently for veterans than for other student subpopulations. They often approach their class responsibilities with a mission mentality, using assignments as "checkpoints" and viewing the final grade as evidence of success (or failure) in meeting their objective.

A doctoral dissertation completed by Williams (2015) attempted to identify the factors influencing a veteran's intent to persist at his or her current institution. Drawing on samples from community colleges and four-year institutions, Williams found that 94.8% of participants expressed an intent to return to their current institution, regardless of financial, relationship, personal, or demographic factors. Among community college veterans in the study, the more academically prepared the student considered himself or herself, the more likely he or she would consider continuing his or her enrollment. Williams suggested that institutions of higher education should "include pre-entry or early transition academic success sessions, online resources or a special session during orientation" (p. 105). Additionally, Williams suggested that higher education should partner with the military to establish educational preparation programs that highlight academic expectations, offer writing and math skills training, and provide information on accessing military educational benefits.

To identify the biggest challenges veterans face on a college campus, Kirchner, Coryell, and Yelich Biniecki (2014) surveyed student veterans who identified the following concerns: balancing other responsibilities with school, transitioning from soldier to student, connecting to others on campus, accessing financial aid, and finding employment (p. 15). However, Kirchner et al. suggested additional research may further validate the need for veteran support to institutional administrators.

To identify factors associated with non-completion, Molina and Morse (2015) used NCES data to study a group of 1.1 million military-connected undergraduates, defined as "National Guard members, reservists, active duty personnel, and veterans" (p. 1). When applying the U.S. Department of Education's index of risk for not completing a college education, Molina and Morse concluded,

"Seven percent of reservists and six percent of National Guard members who were in college had no circumstances associated with not completing college, while all active duty personnel and veterans had at least one factor associated with not finishing college" (p. 15). These factors included delayed college enrollment, no high school diploma, part-time college enrollment, financial independence, presence of dependents, single-parent status, and full-time work while in college (Molina & Morse, 2015, p. 15).

When examining student veterans through a holistic lens, Grimes et al. (2011) indicated that student veterans' experiences are consistent with those of nontraditional students. Therefore, institutions of higher education should establish or adopt services for the nontraditional population. Grimes et al. concluded that student veterans are highly focused on their academic performance, and veterans services offices are more focused on business matters, such as processing educational benefits. This creates a mismatch between institutional priorities and student expectations. Grimes et al. suggested, "Administrators must reevaluate ideas of how to engage today's students and subsequently offer the appropriate support to foster a sense of belonging and promote success for all students" (p. 71).

As many institutions of higher education are focused on better serving student veterans, Vaccaro (2015) warns that although veterans fit the standard profile of nontraditional students, the experience and needs of individual veterans can vary greatly. Vaccaro concluded that student veterans expressed a need to be seen as an individual, not just as a veteran. Their military experiences varied greatly, and what applies to one veteran, may not apply to another. Vaccaro summarizes the concerns expressed by several participants, noting that "the combination of assumptions and stereotypes about student veterans resulted in homogenization, gross generalizations, and inappropriate initiatives by higher education professionals" (p. 356). In her conclusion, Vaccaro suggested that administrators ask student veterans about their experiences through climate studies, program evaluations, and informal conversations (p. 357).

Finally, Bagby, Barnard-Brak, Thompson, and Sulak (2015) conducted a phenomenological study of veteran transition into higher education, with eight of the 11 participants expressing the importance of earning a college degree. One participant, a former Marine, said, "The desire in the back of my mind to pursue my education just started yelling louder and louder" (p. 6). Transitional concerns identified were the lack of structure and sense of community felt in a college environment. One participant was initially nervous about being an older student, but ended up making friends. He said, "I made friends as soon as I got here, which I wasn't sure that I was going to. I guess I am fortunate enough not to look too old"

(Bagby et al., 2015, p. 9). Another veteran noted that he found a connection with students in his major. Bagby et al. (2015) suggested that colleges and universities must reach out and establish relationships with student veterans, regardless of the size of the population. These students are having different experiences than their nonveteran peers, and institutions should remain cognizant of student veterans' perceptions of their environment.

This brief review of the literature highlights the need for further inquiry into the factors that influence student veterans' intent to persist at their current institution of higher education. Several authors cited the lack of empirical research in this area. In several examples, themes and barriers to success were identified, but these themes were generally not confirmed with statistically significant results. This chapter will attempt to quantitatively confirm themes emerging from the literature.

Theoretical Framework

Bean and Metzner (1985) defined nontraditional students as being over the age of 25, not residing on campus, less focused on socialization, and more focused on coursework (p. 488). More recently, scholars have created their own definitions of nontraditional students. St. John and Tuttle (2004) categorized nontraditional students as follows: low income/low socioeconomic status, low-income women, single parents, high school non-completers, military servicemembers, former foster youth, unemployed, and African American men. Student veterans fit the definitions of nontraditional students in the higher education literature (St. John & Tuttle, 2004; Compton, Cox, & Laanan, 2006; Durdella & Kim, 2012; Kirchner et al., 2014; Molina & Morse, 2015).

Bean and Metzer's (1985) Conceptual Model of Nontraditional Undergraduate Student Attrition has been largely accepted as a standard model for identifying factors that contribute to the retention of nontraditional students. The six variables include background, academics, environment, social integration, academic outcomes, and psychological outcomes. Each of these variables have subvariables that contribute to the outlined variables. For the purpose of this study, subvariables were modified to better fit a student veteran's experience and background. Those modifications will be explained in great detail in the methodology section of this chapter.

Research Design and Methodology

This quantitative study analyzed factors that impact the retention of nontraditional students in order to identify and analyze the factors that contribute to student veterans' intent to persist at their current university. Traditional hypothesis testing was performed to determine whether the six variables in the Conceptual Model of Nontraditional Undergraduate Students significantly affect a student veteran's intent to persist.

Students who received veteran educational benefits at the two large, public research universities in the Southern United States were the sample for this study. Both universities have an established veterans center and have been recognized by various publications as being veteran-friendly campuses. One university is in a rural area and had a veteran population of approximately 660 students in fall 2015. The other is in a metropolitan area with a veteran population of approximately 400 students.

The online anonymous survey instrument was designed by the author and created specifically to collect quantitative data that relates to the variables and sub-variables identified by Bean and Metzner (1985). The survey included 101 questions with a variety of response options, including open-ended, multiple choice, or 5-point Likert-type responses ranging from *strongly disagree* (1) to *strongly agree* (5). A final, open-ended question asked participants to share any additional comments about their college experience. Demographic information was also collected. The dependent variable question measured the student veteran's intent to persist. Specifically, the question was "It is likely that I will re-enroll at my current institution in the spring semester."

Questions related to Bean and Metzer's model served as independent variables for the study and included the following:

- **Student background** (i.e., age, residence, previous academic performance, military background, number of deployments, and work hours per week)

- **Academics** (i.e., study habits, academic advising, and course availability)

  » I was confident in my study habits when I started college.

  » My academic advisor has helped me achieve my academic goals.

- **Environment** (i.e., finances, hours of employment, outside encouragement, family responsibilities, and opportunity to transfer)

  » I have had no difficulty in receiving my educational benefits.

  » I have considered dropping out of college due to financial difficulty.

- **Social integration** (i.e., participation in extracurricular activities, peer friendships on campus, relationships with instructors outside of class, and evaluation of those experiences).

  » I have talked to my instructors outside of class.

  » It has been easy to meet and make friends on campus.

- ***Academic outcomes*** (i.e., self-reported GPA)
- ***Psychological outcomes*** (i.e., utility, satisfaction, goal commitment, stress, and personal issues/health)
  - » Completing my degree will help me get the job I want.
  - » I am eager to learn new things in my classes.

The survey was tested and determined to be statistically reliable.

Before the survey was distributed, the research protocol was approved by the Institutional Review Board (IRB) at the author's campus of employment. The criteria for selection of the population was the same at both universities. In an effort to ensure anonymity and designate responses from institution to institution, two identical surveys were created. Each university was sent a link corresponding with the designated survey. The veterans services administrator at each university sent the message and survey link to an e-mail distribution list of students who had self-identified as veterans.

Participants in this study were predominately Caucasian males who were enrolled full time, participating in on-campus instruction for more than half of their courses. Their average age was 30.2 years, and more than half were single with no dependents. Participants predominately worked part time, averaging 15.9 hours per week. In relation to their military service, the clear majority of participants either received honorable or medical discharges. Only 20% were on active duty or members of the National Guard or reserve. Participants served for an average of 6.02 years, and 77% of achieved a rank of E4 or E5, meaning they had been appointed to a leadership role and had received some form of leadership training in order to be promoted. When asked if they had deployed to a combat zone, 61% said yes, averaging 2.01 deployments. Of those who deployed, 47% indicated that they had been directly involved in combat. Academically, 67% of participants self-reported that they had a grade point average of over 3.01, and 6.6% reported a grade point average below 2.0 (see Table 9.1).

The data analysis consisted of a breakdown of demographic characteristics, one-way analysis of variance, and multiple regression. Nominal data were used to determine demographic characteristics. A one-way analysis of variance was used to determine if there was a significant difference between responses at the two universities. There was no significant difference between the two universities, allowing the data to be combined for analysis. Finally, multiple regression was used for each of the variables and subvariables to estimate the statistical impact of each on the dependent variable. A one-way MANOVA revealed no significant multivariate effects for institution (Wilks' $\Lambda = .730$, $F(6, 24) = 1.482$, $p = .226$).

Table 9.1
Participant Demographics

Variable	Institution A (n = 56)	Institution B (n = 30)	Total (n = 86)
Gender			
Female	17%	33%	23%
Male	83%	67%	77%
Ethnicity			
African American	0%	41%	14%
Asian	6%	7%	6%
Caucasian	67%	41%	57%
Hispanic	20%	3%	14%
Other	7%	7%	7%
Mean Age	29.6	32.3	30.2
Classification			
Freshman	11%	17%	13%
Sophomore	19%	23%	20%
Junior	24%	43%	31%
Senior	46%	17%	36%
Enrollment status			
Full-time	96%	83%	90%
Part-time	4%	17%	10%
Primary method of instruction			
Base, extension center, branch campus	4%	7%	5%
Traditional on-campus classes	96%	93%	95%
Credits earned	47.7	42.6	45.9
Credits applied to degree	26.1	30.6	27.8
Housing status			
On-campus	2%	0%	1%
Off-campus	86%	63%	78%
Commute 10 miles or more	86%	37%	21%

continued on page 155

continued from page 154

Variable	Institution A (*n* = 56)	Institution B (*n* = 30)	Total (*n* = 86)
Marital status			
Single	50%	52%	52%
Married	36%	41%	39%
Divorced	14%	7%	8%
Dependents			
No	55%	59%	57%
Yes	45%	41%	43%
Employment status			
Full-time	8%	19%	12%
Part-time (off campus)	36%	26%	32%
Part-time (on campus)	6%	15%	9%
Not employed	50%	44%	47%
Number of hours worked	15.8	16.1	15.9
Military branch			
Air Force	17%	13%	15%
Army	41%	43%	42%
Marine Corps	31%	13%	25%
Navy	11%	27%	17%
Coast Guard	0%	3%	1%
Current status			
Active duty	2%	4%	2%
Honorable discharge	70%	57%	66%
Medical discharge	4%	7%	5%
Individual ready reserve	6%	7%	6%
Active reserve	11%	11%	10%
Active National Guard	6%	14%	8%
Other than honorable discharge	2%	0%	1%
Years of service	6.03	7.07	6.39

continued on page 156

continued from page 155

Variable	Institution A (*n* = 56)	Institution B (*n* = 30)	Total (*n* = 86)
Highest pay grade achieved			
E1	0%	3%	1%
E2	0%	3%	1%
E3	8%	17%	6%
E4	55%	40%	49%
E5	28%	27%	28%
E6	8%	7%	7%
E7	2%	3%	2%
Deployed to combat zone			
Yes	70%	43%	61%
No	30%	57%	39%
Directly involved in combat			
Yes	43%	58%	47%
No	57%	42%	53%
Number of deployments	=1.94	2.17	2.01

Results

Most participants (87.84%) either agreed or strongly agreed that they intended to re-enroll at their current institution in the spring semester. The full regression was $(R = .428)$, $F(6, 56) = 2.090$, $p = 0.069$, indicating that the resulting model was not significantly accurate (see Table 9.2). However, when examining each variable, GPA was a statistically significant predictor variable $(t(56) = 3.199, p = .002)$ of intent to persist. None of the other predictor variables—background $(t(56) = 0.905, p = .370)$, academic $(t(56) = -0.930, p = .356)$, environment $(t(56) = -0.705, p = .484)$, social integration $(t(56) = -0.686, p = .495)$, or psychological $(t(56) = 0.076, p = .585)$—were significant predictors of intent to persist. Among the subvariables, only age $(t(60) = -2.006, p = .049)$ and outside encouragement $(t(66) = 2.700, p = .009)$ were significant predictors of intent to persist.

Table 9.2
Variable Regression Matrix Table

Model	B	Standard Error	β
Constant	1.678	1.792	
Background	0.008	0.009	0.149
Academic	−0.024	0.026	−0.129
Environment	−0.008	0.011	−0.117
GPA	0.669	0.209	.442*
Social integration	−0.011	0.017	0.076

*Note. $R = .428$. Adj. $R^2 = .095$
*$p < 0.05$

Discussion

The results of this study and the previous study by Van Dusen (2011) indicate that generally accepted models of student retention (Bean & Metzner, 1985; Cabrera et al., 1993) should be applied to student veteran populations with caution. These results are consistent with Williams' (2015) analysis that indicated that variables, such as financial, relationship, personal or demographic factors, were not statistically significant predictors of intent to persist. Grimes et al.'s (2011) conclusion that veterans are most focused on their academic performance is supported with the statistical significance of the impact of GPA on intent to persist. Therefore, continued research on this population of students is necessary to gain a better understanding of the factors that influence their persistence at colleges and universities.

When examining the results of the subvariable analysis, two assumptions can be made. The first regarding the negative correlation ($t = −2.006$) of age suggests that the younger the veteran is, the more likely he or she will express an intent to persist. Being closer in age to nonveteran peers may lead to greater comfort in the environment for student veterans. This is consistent with the findings of Bagby et al. (2015) where student veterans expressed concerns about feeling considerably older than traditional students. The second statistically significant subvariable was outside encouragement ($t = 2.700$) — family and close friends' support during the student's educational pursuit, in particular. In the open-ended question at the end of the survey, one student articulated the relationship between GPA and family when he said:

Prior to enlisting, I attended a junior college and in three semesters had a 1.2 GPA. At Institution A, I am now nine hours away from an electrical engineering degree with a 3.6 GPA. The Marines taught me how to channel my energy and focus on something. Most of all, it is my wife and daughter that drive me to do well.

When considering student veterans' focus on GPA and academic performance, institutions of higher education should communicate with families and veterans during the recruitment process about academic resources and support systems to articulate the institutional commitment to the success of student veterans.

Limitations

The data collection was limited to two universities, so it cannot be assumed that the results are generalizable to the wider population of student veterans. Due to time constraints and anonymity, overall retention and graduation were not measured. Future research should look at both intent to persist and actual persistence rates to see if there are gaps between intention and outcomes. Such research should also seek to identify possible barriers to achieving intentions.

Implications

Even though the results of this study indicated that Bean and Metzer's (1985) Conceptual Model of Nontraditional Undergraduate Students is not a good fit for student veterans, college and university administrators can use this study to drive their policies and programs related to student veterans. As Vaccaro (2015) suggested, colleges and universities should communicate with student veterans to better assess their experiences. If several institutions of higher education conducted experiential assessments, themes may emerge that can be empirically measured on a larger scale.

Institutions should consider their message when reaching out to prospective military-connected students. The message should consist of success stories from veterans of various ages and backgrounds, highlighting average GPA, graduation rates, and programs of study enrolling large numbers of veterans. That message can be strengthened by accenting the services available to students to enhance academic performance (e.g., tutoring resources, supplemental instruction, experiential learning programs, disability resources, internships, and career preparation programs). As the institution communicates with currently enrolled student veterans, those messages should be reiterated on a regular basis. The more a student veteran can be reminded of resources available that can enhance their academic performance, the greater the likelihood that the veteran will engage in those resources.

If student veterans see why other successful students made their college choice, they could be more likely to enroll at a specific college. As long as the conversation about how to retain and graduate student veterans continues, this population of students will continue to succeed. When they do, colleges and universities need to share their stories. Additionally, colleges and universities should create targeted recruiting campaigns aimed at families. By sharing messages from a student veteran's family and friends expressing why they encouraged their loved one to enroll at that specific college or university, other families may consider encouraging their loved one to consider college. Additionally, we need to reflect the diversity of veterans in these messages. Marketing campaigns should reflect age diversity in particular so that older veterans see themselves succeeding.

As a guide for other veterans, Bracewell (2014) chronicled his experience from exiting the military through earning his baccalaureate degree in three years. He credits his wife for encouraging him to start school and the support he received from faculty and staff during his journey. Much of the book focused on how his decisions impacted his GPA, both positively and negatively. In his self-published success guide, Bracewell reflected on his personal academic success when he wrote, "I figured out a way to master my own college learning environment and structure once I started my second year of school" (p. 33). He attributed his success to taking possession and control of his educational experience. Bracewell summarized this belief when he wrote, "I strongly believe that the only limit one has is the mind and how they think about situations in life with their mind. I realized if I did not look in the direction where I wanted to be in I would not have been able to make the outcome successful" (p. 50).

This concept was echoed by General Charles Krulak, former commandant of the U.S. Marine Corps, when he discussed the foundational changes in new recruit boot camp. The emphasis was shifted from following orders to developing a Marine's internal locus of control. As described by Duhigg (2016), "Internal locus of control has been linked with academic success, higher self-motivation, and social maturity, lower incidences of stress and depression, and longer lifespan" (p. 23). The shift in the Marine Corps training philosophy has given Marines the tools to adapt to situations and to practice feeling in control of their situation. Locus of control may provide a familiar framework for institutions of higher education to approach conversations about academic success with student veterans.

References

Anderson, M. Goodman, J., & Schlossberg, N. (2012). *Counseling adults in transition: Linking Schlossberg's theory with practice in a diverse world.* New York: Springer.

Bagby, J. H., Barnard-Brak, L., Thompson, L. W., & Sulak, T. (2015). Is anyone listening? An ecological systems perspective on veterans transitioning from the military to academia. *Military Behavioral Health, 3*(4), 219–229.

Bean, J. P., & Metzner, B. S. (1985). A conceptual model of nontraditional undergraduate student attrition. *Review of Educational Research, 55*, 485–540.

Bracewell, K. A. (2014). *A veteran's road to college success.* Publisher: Author.

Cabrera, A. F., Nora, A., & Casteneda, M. B. (1993). College persistence: Structural equations modeling test of the integrated model of student retention. *The Journal of Higher Education, 64*(2), 123–139.

Cate, C. A. (2014). *Million Records Project: Research from Student Veterans of America.* Student Veterans of America, Washington, DC.

Compton, J. I., Cox, E., & Laanan, F. S. (2006). Adult learners in transition. *New Directions for Student Services, 114*, 73–80.

Cook, B. J., & Kim, Y. (2009). *From soldier to student: Easing the transition of service members on campus.* American Council on Education: Washington, D.C.

Duhigg, C. (2016). *Smarter, faster, better: The secrets of being productive in life and business.* New York, NY: Random House.

Durdella, N., & Kim, Y. K. (2012). Understanding patterns of college outcomes among student veterans. *Journal of Studies in Education, 2*(2), 109–129.

Goodman, J., Schlossberg, N. K., & Anderson, M. L. (2006). *Counseling adults in transition: Linking practice with theory* (3rd ed.). New York, NY: Springer.

Griffin, K. A., & Gilbert, C. K. (2015, January/February). Better transitions for troops: An application of Schlossberg's transition framework to analyses of barriers and institutional support structures for student veterans. *The Journal of Higher Education, 86*(1), 71–97.

Grimes, A., Meehan, M., Miller, D., Mills, S. E., Ward, M. C., & Wilkerson, N. P. (2011). Beyond the barricade: A holistic view of veteran students at an urban university. *Journal of the Indiana University Student Personnel Association, 62*–74.

Kirchner, M. J., Coryell, L., & Yelich Biniecki, S. (2014, September). Promising practices for engaging student veterans. *Quality Approaches in Higher Education, 5*(1), 12–18.

Lighthall, A. (2012). Ten things you should know about today's student veteran. *Thought & Action, 80.*

Molina, D., & Morse, A. (2015). *Military-connected undergraduates.* Washington, DC: American Council on Education.

National Center for Education Statistics. (2015). *The condition of education 2015* (NCES 2015–144). Washington, DC: U.S. Department of Education.

New, J. (October 14, 2014). Repeat non-completers. *Inside Higher Education*. Retrieved March 6, 2016, from https://www.insidehighered.com/news/2014/10/07/two-thirds-non-first-time-students-do-not-graduate

Schlossberg, N. K., Waters, E. B., & Goodman, J. (1995). *Counseling adults in transition: Linking practice with theory* (2nd ed.). New York, NY: Springer.

Strawn, P., Draper, A., & Rothenberg, L. (2009). *From military service to student life: Strategies for supporting student veterans on campus*. Washington, DC: The Advisory Board Company.

St. John, E. P., & Tuttle, T. J. (2004). *Financial aid and postsecondary opportunity for nontraditional age, pre-college students: The roles of information and the education delivery systems*. Boston, MA: The Eucational Research Institute.

U. S. Department of Veterans Affairs (2016). *History and timeline*. Retrieved March 6, 2016, from http://www.benefits.va.gov/gibill/history.asp

Vaccaro, A. (2015). "It's not one size fits all": Diversity among student veterans. *Journal of Student Affairs Research and Practice, 42*(4), 347–358.

Van Dusen, R. L. (2011). *A quantitative study of student veterans' intent to persist* (Doctoral dissertation, Texas Tech University).

Williams, D. N. (2015). *Boots on the ground: Examining transition factors for military and veteran student academic success.* (Doctoral dissertation, Iowa State University).

CHAPTER 10

Essential Practices for Student Veterans in the California Community College System

Wayne K. Miller II

This study investigates essential practices for serving enrolled student veterans in the California Community College System, revealing eight essential practices for effectively serving student veterans with and without disabilities. The California Community College System felt a strong need to investigate the difference between staff and student veterans' opinions of essential practices serving student veterans. The study using Modified Delphi design (Skulmoski, Hartman, & Krahn, 2007; Turoff & Hiltz, 1996) achieved consensus between groups of experienced student veteran program directors (practitioners) and student veterans identifying essential practices for helping student veterans with and without disabilities succeed in postsecondary education in California community colleges. A list of essential practices was compiled from research about student veterans with disabilities (Church, 2009a, 2009b; DiRamio & Spires, 2009; Madaus, Miller, & Vance, 2009; Ruh, Spicer, & Vaughn, 2009; Shackelford, 2009; Smith-Osborne, 2009; Tanielian & Jaycox, 2008; Vance & Miller, 2009a, 2009b) and student veterans without disabilities (Ackerman, DiRamio, & Garza Mitchell, 2009; Baechtold & DeSawal, 2009; Branker, 2009; Burnett & Segoria, 2009; Byman, 2007; Cook & Kim, 2009; Ford, Northrup, & Wiley, 2009).

These practices are (see also Table 10.1):

- Each California community college campus must have a veterans resource center.

- Ensure each veteran has access to full learning opportunities.

- Each California community college campus ensures there is physical access to all facilities.

- Get information about my specific veterans' needs from the veterans on my campus.

- Each California community college campus makes sure every student veteran has a vocationally useful education goal.

- Career services on each California community college campus should be able to assist student veterans to prepare for job interviews by helping them translate their military abilities, knowledge, and skills to the "civilian world."

- Each California community college president and staff should support student veteran success.

- Each campus-based student veterans program should collaborate with the disability services office to provide each student with an understanding of his or her rights, especially pertaining to the ADA Amendments Act of 2008 and Section 504 of Vocational Rehabilitation Act of 1973.

The essential practice sections provide recommendations for implementation.

Table 10.1
Chi-Square Results for the Top Eight Essential Practices ($N = 496$)

Rank	Essential practice	n	Times cited	Consensus %	χ^2	p value	df
1	Campus veterans center	454	441	97.1	432.1	< .001	1
2 (tie)	Learning opportunities	447	428	95.7	374.2	< .001	1
2 (tie)	Physical access	447	428	95.7	374.2	< .001	1
2 (tie)	Campus veteran information	447	428	95.7	374.2	< .001	1
5	Vocational goal	454	417	91.9	318.1	< .001	1
6	Career service help	449	413	92.0	316.5	< .001	1
7	Top-down support	457	413	90.4	304.1	< .001	1
8	Understanding rights	448	405	90.4	295.5	< .001	1

Note. For rating this essential practice, student veteran respondents did not use the importance rating. Therefore, 4-point Likert scales were collapsed by combining "essential" and "important" into "Yes" and "not important" and "somewhat important" into a "no" grouping ($n = 19$) for dichotomous analysis of the combined rankings. Not all respondents answered questions for every practice, making for different *n*s.

This study relied heavily on the RAND Corporation's Delphi technique of collecting data from expert panel members in order to forecast outcomes accurately. Delphi participants were selected using a nomination process similar to snowball sampling in which experts were solicited and asked to supply names of other experts if possible (Streveler, Olds, Miller, & Nelson, 2003). In this study, veterans resource managers, the High Tech Center Training Unit director, and the California Community College Counselors Office provided referrals to the expert panel. Essential practices included those previously identified practices (Miller, 2011), which were corroborated by 496 student veterans. However, not every student veteran opined on every practice, resulting in differing N values (see Table 10.1).

Additionally, some of the expert panelists and student veterans included their own comments to the written portion of the study, adding richness to the findings in terms of themes, patterns, and commonalities leading to consensus. Expert panelists and student veterans considered four Likert-scale choices for each of the purported essential practices (i.e., not important, somewhat important, important, or essential). Correlation of practitioners' data indicated that essential practices for student veterans with disabilities were not viewed the same as those for student veterans without a disability. However, the student veteran focus groups made clear they regarded and treated all veterans the same without regard to disability. Thus, practices identified as essential by expert panelists were not consistent with those identified by student veterans.

Gall, Gall, and Borg (2007) state, "the Chi-square (χ^2) test is a nonparametric test of statistical significance used when the research data are in the form of frequency counts for two or more categories" (p. 634). In this study, the research question asks a participant to agree or disagree with a statement for veterans and practitioners. The data indicate there was agreement on certain practices (see Table 10.1), but overall, the study demonstrated that veterans and practitioners disagreed on the degree to which a practice was essential.

Essential Practice #1: Veterans Resource Center

Student veterans ($n = 457$) from California community colleges ranked this practice 454 times with a mean essentiality rating of 3.94 (see Table 10.1) with a narrow standard deviation = 0.379 and a consensus percentage of 94 (Miller, 2014, p. 109). The χ^2 result for this essential practice was statistically significant ($\chi^2 = 831.8$). For rating this essential practice, student veteran respondents did not use the importance rating (see Table 10.1). Chi-square test results for this essential practice were statistically significant ($\chi^2 = 432.1$ for student veterans). Since this is a relatively large sample, the combined analysis yielded good practical significance results ($r = .9756$; with a 95% confidence level), which indicates that California Community College System student veterans deem having a veterans resource center as the highest rated essential practice. Both practitioners and student veterans agreed this was the most essential practice for California community colleges to implement. Either there is or there is not a dedicated, adequately sized veterans resource center on each campus. Where not available there may be competition for existing space; however, in the eyes of both student veterans and practitioners, this is essential to supporting student veteran success.

Essential Practice #2: Access to Learning Opportunities

As indicated in Table 10.1, statistically significant chi-square results identified Essential Practice #2: Access to Learning Opportunities. The practical implications of these statistics are that California Community College System student veterans consider access to learning opportunities a must for all students. A definition of this practice emerged from focus group responses. Several student veterans described "access to learning" as "full learning opportunities," meaning an absence of physical barriers, adequate time between classes to allow mobility-challenged students to arrive on time, lack of harassment from instructors in classes because of veteran status, and respectful and friendly class participation, among others. Implementing this essential practice requires campus administration to review all aspects of class offerings. Treatment in the classroom is problematic. Instructors and students unsupportive of student veterans must not impede student veterans' learning opportunities, nor should student veterans interfere with others' opportunity to learn.

Essential Practice #3: Physical Access

More than 95% of the students (both disabled and abled) surveyed expressed concern for accessibility to campus buildings, personal safety, and campus climate. The school should make sure ANY student with physical mobility limitations can physically access all the facilities that students are entitled to access (Miller, 2014, p. 248):

- I would love to have access to a gym.
- Vets with canes having to navigate through construction of bike racks and new math portables is not really safe or in code.
- I feel often unsafe at *[location removed]*, as there have been three [suicide] incidences in one semester, and NOTHING is being done for vets who are prone to PTSD.
- Serious lack of handicap parking at the schools means a very painful and long walk to your buildings.

Personal observations regarding physical access indicated that student veteran remarks were accurate. The closest handicapped parking was more than 100 yards from the class building, yet closer, non-reserved parking spots were available. These physical limitations affect all students with access issues. A redistribution of handicapped parking would yield a friendlier campus for all. Again, this requires administration to review all aspects of institutional offerings.

Essential Practice #4: Get Information

Colleges collect surprisingly little information from veterans, and participants believed that the characteristics of their unique student population can be different at each campus and can change regularly. Support for this essential practice suggests that campus administrators should gather information each semester to determine the characteristics of currently enrolled student veterans. An important next step is communicating this information appropriately to campus stakeholders and support staff in both academic affairs and student affairs. Some of the enlightening comments from the student veteran participants included:

- Campus staff should know every bit as much about the needs of student veterans as they know about the needs of DSPS [*Disabled Student Program and Services*] students, EOPS [*Extended Opportunity Program and Services*] students, and minority students. There is no valid reason for staff to know less about veterans' needs than they know about the others.

- Misinformation is worse than no information.

- Even some of the staff at my school subscribe to a lot of stereotypes regarding veterans, PTSD, and wounded warriors.

- This is hard if the student vet program staff is headed by someone who has never been a vet themselves and is very out of touch with our needs and mindsets (Miller, 2014, pp. 260–264).

- The development and implementation of a common veterans checklist used by financial aid, disability services, and veterans-certifying services will assist in gathering necessary data with student permission. This will make accurate data available on a timely basis.

Essential Practice #5: Vocationally Useful Goal

Nearly 92% of students surveyed identified this essential practice suggesting a career-minded emphasis, lending support to the notion that student veterans are not interested in classes that do not lead to the end goal of job and career. Wartime service in the military, particularly in combat zones, likely instilled in many veterans the notion that they have indeed achieved the requisite cognitive development and the level of transferable skills needed prior to entering college. As with the general student population and skeptical parents, staff in academic and student affairs may need to place special emphasis on explaining the need for general education classes that support skills that employers want even though not linked to a specific vocation. Students may also need help translating skills learned in the military into civilian job settings. Use of the U.S. Department of Education's Veterans Upward Bound Program (2017) may help prepare student veterans in many subjects, but especially math and English.

The findings also support the idea that student veterans want a college that helps them work toward credentials leading them to a well-paying job, while also allowing them to use their benefits wisely.

- This is important because many veterans have started on their paths to jobs from the military without understanding how their desired career fits into the civilian world and without goals, making these changes can become complicated.

- It's been 16 years since I got out and, in that time, I completed 44 units with no real goal. ... If I had one 16 years ago I might have my bachelor's and not lost my network admin job recently. (Miller, 2014, pp. 255–256)

Having the goal in mind is essential for students using military educational benefits (Post-9/11 Veterans Educational Assistance Act, 2008). Importantly, Veterans Affairs (Post-9/11 Veterans Educational Assistance Act, 2008) does not pay for courses that do not specifically lead to a particular degree. Additionally, a student veteran failing to properly identify a career track may lose future educational benefits. Development of a close working relationship between career services and veterans centers can mitigate the challenges presented by this essential practice and support Essential Practice #6: Career Services.

Essential Practice #6: Career Services

Student veterans deem having a career services professional who can assist them as essential, particularly with information and guidance toward their chosen civilian vocation. Students reflected on other aspects of this essential practice in their comments:

- This is a very important service that so many veterans would benefit from. As it is now, nobody does this adequately for veterans. Ideally, the VA should sponsor or offer this support to veterans. The fact is, though, that while they make an attempt, every veteran I have heard from who describes the VA's attempt at this says it was woefully inadequate.

Interestingly, there appears to be a thread running through the first six practices: Each focuses on the institutional view of students, a narrative based on the perspective of the college or university administration, staff, and faculty. The institutional perspective as narrative is a relatively common phenomenon when studying issues of majority/minority equity and power. Implementation of systems that activate institutional action should be the goal of every California community college.

Essential Practice #7: Top-Down Support

Because 90% of the veterans surveyed cite Essential Practice #7, this population of students view the support of the campus president and staff as essential to their success. Thus, the opinions of student veterans regarding top-down support, while perhaps quite provocative, are worthy of reflection and action:

- Veterans are students who make up a heavy demographic of community colleges. Do not just take our money and leave us to hang and dry.

- Take interest in the veteran student population to succeed or lose accreditation (with the VA).

- Veterans sacrifice a lot for their country and its citizens. I think that the citizens should try to do as much as they can for the veterans in return.

- I think this is important mostly because there are increasingly more veterans and if they are successful students, it helps everyone in the long run.

- Administrators should be required to get training on VA programs and how they have a mutual benefit for both the school and the veteran.

- This is needed. Veterans will be successful either way, but it helps a lot knowing the higher-ups have your back and support you. It's sad when veterans have to put in their own Veterans Day and Memorial Day celebrations. This should be changed and every college should follow suit. It's the least they can do. (Miller, 2014, pp. 265–269)

Presentations by these top college administrators on the value of student veterans to the institution and community are a visible demonstration of institutional purpose and intent. Equally important is the physical presence of top institution administrators at the veterans center. Occasional visits to the center by these individuals would be a physical demonstration of support.

Essential Practice #8: Understanding Rights

Of all the essential practices cited by student veterans in this study, this was the most surprising. Ninety percent of veterans felt a need to understand better their rights in terms of benefits, disability support, and privacy. On the other hand, it was disturbing to learn how many student veterans did not apply for Pell Grants mostly due to lack of information about financial support opportunities. Some of the student comments included:

- I didn't know that I could use both [Pell Grant and Post-9/11 GI Bill].

- The Privacy Act 1974 [related to] assistance with veterans [and] ethnicity is truly challenging.

- I was not sent to campus disability services, I was sent to transfer counseling, then back to the vet center on campus, then back to transfer counseling, then finally after much defeat, was granted extra time, by suggestion of Dr. [name removed]. (Miller, 2014, pp. 307–308)

While on a tour of a campus of a veterans resource center at one of the community colleges, academic assistive technology equipment (e.g., operational screen magnifier) normally seen in a disability services lab was present. Inquiries into how this equipment arrived in the center indicated it was stored in this room simply because there was space available. Apparently, on their own and without prompting or permission, student veterans in the center began to use the machine and, realizing that it made print larger, trained other student veterans on its use and value for reading.

The adoption of the screen magnifier by student veterans on this campus challenges the status quo in disability services and raises the question of whether use of assistive technologies should be limited only to those with documented disabilities. Universal use of assistive technology by all students is not a new idea. For example, Edyburn (2004) noted:

There are a considerable number of students whose performance fails to meet the expected standards. As a result, why are students without disabilities denied the opportunity to use appropriate technologies that could enhance their performance? Isn't everyone entitled to the tools they need to be successful? (p. 19)

Student veterans are an interesting postsecondary student population to consider for the use of assistive technology, whether disabled or not, for two main reasons. First, many veterans report experiencing academic "rustiness" when enrolling in college (DiRamio, Ackerman, & Mitchell, 2008) and could benefit from the assistive technology tools normally designated for use by students with disabilities. Second, research concerning the help-seeking attitudes of veteran students by DiRamio and colleagues (2015) report many are reluctant to ask for help, including academic support, likely due to the strong influence of military culture, which often equates asking for assistance as an indicator of weakness. By housing a disability services counselor in the veterans resource center with a separate office in which to conduct confidential discussions, Salt Lake Community College (Salt Lake City, Utah) demonstrates how improvements in this area are both possible and practical.

Other Noteworthy Considerations

Another finding in this study was that the student veteran's branch of service turned out to be important in understanding need. For student affairs educators and other helping professionals on campus, understanding this mix is important because each branch of service can offer a dramatically different military experience, with many students in some branches having experienced combat duty while those in other branches did not. Kleykamp (2006) posits that considering military rank and resulting experiences yields important insights into the likely personal development level of the former servicemember and his or her abilities, for example, to work with groups in class. To give campus staff a better understanding about this important consideration, Table 10.2 offers self-reported discharge ranks for California community college veterans.

Interestingly, data collected from participants in student veteran focus groups and those who responded via survey demonstrated that gender appeared not to be an issue for student veterans. Female veterans were at least as vocal and outspoken as male veterans. This is an important anecdotal finding as the composition of the U.S. military has changed significantly in the last decade, and female military personnel are as likely to find themselves in combat situations as males. Most female veterans in the study wanted all others to view them simply as veterans without regard to gender.

Table 10.2
CCCS Student Veteran Self-disclosed Discharge Ranks

| Rank | Branch of Service | | | | *n* |
	Army	Navy	Marines	Air Force	
E1 – E2	Private	Seaman	Private	Airman Basic	22
E3	Private 1st Class	Seaman	Lance Corporal	Airman 1st Class	54
E4	Corporal/Specialist	Petty Officer 3rd Class	Corporal	Senior Airman	150
E5	Sergeant	Petty Officer 2nd Class	Sergeant	Staff Sergeant	159
E6	Staff Sergeant	Petty Officer 1st Class	Staff Sergeant	Technical Sergeant	51
E7	Master Sergeant	Senior Chief Petty Officer	Master Sergeant	Senior Master Sergeant	24
E8 – E9	Sergeant Major/Command Sergeant Major	Master Chief Petty Officer	Sergeant Major	Chief Master Sergeant	12
Officer					9
Other					11

Where Do We Go From Here?

In conclusion:

The degree to which institutions can harness their resources to achieve their objectives will depend upon the clarity of these objectives and the institution's willingness to set priorities and solve its problems. This requires assessing current status, designing a change process, developing and educating senior leaders, and the obligation and nimbleness to make significant widespread change at all levels (American Council on Education, 2017).

Even though the Chancellor's Office of the California Community College System authorized this study for their system, the findings certainly have applicability to colleges across the nation. It is likely that the essential practices identified are universally important. In fact, the implementation, or lack thereof, may influence the impact on the Post-9/11 GI Bill's success or failure. These findings also support the idea of new policies within the military's educational benefits and a future iteration of the GI Bill. Ongoing research into the impact of this legislation should continue both to inform the impact of military service on society and to inform educators about how to make the postsecondary experience for veterans efficacious in influencing society without regard to the institutional or academic views of politics.

References

Ackerman, R., DiRamio, D., & Garza Mitchell, R. (2009). Transitions: Combat veterans as college students. In R. Ackerman & D. DiRamio (Eds.), *Creating a veteran-friendly campus: Strategies for transition success* (New Directions for Student Services, No. 126, pp. 5–14). San Francisco, CA: Wiley & Sons. doi:10.1002/ss.311

American Council on Education (2017). *Higher education topics: Institution effectiveness.* Washington, DC: Retrieved from http://www.acenet.edu/higher-education/topics/Pages/Institutional-Effectiveness.aspx

Baechtold, M., & DeSawal, D. (2009). Meeting the needs of women veterans. In R. Ackerman & D. DiRamio (Eds.), *Creating a veteran-friendly campus: strategies for transition success* (New Directions for Student Services, No. 126, pp. 35–43). San Francisco, CA: Wiley & Sons. doi:10.1002/ss.314

Branker, C. (2009). Deserving design: The new generation of student veterans. *Journal of Postsecondary Education and Disability, 22*(1), 59–66.

Burnett, S., & Segoria, J. (2009). Collaboration for military transition from combat to college: It takes a community. *Journal of Postsecondary Education and Disability, 22*(1), 53–58.

Byman, D. (2007, December 14). Veterans and colleges have a lot to offer each other. *The Chronicle of Higher Education, 54*(16), p. B5.

Church, T. (2009a). The growing number of veterans returning to campus. In M. Vance & L. Bridges (Eds.), *Advising students with disabilities: Striving for universal success* (2nd ed., pp. 91–100). Manhattan, KS: NACADA.

Church, T. (2009b). Returning veterans on campus with war related injuries and the long road back home. *Journal of Postsecondary Education and Disability, 22*(1), 43–52.

Cook, B., & Kim, Y. (2009). *From soldier to student: Easing the transition of service members to campus.* Washington, DC: The American Council on Education.

DiRamio, D., Ackerman, R., & Mitchell, R. (2008). From combat to campus: Voices of student-veterans. *NASPA Student Affairs Administrators in Higher Education Journal, 45*(1), 73–102.

DiRamio, D., Jarvis, K., Iverson, S., Seher, C., & Anderson, R. (2015). Out from the shadows: Female student veterans and help-seeking. *College Student Journal, 49*(1), 49–68.

DiRamio, D., & Spires, M. (2009). Partnering to assist disabled Veterans in transition. In R. Ackerman & D. DiRamio (Eds.), *Creating a veteran-friendly campus: Strategies for transition success* (New Directions for Student Services, No. 126, pp. 81–88). San Francisco, CA: Wiley & Sons. doi:10.1002/ss.319 .

Edyburn, D. L. (2004). Rethinking assistive technology. *Special Education Technology Practice, 5*(4), 16–23.

Ford, D., Northrup, P., & Wiley, L. (2009). Connections, partnerships, opportunities, and programs to enhance success for military students. In R. Ackerman & D. DiRamio (Eds.), *Creating a veteran-friendly campus: Strategies for transition success* (New Directions for Student Services, No. 126, pp. 45–54). San Francisco, CA: Wiley & Sons. doi:10.1002/ss.317

Gall, M., Gall, J., & Borg, W. (2007). *Educational research: An introduction* [8th ed]. Boston, MA: Pearson International.

Kleykamp, M. A. (2006). College, job, or the military? Enlistment during times of war. *Social Science Quarterly, 187, 87*(2), 272–290.

Madaus, J. W., Miller, W. K. II, & Vance, M. L. (2009). Veterans with disabilities in postsecondary education. *Journal of Postsecondary Education and Disability, 21*(1), 10–17.

Miller, W. K. II (2011). *Essential practices in student veterans programs: Serving veterans and veterans with disabilities in higher education. A Delphi study.* (Doctoral dissertation). ProQuest Dissertations and Theses database (Publication No. AAT 3504775). University of Connecticut.

Miller, W. K. II (2014). *Essential practices in serving student veterans in the California community college system.* Retrieved from http://extranet.cccco.edu/Portals/1/SSSP/VETS/Essential%20Practices%20for%20Serving%20Veterans.pdf

Post-9/11 Veterans Educational Assistance Act of 2008, Pub. L. No. 110–252, 122 Stat. 2323 (2009). Retrieved from http://www.law.cornell.edu/uscode/html/uscode38/ usc_sec_38_00000101----000-.htmldiramiop

Ruh, D., Spicer, P., & Vaughan, K. (2009). Helping veterans with disabilities transition to employment. *Journal of Postsecondary Education and Disability, 22*(1), 67–74.

Shackelford, A. L. (2009). Documenting the needs of student veterans with disabilities: Intersection roadblocks, solutions, and legal realities. *Journal of Postsecondary Education and Disability, 22*(1), 36–42.

Skulmoski, G., Hartman, F., & Krahn, J. (2007). The Delphi method for graduate research. *Journal of Information Technology Education, 6,* 1–21.

Smith-Osborne, A. (2009). Does the GI Bill support educational attainment for veterans with disabilities? Implications for current veterans in resuming civilian life. *Journal of Sociology & Social Welfare, 36*(4), 111–125.

Streveler, R., Olds, B., Miller, R., & Nelson, M. (2003). *Using a Delphi study to identify the most difficult concepts for students to master in thermal and transport science.* Paper presented at the annual meeting of the American Society of Engineering Education, Nashville, TN. Retrieved from: http://www.thermalinventory.com/images/Papers/2003DelphiStudy.pdf

Tanielian, T., & Jaycox, L. H. (Eds.). (2008). *Invisible wounds of war: Psychological and cognitive injuries, their consequences, and services to assist recovery.* Santa Monica, CA: Rand Corporation.

Turoff, M., & Hiltz, S. (1996). Computer based Delphi processes. In M. Adler & E. Ziglio (Eds.), *Gazing into the oracle: The Delphi method and its application to social policy and public health* (pp. 56–88). Philadelphia, PA: Kingsley.

U.S. Department of Education. (2017). *Programs: Veterans Upward Bound Program.* Washington, DC: Author. Retrieved from https://www2.ed.gov/programs/triovub/index.html

Vance, M., & Miller, W. K., II. (2009a). Serving wounded warriors: Current practices in postsecondary education. *Journal of Postsecondary Education and Disability, 21*(1), 18–35.

Vance, M. & Miller, W. K., II. (2009b). *Essential practices in academic advising.* Unpublished data.

SECTION THREE

SUMMARY, IMPLICATIONS, AND
RECOMMENDATIONS

CHAPTER 11

★★★★★★★★★★★★★★★★★★★★★★★★★★★★★★★★★★

What's Next? Charting the Course Before Moving Off the Radar

David DiRamio

Early in 2016, I had the privilege of delivering a keynote speech at a student success conference hosted by a university in Michigan. While preparing to give that talk, it dawned on me that while efforts to support student veteran success on college campuses across the nation were continuing along at a business-as-usual pace, they were also at a critical point in time. This turning point, as I see it, is occurring because post-9/11 student veteran enrollment likely peaked sometime in the fall semester of 2014 and, perhaps more importantly, absent another scandal like the VA health care crisis, advocacy and support on behalf of veterans is fading as the subject moves off the general public's radar. If this is true and interest in veterans is waning, what are the implications for student veterans and what should the higher education community be doing to support this population, even in the face of declining enrollment numbers?

In this chapter, seven areas of concern are identified and labeled as unfinished business relative to support services for student veterans. Efforts to address these seven items should continue, resume or, in some cases, begin in order to provide support for current and future veterans in higher education, particularly while there is still authentic support from senior administrators, trustees, and policy makers. Few people are against veterans or veterans' issues, but tepid support is very different from the type of support needed to sustain genuine advocacy and influence policy formation or changes. These seven areas of unfinished business include staffing and collaboration; faculty and staff training; evaluating military schooling for college credit; preparing students for the transition into the workforce; reaching out to specific populations of military-connected students; exploring the nexus of traumatic brain injury, mental health, and substance abuse; and addressing educational inequity.

Staffing Needs and Collaboration

It has been nearly a decade since the first veterans of the wars in Iraq and Afghanistan began enrolling in college using new GI Bill educational benefits, and yet many schools still have inadequately staffed veterans affairs offices (McBain, Cook, Kim, & Snead, 2012). Where enrollment numbers do not necessitate the need for a physical space or office, low staffing is understandable. However, at institutions with hundreds of military-connected students who are receiving GI Bill and other educational benefits, there is need for much more than a VA benefits-certifying official. As has been well-established in the literature, the needs of student veterans go well beyond the processing of financial aid paperwork to include academic, social, and health-related support (Elliott, Gonzalez, & Larsen, 2011; Whiteman, Barry, Mroczek, and MacDermid Wadsworth, 2013). Responsibility for processing VA educational benefits at a typical college or university is extremely challenging, and the paperwork required to support each student is complex and tedious. Frankly, the onerous duty of certification each semester could easily take up all the time of a competent staffer, thus leaving little time for the other important support services that can and should be offered to student veterans.

The American Council on Education recommends 1% to 3% enrollment of student veterans as the tipping point for offering support services in a formal, intentional way (Cook & Kim, 2009). Based on my own observations and research conducted in the past five years, including a secondary analysis of the American Council on Education's From Soldier to Student data (Cook & Kim, 2009; DiRamio & Jarvis, 2011; McBain et al., 2012), I have developed a formula for estimating staffing needs based on student enrollment numbers. Estimates noted in Figure 11.1 may be used as a starting point for serious discussions about staffing with a college president, a senior student affairs officer, and/or other senior officials involved in final hiring decisions.

Another reason that staffing needs can be so variable is related to how effective collaboration is among campus units. When units such as financial aid, career services, the registrar's office, academic support, and the counseling center partner to support student veteran success in a unified manner, the synergy can have a significant positive effect on easing the workload of the veteran support staff and may have implications for staffing requirements. In Chapter 6, "Navigating Toward Academic Success," Kees and colleagues offer a detailed description of their nationwide peer-support program. Such programs can provide needed services to students while easing the burden placed on personnel and budgetary

Larger campuses with > 5,000 students (total enrollment)
100 to 199 using benefits = One (1) FT staff + 1-2 VA work study
200 to 399 using benefits = Two (2) FT staff + 2-3 VA work study
400 to 599 using benefits = Three (3) FT staff + 3-4 VA work study
600 or more using benefits = Four (4) FT staff + 5-6t VA work study

Smaller campuses with < 5,000 students (total enrollment)
50+ using benefits? One (1) FT staff + VA work study
< 50 using benefits? Variability is too large to estimate staffing

Figure 11.1. Estimate of staffing needs based on student veteran enrollment.

resources. Community colleges and others who routinely face tight budgetary constraints should consider how a collaborative approach might work effectively to support the efforts of their VA benefits-certifying official.

In Chapter 9, "Where Do They Fit?" Van Dusen applied a model for attrition that included a campus environment component, which includes programming and services provided by the institution. Although environment in the aggregate was not significant in the findings, elements of environment, including communication and messaging, were worth noting. Colleges and universities should consider their message when reaching out to prospective military-connected students to include stories of encouragement and academic success. Encouragement, albeit from the outside, was indeed a significant factor in Van Dusen's study of retention rates.

Faculty and Staff Training

Much of the research literature about student veterans published during the past decade included recommendations for colleges and universities to conduct faculty and staff training for working with veterans (American Council on Education, 2010), including Chapters 2 (Morse & Molina) and 5 (Molina & Ang) of this volume. Less than half (47%) of the schools surveyed in From Soldier to Student II had conducted faculty–staff training though another 20% pledged to do so by 2017 (McBain et al., 2012). More recent national data on training efforts are not available; however, based on my own observations, I suspect the percentage of schools providing training for faculty and staff has not increased as promised and, in some instances, actually waned. Training done well provides faculty and staff with important information about the student veteran population's transitional and educational needs, as well as best practices for supporting them both in and out of the classroom. Understanding and acknowledging that the characteristics exhibited by veterans when compared with younger, traditionally aged students are differences, not deficits, can go a long way in creating an inclusive, welcoming environment, which is helpful to many veterans.

There is an adage in the student veteran support community: When designing training, appeal to faculty members through their hearts and administrators through their wallets. The financial appeal to administrators is simple and straightforward: Each student using GI Bill benefits is a mini-federal grant with up to 36 months of continuous funding. Faculty members, on the other hand, are less concerned about tuition and educational benefits. In my experience, most faculty want to know why there is an edge to many of the veterans in their classes and how can they set aside their ambivalence about or sometimes-fervent opposition to war to present a welcoming attitude to servicemembers.

I emphasize two related themes for faculty members as part of the training curriculum that I use. First, I reassure professors that the edgy disposition they have sensed may indeed be the way that a student who comes from a military culture expresses the need for help, whether it be for academic assistance or other matters, such as frustration with school, difficulties transitioning to civilian life, psychological challenges, or some combination of these. In military culture, one does not ask for help except within the close-knit unit in which he or she serves. Asking for help is, with few exceptions, a sign of weakness and, as one can imagine, weakness is not a virtue highly regarded in the military.

Second, I make faculty members aware that a majority of the student veterans with whom I have worked and interviewed over the years view their professors as officers, which comes with a mixed bag of connotations ranging from deep respect to high expectations. A professor's style may clash with the student veteran's "professor–officer" expectations and lead to frustration or confrontation. There are no pat answers to resolve these sorts of issues, but in my experience, training to make faculty aware of the dynamics at play certainly seems to help. If faculty and staff investigate and make themselves aware of the resources available for assisting student veterans, that effort will go a long way in allowing them to make informed referrals for students who are facing crisis and are having trouble asking for help.

Transfer Credit for Military Schooling

Of all the unfinished business items, credit for military education may be thorniest of issues. At the institutional level, each academic program reserves the right to accept or reject transfer credits regardless of the source. For most of the student veterans with whom I have spoken, the bottom line is that a veteran will accept whatever decision is made regarding the applicability of their military schooling as long as he or she feels that officials from the program, college, and/ or university have made a good-faith attempt to fairly evaluate the military transcript.

Good faith and fair evaluation are key, as suggested by a 2011 Department of Defense (DOD) Memorandum of Understanding (MOU) to all colleges and universities receiving DOD-funded tuition remittances for currently enrolled active-duty military personnel. One tenet of the MOU requires institutions to "review, and where possible, accept transfer credits for military training and experience" (U.S. Department of Defense, 2011). While the MOU only applies to active-duty personnel, I have long suspected that federal officials are seeking ways to apply this to veterans as a cost-saving strategy for a Post-9/11 GI Bill program that exceeded expenditures of $42 billion in 2014.

Consortium building among institutions and states appears to be a worthy top-down strategy to attack the issue of military credit. For example, the accrediting body known as the Midwestern Higher Education Compact (MHEC), with funding from the Lumina Foundation, is supporting the Multi-State Collaborative on Military Credit (MCMC), which is:

> an Interstate partnership of 13 states (Illinois, Indiana, Iowa, Kansas, Kentucky, Michigan, Minnesota, Missouri, Nebraska, North Dakota, Ohio, South Dakota, and Wisconsin) to advance best practices ... with special reference to translating competencies acquired through military training and experiences into milestones toward completing a college degree or earning a certificate or license. (Midwestern Higher Education Compact, 2016, p. 1)

The process for evaluating experiential credit for military training and service experiences goes beyond the scope of this chapter, but the topic is certainly on the minds of registrars and their staffs across the nation. MCMC has made headway in this area, particularly with respect to licensure and certification. By working with licensing boards and industry associations, MCMC has streamlined the process for military-connected students to apply training and service experiences toward a license or certificate and eliminated the need for community, technical, and vocational colleges to interpret each student's military record for this purpose (American Council on Education, 2015).

For larger institutions, starting with a single college or program within the institution (i.e., liberal arts or business) and working with that college's associate dean for academics to see if any programs within that college would be amenable to a more standardized approach to evaluating student veteran military transcripts is advisable. A willingness to consider accepting some military schooling for credit toward a major(s), not simply as general elective credits that would not likely help a student veteran's educational attainment goals, is the goal of such evaluation processes. Similar to the work described in Chapter 5, "Serving Those Who Served" (Molina & Ang), the American Council on Education has taken a leadership role in attempting to provide examples for registrars interpreting military school transcripts of their student veterans.

The ACE College Credit for Military Service website and its online resources (American Council on Education, 2016) are a good place to start. Advocates for military-connected students could use the ACE guide to walk academic deans through an example of an official military course and recommendations for applying credit toward a program's major. This type of exercise lays the groundwork for a cooperative effort, a pilot program of sorts, with selected colleges and programs to provide student veterans the option of choosing a major that is more inclusive of credit for military schooling. The registrar is a key partner in these efforts and vital to the success of this type of initiative. Again, in my experience, student veterans are looking for a good-faith attempt from the institution to offer more credit-friendly programs and, should a student choose to stick with a major like engineering that will not typically accept any military schooling for credit, he or she will be satisfied with that choice and be appreciative of the effort by the institution to offer alternatives.

Workforce Preparedness

Many companies listed in the Fortune 100 have some form of an initiative to hire veterans because it makes smart business sense and shows good corporate responsibility and because veterans possess skills, abilities, and attributes only found in military service. It turns out, however, that employers are underwhelmed with the preparedness of our veteran population to enter the civilian workforce. In fact, 50% of the 429 hiring professionals surveyed by the Society for Human Resource Management (SHRM) reported making specific efforts to hire veterans, but a surprisingly high 60% in the same study indicated that many veterans have difficulty adapting to workplace culture (SHRM, 2010).

In my experience, many veterans attending college today need to learn to adapt themselves to a civilian corporate culture, which is markedly different from military culture, particularly during a time of war. A student veteran will likely tell you that he or she needs no training for transferable skills development and corporate culture preparedness, perhaps even citing examples of events, some gritty and very intense, that he or she experienced during active duty. As discussed in Chapter 1, "Data-Driven Inquiry" (Zoli, Maury, & Fay), students need help translating those experiences into skills valued by civilian employers.

Time limits on education benefits may mean that servicemembers enroll in college not long after discharge and proceed to complete courses as quickly as possible without participating in any cocurricular or out-of-the-classroom experiences offered by a college. For some students, this narrow focus on coursework will have a negative impact on the transition to civilian life and employment after graduation, as opportunities to develop socially and cognitively and to identify and cultivate transferable skills valued by employers may be limited. One way that student affairs educators, especially those in the career counseling and academic advising fields, can assist students with military experience to acquire the requisite employment skills is to create opportunities for academic and social development in the broader campus community and to encourage students to become engaged in some form beyond the college classroom. Participation in the student veterans organization on campus is obviously one option, but educators should help students find experiences that are well-suited to their personal interests and educational goals. Frankly, it is part of what employers want: the dynamic and dedicated servicemember with a bit of the military cultural edge shaved off who is ready to perform capably in private business, global industry, public service, and/or civilian corporate culture.

It is worth noting the contribution that Student Veterans of America (SVA), a nonprofit coalition of student veteran groups on college campuses across the globe, has made by funding research that includes analysis of the matriculation patterns of more than 100,000 veterans in college. A description of the research and findings that SVA is producing with support from its partners is described in Cate's Chapter 8, "Academic Outcomes and the Million Records Project."

Related Subpopulations

For many, the stereotypical image of a military-connected individual is a male combat veteran. My own coauthored research has confirmed that gender and whether one served in combat is of paramount significance in military culture (Iverson, Seher, DiRamio, Jarvis, & Anderson, 2016). Perhaps because of this emphasis, most of the women we interviewed simply wished to be called veterans, with no distinction by gender. Miller noted a similar finding in Chapter 10, "Essential Practices for Student Veterans," suggesting "female veterans were at least as vocal and outspoken as male veterans" in his focus groups with students in a community college setting. Yet, gender bias—whether subtle or more outright—persists and is part of the narrative that many of the women who have served (e.g., 280,000 returning from deployments in Iraq and Afghanistan in the last decade) bring with them to our campuses. Moreover, inequities seem to persist on campus. For example, Molina and Morse (2015) discovered that female undergraduate veterans accrued significantly more debt in school than their male counterparts. Clearly, supporting this important student group, including research investigating financial need and other disparities, is a top priority as veterans move off the nation's radar. However, a more serious issue looms.

Concerns about misogyny and aggression against women in the military have been prominent in recent years. Military-connected women may perceive they are transitioning to a more welcoming and safer environment in moving to higher education. Yet, high-profile incidents at prestigious schools such as Stanford University (D'Onofrio, 2016), Baylor University (Braziller, 2016), and Wesleyan University (Barthel, 2015) and ramped up Title IX enforcement have highlighted the need for education about and policy reform in response to sexual violence at colleges and universities, as well. As part of the higher education ethos of rallying against the marginalization of student subpopulations and ensuring a safe campus environment that is free of oppression and threat (real or perceived), I challenge the higher education community to give extra consideration and thoughtfulness to this noteworthy group of women.

Another population of military-connected college students are the children of veterans using military educational benefits transferred from their parents. Their enrollment numbers are impressive and at some schools exceed the number of servicemembers enrolled. Research findings suggest that because of their experiences living in a military family, children of servicemembers have characteristics that are different from typical undergraduate students. One theme that seems to resonate with this student group is that they do connect well with each other, and student affairs educators should help them do so. Several schools have student organizations formed by these dependent children of military families, and they reap the benefits of participation in cocurricular activities, including social and philanthropic efforts, just like non-veteran students in the general population.

Mental Health and Substance Abuse

With all due respect to those who have been injured in service to our country, the signature injury of the wars in Iraq and Afghanistan is traumatic brain injury (TBI) due to a concussive blast. Unfortunately, the signature cure for many veterans who have returned with a variety of untreated problems (both physical and psychological) is self-medication using drugs and alcohol (Jakupcak et al., 2010). Interestingly, Whiteman and Barry (2011) reported that hazardous drinking was positively associated with coping motivations among student veterans but there was no connection among students without military service.

In related research referenced in Chapter 4, "Mental Health and Academic Functioning," Barry, Whiteman, MacDermind Wadsworth, and Hitt (2012) reported that student veterans consumed alcohol at about the same levels as younger, non-veteran students. However, binge-drinking habits were markedly higher than in traditional-aged college students and were associated with indicators of problem drinking and mental health symptoms, such as depression/anxiety and PTSD. As Barry and colleagues (2012) noted, "Relative to civilians and independent of college enrollment status, military personnel heavily use alcohol and binge drink at markedly higher rates" (p. 2). Campuses that offer collegiate recovery community meetings and sober social activities for students from both veterans groups and the general population are leading efforts nationally to assist college students battling addiction (Harrington Cleveland, Harris, Baker, Herbert, & Dean, 2007).

The lack of leadership and an absence of effective mental health policy in our society, in general, and higher education, specifically, make addressing the matter of substance abuse among veterans both alarming and urgent. Clearly, this is a critical piece of our unfinished business. We must continue to sound the alarm by requesting campus policies and student programming that emphasize increased resources for treatment and education.

Educational Equity

Educational opportunity is an important theme in the American narrative. Our nation's colleges and universities strive to empower students through their educational journey to pursue a pathway to socioeconomic opportunity (see Chapter 2 by Morse and Molina). However, our nation continues to struggle with inequity to opportunities that persist along socioeconomic and demographic lines. One would think that the Post-9/11 GI Bill might mitigate the educational inequities that veterans face, but their college-going profile is remarkably similar to that of traditionally underserved populations, with overrepresentation in the for-profit sector and underrepresentation in the private, nonprofit sector. Moreover, student veterans are graduating with more debt than anticipated because, although the new GI Bill is deservedly generous, unmet financial need is an issue for many.

The debt accrued by student veterans based on their unmet financial need, despite receiving military educational benefits, is alarming. Molina and Morse (2015) found that 40% of Latino student veterans accrued loan debt that averaged $5,275 and more than 53% of African American student veterans accrued loan debt that averaged $7,459. By comparison, White student veterans averaged $4,246 in loan debt. Before interest in the challenges facing veterans in college fades, more should be done to assist student veterans with the unmet financial need that extends beyond what the Post-9/11 GI Bill provides. Many student veteran organizations have established scholarships for veterans as part of their philanthropic efforts.

Attention also needs to be paid to where military-connected students are pursuing their educations amid concerns of the viability of degrees awarded by for-profit postsecondary institutions. Cate (2014) found that nearly 13% of student veterans graduated from proprietary (for-profit) institutions, which is closer to the 2013 enrollment patterns of African American students in the for-profit sector (15.8%) and nearly 60% higher than the general population of all students (8.1%). Similarly, while 19.5% of all students attended private, nonprofit colleges and universities, only 10.7% of student veterans did so, which is actually lower than the lowest underrepresented student population (i.e., Latina/os at 11%).

Conclusion

It is important to put policies in place before issues fade out and veterans move off the radar. I encourage the higher education community to act now and reach out to senior administrators and policy makers with considerations for what will be needed to support student veteran success for the next five to 10 years. Remember that student veterans are their own best advocates and, while still partially in the limelight, their requests resonate with our top officials with more influence than the voices of faculty members and staffers. A lesson learned from Lang and O'Donnell's Chapter 7, "Completing the Mission II," is to keep in mind that, as with any higher education program or initiative in today's assessment and evaluation environment, one needs data to support policymaking. In a cynical sense, no one wants to be on the wrong side of a veterans' issue in the current sociopolitical climate. However, setting cynicism aside, supporting the postsecondary pursuits of this generation of men and women who have served our country in war, helping to preserve the freedoms that we all enjoy, remains the right thing to do.

References

American Council on Education. (2010). *Ensuring success for returning veterans.* Washington, DC: Author.

American Council on Education. (2015). *Quick hits: Credit mobility and postsecondary attainment.* Retrieved from http://www.acenet.edu/news-room/Pages/Quick-Hits-Credit-Mobility-and-Postsecondary-Attainment.aspx

American Council on Education. (2016). *College credit for military service.* Retrieved from http://www.acenet.edu/news-room/Pages/Military-Guide-Online.aspx

Barry, A. E., Whiteman, S., MacDermid Wadsworth, S., & Hitt, S. (2012). The alcohol use and associated problems of student service members/veterans in higher education. *Drugs: Education, Prevention & Policy, 19*(5), 415–425.

Barthel, M. (2015, March 31). Where all the frat houses are coed. *The Atlantic Monthly.* Retrieved from www.theatlantic.com/education/archive/2015/03/wesleyan-coed-frats/389177/

Braziller, Z. (2016, October 28). Horrifying details of Baylor sexual assault scandal revealed. *New York Post.* Retrieved from nypost.com/2016/10/28/horrifying-details-of-baylor-sexual-assault-scandal-revealed

Cate, C. A. (2014). *Million Records Project: Research from Student Veterans of America.* Washington, DC: Student Veterans of America.

Cook, B. & Kim, Y. (2009). *From soldier to student: Easing the transition of service-members on campus.* Washington, DC: American Council on Education.

DiRamio, D., & Jarvis, K. (2011). *Veterans in higher education: When Johnny and Jane come marching to campus* (ASHE Higher Education Report, 37.3). San Francisco, CA: Wiley.

D'Onofrio, K. (2016, June 8). Campus rape culture: Outrage over light sentence in Stanford sexual assault. *Diversity Inc.* Retrieved from www.diversityinc.com/news/stanford-rape-brock-turner/

Elliott, M., Gonzalez, C., & Larsen, B. (2011). U.S. military veterans transition to college: Combat, PTSD, and alienation on campus. *Journal of Student Affairs Research and Practice, 48*(3), 279–296.

Harrington Cleveland, H., Harris, K. S., Baker, A. K., Herbert, R., & Dean, L. R. (2007). Characteristics of a collegiate recovery community: Maintaining recovery in an abstinence-hostile environment. *Journal of Substance Abuse Treatment, 33*(1), 13–23.

Iverson, S. V., Seher, C. L., DiRamio, D., Jarvis, K., & Anderson, R. (2016). *NASPA Journal About Women in Higher Education, 9*(2), 152–168.

Jakupcak, M., Tull, M. T., McDermott, M. J., Kaysen, D., Hunt, S., & Simpson, T. (2010). PTSD symptom clusters in relationship to alcohol misuse among Iraq and Afghanistan war veterans seeking post-deployment VA health care. *Addictive Behaviors, 35,* 840–843.

McBain, L., Cook, B., Kim, Y., & Snead, K. (2012). *From soldier to student II: Assessing campus programs for veterans and service members.* Washington, DC: American Council on Education.

Midwestern Higher Education HEC. (2016). *Multi-state collaborative on military credit.* Retrieved from http://www.mhec.org/multi-state-collaborative-on-military-credit

Molina, D., & Morse, A. (2015). *Military-connected undergraduates: Exploring differences between National Guard, reserve, active duty, and veterans in higher education.* Washington, DC: American Council on Education & NASPA – Student Affairs Administrators in Higher Education. Retrieved from http://www.acenet.edu/news-room/Documents/Military-Connected-Undergraduates.pdf

Society for Human Resource Management. (2010). *Employing military personnel and recruiting veterans.* Retrieved from www.shrm.org/Research/SurveyFindings/Documents/10–0531_Military Program Report_FNL.pdf

U.S. Department of Defense. (2011). *Voluntary education partnership memorandum of understanding (MOU).* Retrieved from http://www.dantes.doded.mil/educational-institutions/dod-mou.html#sthash.vTz5NXgB.dpbs

Whiteman, S., & Barry, A. (2011). A comparative analysis of student service member/veteran and civilian student drinking motives. *Journal of Student Affairs Research and Practice, 48,* 297-313.

Whiteman, S., Barry, A., Mroczek, D., & MacDermid Wadsworth, S. (2013). The development and implications of peer emotional support for student service members/veterans and civilian college students. *Journal of Counseling Psychology, 60*(2), 265–278.

ABOUT THE AUTHORS

Tanya Ang is director for Veterans' Programs at the American Council on Education (ACE) and oversees veterans initiatives, such as the Toolkit for Veteran Friendly Institutions and the Severely Injured Service Members program. She also works collaboratively with institutions of higher education and other organizations to disseminate and promote best practices in serving military and student veterans on campus. Prior to her role in Veterans' Programs, Ang served as a senior program manager in ACE's Military Programs working, with evaluation teams to provide credit recommendations on servicemembers' military transcripts. Ang has worked in higher education for more than 13 years in a variety of roles, including administrative analyst for the Vice President of Student Affairs Office at California State University, Fullerton.

Adam E. Barry currently serves as an associate professor in the Department of Health & Kinesiology at Texas A&M University (TAMU). Barry served as a coprincipal investigator on an NIAAA-funded grant that explored whether student veterans' alcohol-related cognitions and patterns of use differ from those of their nonmilitary peers and whether they experienced a greater proportion of negative outcomes (i.e., mental health, social, and academic) as a result of their alcohol use. Peer-reviewed journals featuring his scholarly work include *Addiction, Addictive Behaviors, American Journal of Public Health, Health Education & Behavior, Journal of School Health*, and *Journal of Studies on Alcohol*. Barry has a bachelor's and master of science in health education from Florida State University, as well as a PhD in health education from TAMU.

Chris Andrew Cate is vice president of research for Student Veterans of America (SVA). Cate graduated from the University of California at Santa Barbara with a master of arts in research methodology in 2009 and a doctorate in special education, disability, and risk studies in 2011. His dissertation examined student veterans' college experiences and academic performance. He has worked with SVA since June 2010 and joined SVA's professional staff in September 2012. Cate created the concept of matching Department of Veterans Affairs education benefit data with the National Student Clearinghouse degree attainment data, leading to the partnership between the VA, the Clearinghouse, and SVA and the Million Records Project. In addition, Cate is responsible for analyzing the Million Records Project for SVA and producing reports on the findings and results. Cate's future research will build on the results of the Million Records Project to look at student veterans' persistence, school transfers, and retention as well as completion among Post-9/11 GI Bill veterans. The research will also include how campus environments, such as campus policies, programs, and services, influence student veterans' academic outcomes. This is the first step in assessing the return on investment of the Post-9/11 GI Bill.

James S. Cole is an associate research scientist at the Center for Postsecondary Research, Indiana University School of Education in Bloomington, Indiana. Cole is the project manager for the Beginning College Survey of Student Engagement (BCSSE) and provides research and data analysis support to various projects with the National Survey of Student Engagement (NSSE). He earned his PhD in educational psychology (with an emphasis in motivation) from University of Missouri. Prior to his current position, Cole worked at California State University East Bay Concord Campus, Northern Arizona University, and Sterling College (Vermont). His research interests include first-year programs and engagement and data quality in survey research.

David DiRamio is associate professor of higher education administration at Auburn University. Since his first coauthored article, "From Combat to Campus," was published in the *NASPA Journal* in 2008, DiRamio has emerged as a nationally known researcher reporting about student veterans. His scholarly works include a 2011 coauthored book, *Veterans in Higher Education*, which applies well-known theories and models of college student development to the contemporary phenomenon of the student veteran, and *Creating a Veteran-Friendly Campus* (2009), a coedited *New Directions for Student Services* volume that details best practices and how campus leaders can help student veterans succeed. DiRamio received both BS and MBA degrees from the State University of New York at Buffalo and a PhD in educational leadership from the University of Nevada, Las Vegas. DiRamio is a U.S. Navy veteran.

Daniel L. Fay is an assistant professor of public administration in the Department of Political Science and Public Administration at Mississippi State University. His research interests include organizational theory, diversity issues in public management, veterans' policy, policy diffusion, and higher education policy and management. His work appears in *Research in Higher Education, Social Science Quarterly,* and *The Journal of Technology Transfer*. Prior to joining the faculty at Mississippi State University, Fay served as a visiting assistant professor in the Department of Public Administration and Policy at the University of Georgia and a postdoctoral associate at Syracuse University. His veterans' research has received external funding from the National Science Foundation and a Google Impact Award. He received his PhD in public administration and policy from the School of Public and International Affairs at the University of Georgia, his MPA with a specialization in higher education administration from the University of Georgia, and his bachelor of arts in English from the University of Florida.

Michelle Kees is an associate professor in child and adolescent psychiatry at the University of Michigan, has dual clinical and research without compensation appointments at the Ann Arbor Veterans Affairs Medical Center, and is a lead investigator with Military Support Programs and Networks (M-SPAN). Kees is the principal investigator for PAVE (Peer Advisors for Veteran Education) and of HomeFront Strong, a resiliency intervention for military spouses and children. She is a co-investigator on a longitudinal study examining risk and resiliency in National Guard soldiers and family members over the transitions of deployment.

Amanda Kraus received her MA and PhD from the University of Arizona (UA) in higher education. She currently serves as associate director at the UA Disability Resource Center. Kraus is also assistant professor of practice in the Center for the Study of Higher Education at UA, where she coordinates the M.A. program and instructs courses on student services, student development, and disability. In her previous role on campus, she directed a federal grant that researched how disabled veterans experience higher education and developed initiatives for their successful integration to college. She is passionate about social justice and access; this is reflected in her work on campus, teaching, and community involvement. Kraus was recently recognized as one of Tucson's Top 40 Under 40 by the *Arizona Daily Star* and Tucson Hispanic Chamber of Commerce.

Wendy A. Lang is the founder and director of Operation College Promise (OCP), a national policy, research, and education program supporting the postsecondary advancement of our nation's veterans. In 2011 and 2013, Lang published landmark research on student veterans' progress toward degree attainment in the post-9/11 era. The "Completing the Mission" reports have been widely cited in various articles and journals. Lang's work with OCP has been featured in *The New York*

Times, USA Today, The Philadelphia Inquirer, The Chronicle on Higher Education, Inside Higher Ed, Military Advanced Education, NBC, Fox News, NPR, and CNN, among other local and media outlets. OCP is housed on the campus of Thomas Edison State College (TESC). Lang worked in state government for 10 years including serving as Senator John H. Ewing's Chief of Staff, staffing both the Senate Education and Women's Issues Committees, and later, filling an appointment as Governor Christine Todd Whitman's education policy advisor. She ran her own independent consulting business from 2000 to 2005. Lang received her BA in political science and MA in international relations from Drew University.

Rosalinda Maury is director of survey research at Syracuse University's Institute for Veterans and Military Families. She brings extensive experience in survey development and worldwide data collection and has been responsible for developing, implementing, and managing surveys for data collection for organizations including VAnalytic, Metrica, U.S. Coast Guard, U.S. Air Force, and Texas State University. Her work has been featured in numerous publications on topics including job performance, effects of personal financial mismanagement behaviors, training needs assessment, workload assessment, organizational restructuring, job and occupational analysis and equal pay for equal work. Maury holds master's and bachelor's degrees in psychology from the University of Texas at San Antonio.

Chrysta Meadowbrooke is the research specialist for M-SPAN, working on research and evaluation for PAVE and other military- and veteran-focused programs. She has several years of experience on community-based health and clinical projects, performing both qualitative and quantitative data collection and analysis.

Wayne K. Miller II earned his PhD from the University of Connecticut in special education. He has researched student veterans issues since 2009. He is the director of Veterans Upward Bound at Weber State University in Ogden, Utah.

Dani Molina is director of the Veterans Resource Center at the California State University, Los Angeles. As director, Molina manages programs and services centered on supporting the higher education access and success of military-connected students. Molina holds a doctorate in higher education and organizational change from UCLA. He is an Army veteran and served during Operation Iraqi Freedom (OIF-1).

Andrew Q. Morse is a consultant and project director with Keeling & Associates, LLC. He previously was director for policy research and advocacy with NASPA – Student Affairs Administrators in Higher Education's Research and Policy Institute. He earned his bachelor's degree in psychology from the University of Northern Iowa. Morse earned a master of science in college student personnel and holds a doctorate in higher education administration from the University of Tennessee, Knoxville.

R. Cody Nicholls is the assistant dean of students for military and veteran engagement at the University of Arizona. Nicholls is a nine-and-a-half-year veteran of the U.S. Army Reserves. During his tenure in the service, he completed deployments to Iraq (2004–2005) and Kuwait (2008–2009) and one state side mobilization immediately following 9/11 (2001–2002). Nicholls is currently ABD in higher education with a major concentration in organization and administration and a minor concentration in entrepreneurship from the Eller College of Management at the University of Arizona.

Tom O'Donnell is assistant dean of students/veteran affairs at Stockton University in New Jersey, where he developed the Veteran Affairs Program. O'Donnell graduated from the University of Nebraska where he studied psychology and crisis intervention and received an MS in education and contemporary civilization from Kean University. He taught and developed leadership and education courses at Kean University and became director of student development, a position in which he served for 15 years. He came to Stockton University in 1999 and continues to develop academic courses in leadership and veteran affairs. O'Donnell serves on several regional and national veterans boards and lectures nationally on leadership and veterans affairs.

Brittany Risk is the program coordinator for PAVE. She coordinates and oversees all aspects of the implementation of the PAVE Program. Prior to her work with M-SPAN, Risk was a project coordinator at the Department of Veterans Affairs on grants that focused on veterans' mental health, substance abuse, and suicide.

Jane L. Spinner is project officer for strategic initiatives at the University of Michigan Depression Center and Department of Psychiatry. She oversees the design, development, and implementation of major projects and initiatives that address the mental health needs of special populations, including the portfolio of military and veteran-focused programs at M-SPAN. Spinner has more than 20 years of experience in the health care field, with a background as a clinician, health care business executive, and entrepreneur.

Marcia Valenstein is professor of psychiatry at the University of Michigan and a research scientist at the Ann Arbor Veterans Affairs Medical Center in health services research and development. She has worked as a clinical psychiatrist in the VA for more than 25 years and has been principal investigator on multiple federally and foundation-funded grants. She has more than 165 articles or book chapters published or in press. Valenstein is a national expert on peer programs and was a key member in the team that conceptualized and implemented PAVE.

Ryan L. Van Dusen is dean of student development at Bethany College in Lindsborg, Kansas, and has worked in higher education since 2002. He has held positions in student activities, residential life, student conduct, and veterans services at Independence (Kansas) Community College, New Mexico State University, Texas Tech University, and the University of Memphis. He was previously the director of Military & Veterans Programs at Texas Tech. Prior to working in higher education, Van Dusen served in the U.S. Army from 1998–2002 as a 19K (armor crewman) and achieved the rank of sergeant (E5). He was stationed at Ft. Riley, Kansas, and Camp Casey, South Korea. Van Dusen earned a bachelor of arts in history and a master of arts in communications studies from Edinboro University of Pennsylvania. He also earned an MBA from the University of Memphis and holds a doctorate in higher education from Texas Tech University. His research interests include veterans in higher education, nontraditional student retention, and leadership in higher education.

Shelley MacDermid Wadsworth currently serves as professor and director of the Military Family Research Institute at Purdue University. MacDermid Wadsworth's research broadly examines the relationships between work conditions and family life, with a special focus on military-connected families. Her work has been supported by a variety of funding agencies including the Department of Defense. She is extensively published and is a fellow of the National Council on Family Relations.

Shawn D. Whiteman currently serves as an associate professor at Purdue University. Whiteman's research examines how siblings directly and indirectly act as sources of social influence and social comparison within families and how their family experiences foster similarities and differences in their relationship qualities, attributes, and adjustment. In addition, he has published extensively on the mental and physical health of student servicemembers/veterans, served as coprincipal investigator on an NIAAA-funded grant specific to student veterans, and frequently collaborates with the Military Family Research Institute at Purdue University. Whiteman has a PhD in Human Development and Family Studies from the Pennsylvania State University.

Corri Zoli is director of research at Syracuse University's (SU) Institute for National Security and Counterterrorism and a research assistant professor in SU's Maxwell School of Citizenship and Public Affairs. Her research focuses on global security issues at the intersection of cultural studies and security policy, with additional interests in gender and identity, terrorism, critical theory, globalization, and veterans in higher education. Notably, since 2009, Zoli's research on veterans' educational aspirations—with emphasis on technical fields and engineering (STEM)—has been supported by both the National Science Foundation and Google (in partnership with the IVMF), which has led to one of the most comprehensive national datasets on servicemembers' educational goals and needs.

INDEX

NOTE: Page numbers with italicized *f* or *t* indicate figures or tables respectively.

A

academic adjustment or functioning
  California Community College System and, 171
  military-affiliated college students and, 68
  peer support and, 61
  peer support study measures of, 64
  of retention rate study participants, 152
academic advising. *See also* pre-enrollment advising
  servicemembers on helpfulness of, 7
Academic Motivation Scale, 64, 66*t*
academic outcomes research. *See also* graduation rates
  conclusion, 145
  federal databases and, 138–141
  Million Records Project and, 141–144
  past research, 136–138
  population-level data for, 135–136
  retention rate study participants and, 153
academics. *See* academic adjustment or functioning

academic-veterans communities, 4
access to full learning opportunities, in California Community College System, 163, 164*t*, 166
active duty personnel. *See also* military-affiliated college students
  non-completion risk factors for, 34*f*, 35
  undergraduate STEM participation and, 33, 33*f*
African Americans. *See also* Black student veterans; race
  as nontraditional students, 151
  retention rate study and, 154*t*
  as student veterans, loan debt of, 188
age of veterans
  first degree completion and, 143–144, 144*t*
  retention rates and, 157
alcohol abuse, 187
American Council on Education (ACE)
  College Credit for Military Service website, 184
  formation and programs of, 79–81, 89
  on Post-9/11 GI Bill and enrollment, 28
  pre-enrollment advising and, 85
  From Soldier to Student, 180
  From Soldier to Student II, 124, 126, 181

on support services for student veterans, 180

on veteran assistance with transition to college, 95

The American Freshman: National Norms Fall 2012, 122

Americans with Disabilities Act (ADA)

amendments (2008), 164

compliance, veterans lounges and, 129

amputations, 41

anxiety

generalized, military-affiliated college students and, 60

peer support and, 61

untreated, Peer Advisors helping with, 104–105

armed services. *See also* disabled student veterans; military-affiliated college students; student veterans

desire to return to, 18–19

reasons for joining, 7, 8*t*

reasons for leaving, 18, 20*t*

assistive technologies, California Community College System and, 170–171

associate degrees, student veterans and, 142

attrition. *See* retention rates

Aud, S., 25

B

bachelor's degrees, student veterans and, 142

Bagby, J. H., 150, 151, 157

Barazandeh, G., 50

Barnard-Brak, L., 150

Barry, A. E., 187

Basic Allowance for Housing (BAH), as VA benefit, data tracking under, 139

Baylor University, 186

Bean, J. P., 148, 151, 152

belonging, sense of

peer support and, 96

student veterans and, 148–149

veteran transition to higher education and, 150–151

benefits. *See* GI Bill benefits; Post-9/11 GI Bill; Vocational Rehabilitation and Employment

Black student veterans. *See also* African Americans

loan debt of, 31, 31*f*

unmet financial need and, 29, 29*f*

Borg, W., 165

Bracewell, K. A., 159

Bradley Commission on Veterans' Benefits in the United States, 16

Brief Symptom Index, 65

Buddy-to-Buddy program, 96

Burgo-Black, A. L., 70

C

Cabrera, A. F., 148

California Community College System study

access to full learning opportunities in, 166

career services, 168–169

conclusion, 172–173

information on veterans' needs, 167

overview of essential practices for student veterans in, 163–165, 164*t*

physical access to facilities of, 166–167

self-reported discharge ranks of student veterans in, 171, 172t
top-down support, 169–170
understanding student veterans' rights, 170–171
veterans resource center, 165–166
vocationally useful educational goals, 168
campus climate, disabled student veterans on, 49–50
Campus Teams. See also Peer Advisors for Veteran Education
composition and role of, 97–98
implementation challenges for, 106–107
implementation support for, 101–102
online tracking by, 103–104
PAVE success and, 108
program evaluation and, 102–103
tailored work plan of, 100
tiered model and, 98f
voices of, 106
career development. See also employment issues
capitalizing on military experiences and, 51–52
counseling and, 124
engagement patterns interview protocol, 56
opportunities geared toward graduating veterans and, 125
career services, in California Community College System, 164, 164t, 168–169
Casteneda, M. B., 148
Cate, C. A., 147, 188
Certificate for Veterans Service Providers (CVSP), 119, 128

CES-D, 65
Chapter 31 (Vocational Rehabilitation and Employment [VR&E]), 105
Chapter 33. See Post-9/11 GI Bill
character formation, military service and, 17–18, 19t
children of veterans, educational benefits transferred from parents of, 186
Chi-square test, 165
civilian college students, on military-affiliated college students, 59–60
civilian reintegration, as challenge or barrier to transition and, 11, 11t
class registration, military education benefits processing and, 125
Cold War GI Bill, 137
collaborative learning
disabled student veterans on, 48–49
disabled student veterans vs. other student groups and, 46t
engagement patterns interview protocol, 56
collaborative support, military-affiliated college students and, 81–82, 180–181
The College of New Jersey, 118
College Self-Efficacy Inventory, 64
College Stress Scale, 64, 66t
Combat Papers, 128
communication
of campus and community resources for military-connected students, 82–83
of success stories with enrolled student veterans, 158–159
community, sense of. See belonging, sense of

community colleges. *See also*
California Community College
System study
    disabled veteran engagement
    patterns study and, 50
comorbidity of invisible injuries, 41
Complete College America, *Time is the Enemy* report by, 26
Conceptual Model of Nontraditional
Undergraduate Student Attrition
(Bean and Metzer), 151, 152, 158
connectedness, sense of. *See also*
belonging, sense of
    peer support and, 96
Cooperative Institutional Research
Program, 122
Coryell, L., 149
cost of higher education
    average loan amount and, 31–32,
    31f, 32f
    low-income students and, 26
    student debt and, 36
    unmet, race or ethnicity or gender
    and, 29–31, 29f
counseling
    Peer Advisors connecting student
    veteran with, 105
    provisions for, 94
Counselors Office, California Community College System, 165
credits, military transfer
    evaluation and acceptance of,
    182–183
    recruiting military students and,
    124
    tracking, 148
credits, percentage earned versus pursued, Graduation Probability Indices
and, 119

D

critical thinking, engagement patterns
interview protocol, 56
cultural barriers, transition and,
12–17, 14t, 15t

data-driven inquiry, 3–6
Defense Centers of Excellence for
Psychological Health and Traumatic
Brain Injury, 96
Defense Department. *See* U.S.
Department of Defense
degree attainment study
    additional research suggestions,
    126–127
    conclusion, 129–130
    grade point averages and, 121,
    121f
    method, 120
    overview, 119
    participants, 120–121
    participating institutions, tuition
    and enrollment for, 133
    persistence rate and, 122–123,
    123f
    programs and services and,
    123–126
    Stockton University case,
    127–129
    success rate and, 122
delayed college enrollment,
non-completion risk and, 150
Delphi technique, Rand Corporation, 164–165
demographics
    diversity beyond, 16–17
    inequality and, 25–27
    of peer support study participants,
    63

policy and practice implications and, 35–36

of retention rate study participants, 152, 153, 154–156*t*

of servicemembers' perspectives study, 5–6, 6*t*

DePaul University, 121

dependents. *See also* family

non-completion risk and, 150

depressive disorders or symptoms

military-affiliated college students and, 60

peer support and, 61

peer support study measures of, 65, 67*t*

DiRamio, D., 60, 70, 171

disability services office, campus-based student veterans program and, 164

disability studies, as academic discipline, 43

disabled, aversion to identifying as, 42–43, 51

Disabled Student Program and Service, California Community College System, 167

disabled student veterans

on campus climate, 49–50

on collaborative learning, 48–49

conclusion, 52–53

Discussion with Diverse Others scale and, 47–48

engagement patterns interview protocol, 55–56

engagement patterns study findings, 45–50

engagement patterns study limitations, 50

engagement patterns study overview, 44–45

essential practices, in California Community College System, 163, 164*t*

other student groups compared with, 46*t*

on perceived gains, 45–47

rights of, California Community College System and, 164, 164*t*, 170–171

scope of disabilities among, 41

semi-structured interview questions on, 55

on student–faculty interaction, 49

study discussion and implications, 51–52

discipline, military service and development of, 17–18, 19*t*

Discussion with Diverse Others (DO) scale, 47–48

diversity

among servicemembers, 35

beyond basic demography, 16–17

disabled student veterans on interacting with, 46*t*, 47–48

engagement patterns interview protocol, 56

DoD. *See* U.S. Department of Defense

Duhigg, C., 159

Durdella, N., 148–149

E

Eakman, A. M., 61

Education Department (ED). *See* U.S. Department of Education

education interruptions, data collection and, 140

education issues
   as challenge or barrier to transition and, 11*t*
   Peer Advisors helping with, 104–105
   student veterans' concerns about, 104
Educational Degree Behaviors Self-Efficacy Scale, 64
Edyburn, D. L., 170–171
Emergency Council on Education, 79–80
employment issues. *See also* career development; career services
   as challenge or barrier to transition and, 11, 11*t*, 12
employment status, cost of higher education and, 26
enrollments, veteran, changing levels of, 147
environment. *See also* family; financial issues
   for retention rate study participants, 152
Espinosa, L., 26
ethnicity
   average loan amount and, 31*f*
   college affordability and, 87
   income of undergraduate veterans and, 27–28, 28*f*
   peer support study and, 69
   STEM fields and, 25–26
   unmet financial need and, 29–31, 30*f*
   unused GI Bill benefits and, 29, 29*f*
Executive Order 13607 (2012), 118, 140, 141
Extended Opportunity Program and Services, California Community College System, 167

F

faculty
   assumptions on servicemembers by, 13
   capitalizing on military experiences by, 51
   mentoring team at Stockton University and, 128
   as officers, student veterans' view of, 182
   training for, 36–37, 83, 181–182
family. *See also* environment
   balancing work and, 149
   characteristics, cost of higher education and, 26
family support
   military-affiliated college students and, 62, 65
   retention rates and, 157–158
   servicemembers on helpfulness of, 7, 9*t*
federal student aid. *See also* GI Bill benefits; Pell Grants; Post-9/11 GI Bill
   DoD and VA education benefits and, 87
financial aid, 86–87
financial independence, non-completion risk and, 150
financial issues. *See also* cost of higher education
   as challenge or barrier to transition and, 11*t*, 12
   challenges for student veterans and, 94, 149
   educational equity and, 187–188

funding sources, 13*t*
understanding, 36
Yellow Ribbon, Choice Act and,
124–125
for-profit institutions
disabled veteran engagement
patterns study and, 50
student veteran graduates from,
188
Fortune 100 companies, veteran
hiring by, 184
four-year institutions, student veterans and, 143
Framework for Veterans' Success, 119
fresh start, servicemembers on new
identity and, 14–15
friends support
military-affiliated college students
and, 62, 65
retention rates and, 157
servicemembers on helpfulness
of, 7, 9*t*
From Soldier to Student (ACE), 180
From Soldier to Student II (ACE),
124, 126, 181
full-time work during college enrollment, non-completion risk and, 150

G

Gall, J., 165
Gall, M., 165
gender. *See also* women
average loan amount and, 32*f*
unmet financial need and, 29–31,
30*f*
unused GI Bill benefits and, 29,
29*f*
GI Bill. *See also* Cold War GI Bill;
Post-9/11 GI Bill

academic outcomes and data
tracking, 135
California Community College
System study and, 172–173
enrollment statistics and, 147
income of undergraduate veterans
and, 28
research on economic effects of,
136
GI Bill benefits
pre-enrollment advising and,
84–86
processing assistance for, 7
student veterans' concerns about,
104
unmet financial need and, 29–31,
29*f,* 30*f,* 86–87
unused, campus culture and, 14
unused, race or ethnicity or
gender and, 29
veterans on post-service plans
and, 3
World War II and use of, 16, 80
Gilbert, C. K., 148
Gloria, A. M., 64
government websites. *See also* online
tools or sources
servicemembers on helpfulness
of, 7, 9*t*
grade point average
degree attainment study and, 120,
121*f*
family support, retention rates
and, 157–158
Graduation Probability Indices
and, 119
military-affiliated college students
at Stockton Univ. and, 129
peer support and, 61, 62

retention rate study participants and, 153

student veterans and, 148–149

Graduation Probability Indices (GPI), 119, 120, 122

graduation rates. *See also* academic outcomes research

difficulties in tracking, 147

military-affiliated college students at Stockton Univ. and, 129

grants, for student veterans, VA data tracking limits with, 139

Griffin, K. A., 148

Grimes, A., 150, 157

H

handicapped parking, at California Community College System, 166–167

health issues, as challenge or barrier to transition and, 11, 11*t*, 12

hearing loss, 41

help, asking for

PAVE's Campus Teams and, 107

reluctance of student veterans in, 171

as sign of weakness in military culture, 96, 101, 106, 182

Henry, K. L., 61

high school diploma, lack of, noncompletion risk and, 150

High Tech Center Training Unit, California Community College System, 165

higher education

capitalizing on military experiences and, 51–52

challenges and barriers to transition and, 10–12, 11*t*

cultural barriers to, 12–17

disability in, 42–44

leadership support for military-connected students in, 81

opportunity linked to, 25

postservice transition and, 7–10, 8*t*, 9*t*, 10*t*

servicemembers on favorite parts of, 21

servicemembers on goals for, 6*t*

Higher Education Act (1965), 137

Hildebrandt, M. J., 69

historically Black colleges and universities (HBCUs), disabled veteran engagement patterns study and, 50

Hitt, S., 187

Hunt, S. C., 70

I

identity and identification. *See also* stigma or stereotypes

as individual not just as a veteran, 150

new, servicemembers on fresh start and, 14–15

veteran with disability and, 42–43, 51

veterans as protected class under federal law and, 140

women as veterans without gender distinction, 185–186

inclusiveness, nomenclature and, 59

income. *See also* financial issues

undergraduate veterans and, 27–28, 28*f*

inequality

conclusion, 37

demographic or socioeconomic status and, 25–27

higher education and, 25

opportunity and, 27–32
policy and practice implications
and, 35–37
service background differences
and, 32–35
information on veterans' needs, in
California Community College
System, 163, 164t, 167
Institute for National Security and
Counterterrorism (INSCT), Syracuse University, 4
Institute for Veterans and Military
Families (IVMF)
    social media, survey and, 5
    Syracuse University, 4
institutional practices
    academic support, 87–88
    American Council on Education
    and, 79
    conclusion, 89
    critical areas for support, 84–88
    financial aid, 86–87
    graduate and professional school,
    88
    history of serving those who
    served, 79–81
    lessons learned from, 81–84
    NCES survey on military-affiliated
    college students and, 94
    pre-enrollment advising, 84–86
    student veterans' needs and, 148
Institutional Review Board (IRB),
153
Integrated Model of Student Retention, 148
Integrated Postsecondary Education
Data System (IPEDS), 139–140
internal locus of control, Marines'
on, 159

international experiences, military
service and, 17
invisible injuries, 41. See also posttraumatic stress disorder; traumatic
brain injuries

J

jobs. See also career development
    finding, as challenge for student
    veterans and, 149
    postsecondary credential for, 25
Johnson, Lyndon B., 137
Journal of American College Health, 59

K

Kean University, 118
Kees, M., 180
Kim, Y. K., 148–149
Kirchner, M. J., 149
Kleykamp, M. A., 171
Kognito (training program), 83
Korean War, GI Bill and academic
    outcomes after, 136–137
Krebs, R. R., 16
Kresge Foundation, 80–81
Krulak, Charles, 159

L

Lang, W. A., 121, 188
Latino student veterans
    adjusted gross income of, 27
    loan debt of, 31, 31f, 188
    unmet financial need and, 29, 29f
leadership, military service and devel-
    opment of, 17, 18, 19t
length of service, servicemembers
    on, 6t
links to resources, PAVE program
    and, 99

logging records, in PAVE program, 103–104

Lumina Foundation, 183

M

MacDermid Wadsworth, S., 187

marketing campaigns, of success stories with enrolled student veterans, 158–159

medical documentation, as context for disabled student veterans, 42

Meet and Greet, for department heads and veterans, 125

mental health
    challenges for student veterans and, 93–94
    counseling, provisions for, 94
    military-affiliated college students and, 60
    Peer Advisors helping with, 105
    peer support study measures of, 65
    services, military-affiliated college students and, 70
    signs and symptoms, PAVE training on, 100–101
    as student veteran challenge, 104
    substance abuse among veterans and, 186–187

Metzner, B. S., 148, 151, 152

Middleton, M. J., 69

Midwestern Higher Education Compact (MHEC), 183

Military Ally (training program), 83

military occupational specialties (MOS)
    interest in education and, 8–9, 9t
    STEM fields and, 20, 21t
    veterans on post-service plans and, 3

military service, servicemembers on experience of, 17–22, 19t

military undergraduates, use of term, 59

military-affiliated college students. *See also* disabled student veterans; peer support study; servicemembers; student veterans
    on civilian college students, 59–60
    collecting data on and outcomes data on, 83–84
    involving in program development, 70–71, 82
    other college community members and, 68–69
    peer support and, 61–62
    pre-enrollment advising for, 84–86
    Stockton University and, 127–129
    use of term, 59

Million Records Project (MRP)
    academic outcomes and, 141–144, 145
    creation of, 136
    graduation rates studies using, 109

mixed-methods protocol, for disabled student veterans' engagement patterns study, 44–45, 55–56

mobile application, campus-tailored, PAVE implementation and, 102

mobility impairment, 41

Modified Delphi design, California Community College System study and, 163

Molina, D., 33, 149, 188

Montclair State University, 118

Montgomery GI Bill for Active Duty and Veterans (MGIB-AD), 13t
Montgomery GI Bill for Selected Reserves (MGIB-SR), 13t
Montgomery GI Bill (MGIB), 93, 137, 138
   Million Records Project and, 141–142
Morse, A., 33, 149, 188
mortality, decreased rates in, peer support and, 61
Multi-State Collaborative on Military Credit (MCMC), 183
myths about servicemembers, 15t. *See also* stigma or stereotypes
   propagation of, 12–13, 15

N
NASPA, 86
National Center for Education Statistics (NCES)
   on employment status, dependents and postsecondary credentials, 26
   on graduation rates for veteran vs. civilian students, 147–148
   on military-affiliated college student enrollment, 94
   non-completion factors and, 149
   on non-completion risk factors, 34
   postsecondary student academic databases of, 139
National Guard, undergraduate STEM participation and, 33, 33f
National Postsecondary Student Aid Study (NPSAS), 27
   service background differences and, 32–35
National Science Foundation (NSF), 4

National Student Clearinghouse, 122
   Million Records Project and, 141
National Survey of Veterans (NSV, 2010), 137–138
National Survey on Student Engagement (NSSE)
   Collaborative Learning (CL) scale, 48–49
   College Student Report, 44
   disabled student veteran data and, 42
   Discussion with Diverse Others scale, 47–48
   Perceived Gains (PG) scale, 45–47
   Student–Faculty Interaction (SF) scale, 49
National Team. *See also* Peer Advisors for Veteran Education
   housing and role of, 97
   implementation challenges for, 106–107
   implementation support by, 101–102
   online tools, 102
   program evaluation and, 102–103
   tiered role for training and implementation and, 98f
National Training Conference (PAVE 2016), 108
National Veteran Education Success Tracker (NVEST) Project, 144, 145
Native Americans, peer support study and, 69
NCES. *See* National Center for Education Statistics
Nellum, C., 26
nemo resideo ("leave no one behind"), peer support and, 95
Ness, B. M., 69

New Jersey Association of State Colleges and Universities (NJASCU), 118, 127

New Jersey City University, 118

non-completion risk factors, service background differences and, 34, 34f

nontraditional students, definitions for, 151

Nora, A., 148

O

Obama, Barack, 118, 140

O'Donnell, T., 187

online tools or sources
College Credit for Military Service website, 184
Operation College Promise as, 118
PAVE implementation and, 102, 108–109
servicemembers on helpfulness of, 7, 9t
for student veterans, 125

Operation College Promise (OCP). *See also* degree attainment study
Certificate for Veterans Service Providers and, 119, 128
faculty and staff training and, 83
founding of, 118, 127
progress to degree attainment study and, 119–127
recruiting additional schools for, 126
veterans' support services survey by, 125

Operation Enduring Freedom/Operation Iraqi Freedom, 59

opportunity
as American theme, 25

inequality and, 27–32

opt-out policy, PAVE's National Team on, 107

orientation, new student veterans, 125

outreach, PAVE program and, 99

P

part-time college enrollment, non-completion risk and, 150

Pat Tillman Foundation (PTF), 119. *See also* degree attainment study

Peer Advisors. *See also* Peer Advisors for Veteran Education
Campus PAVE Teams and, 98–99
helping with benefits questions, 105
helping with educational issues, 104–105
helping with mental health concerns, 105
implementation challenges for, 106–107
implementation support for, 101–102
online tracking by, 103–104
PAVE success and, 108
training, 99–100
training on support for, 101
voices of, 106
welcoming into the community, 104

Peer Advisors for Veteran Education (PAVE)
challenges for student veterans and, 93–94
conclusion, 109–110
expansion of, 108–109
formation and goals of, 96–97

funding and support for, 110
impact of, 103–106
implementation challenges, 106–107
online tools, 102
overview, 93
partner campuses, 109*f*
power of peers, 95–96
program elements, 99–103, 100*f*
program evaluation, 102–103
program success factors, 107–108
support for academic institutions and, 94–95
tiered model of, 97–99, 98*f*
training, 99–101
peer support
challenges for student veterans and, 94
general population implications for, 61
military-affiliated college students and, 60–62
PAVE program and, 99
power of, 95–96
peer support study
conclusion, 69–71
discussion, 68–69
measures, 63–65
participants, 62–63
procedure, 63
results, 65, 66–67*t*
peers, opportunities for student veterans to connect with, 148
Pell Grants, 170
Pell Institute for the Study of Opportunity in Higher Education, 26
PennAHEAD, 26
Perceived Gains (PG)
disabled student veterans on, 45–47
disabled student veterans vs. other student groups and, 46*t*
semi-structured interview questions on, 55
persistence rate
in progress to degree attainment study, 122–123, 123*f*
student veterans and, 149
personal contacts with university or college individuals, servicemembers on helpfulness of, 7, 9*t*
physical access to facilities, in California Community College System, 163, 164*t*, 166–167
physical health, improved, peer support and, 61
policy and practice implications
demographic and socioeconomic characteristics and, 35–36
training for faculty, staff, and students, 36–37
understanding affordability, unmet financial need, and student debt and, 36
Post-9/11 GI Bill (2008)
ACE advocacy for passage of, 80
California Community College System study and, 172–173
data tracking under, 139
enrollment under, staffing needs and collaboration and, 180–181
as funding source, 13*t*
higher education enrollment and, 28
Million Records Project and, 141–142
National Veteran Education Success Tracker Project and, 144

passage of, 117
Peer Advisors helping with questions about, 105
Pell Grants and, 170
people benefited by, 93
persistence rate and, 123
progress to degree attainment study and, 120
servicemember education and, 79
student outcomes measures under, 140
transfer credit for military schooling and, 183
unmet financial need and, 87, 187–188
postservice transition
challenges or barriers to, 10–12, 11t
higher education and, 7–10
room for improvement in, 125–126
as student veteran concern, 149
posttraumatic stress disorder (PTSD)
disabled student veterans and, 41
faculty and staff training on, 83
maximizing higher education objectives and, 129
military-affiliated college students and, 60
as student veteran challenge, 93–94
symptoms, peer support and, 61, 62, 69
veterans at California Community College System and, 166
Powers, J. T., 121
pre-enrollment advising, 84–86, 149. See also academic advising

presidents
California Community College System, support for student veteran success by, 164
Principles of Excellence, Executive Order 13607 (2012) on, 118
Privacy Act (1974), 170
private, nonprofit institutions
student veteran enrollment in, 143, 143t
student veteran graduates from, 188
problem solving, engagement patterns interview protocol and, 56
proprietary schools
student veteran enrollment in, 143, 143t
student veteran graduates from, 188
protected class, federal law on, 140
psychological outcomes, retention rate study participants and, 153
psychosomatic symptoms, peer support study measures of, 65, 67t
public institutions, student veteran enrollment in, 143, 143t

R

race
average loan amount and, 31f
college affordability and, 87
income of undergraduate veterans and, 27–28, 28f
peer support study and, 69
STEM fields and, 25–26
unmet financial need and, 29–31, 30f
unused GI Bill benefits and, 29, 29f

Radford University, 124
Ramapo College, 118
RAND Corporation
    Delphi technique, 164–165
    on challenges for student veterans, 94
    on DoD and VA education benefits, 87
    on peer support, 95
    on Post-9/11 GI Bill and enrollment, 28
reenrollment process, policies governing, 126
referrals, PAVE program on, 100
Reserve Education Assistance Program (REAP), 13t
reservists, undergraduate STEM participation and, 33, 33f
retention rates
    discussion, 157–158
    Graduation Probability Indices and, 119
    literature review, 148–151
    military-affiliated college students at Stockton Univ. and, 129
    peer support and, 61
    research design and methodology, 151–153
    of student veterans, overview, 147–148
    study implications, 158–159
    study limitations, 158
    study participant demographics, 152, 153, 154–156t
    study results, 156, 157t
    theoretical framework, 151
Robinson Kurpius, S. E. R., 64
ROTC programs, servicemember education and, 13

Rowan University, 118

S

salaries, higher education, tuition prices, student debt and, 26
Salt Lake Community College, 171
Schafer, W., 64
Schelly, C., 61
scholarships, for student veterans, VA data tracking limits with, 139
school enrollment, survey respondents and, 6, 6t, 8
Seal, K. H., 70
self-efficacy
    peer support and, 62, 66t
    peer support from other military members and, 65
self-esteem, peer support and, 61
self-harm, military-affiliated college students and, 60
self-reflection, campus culture concerns and, 14–15
Service to School program, 85
ServiceMember and Veteran Academic Advising Summit (2014), 85–86
servicemembers. See also disabled student veterans; military-affiliated college students; student veterans
    demographics of survey responders, 5–6
    diversity among, 35
    on helpful resources, 9t
    on military service impact on their education, 9–10, 10t
    on myths concerning, 12–13
    non-completion risk factors for, 34–35, 34f
Servicemen's Readjustment Act

(1944), 80, 147, 117. *See also* GI Bill

Serving Those Who Serve: Higher Education and America's Veterans (presidential summit), 80

Serving Those Who Serve Initiative
ACE's comprehensive agenda for, 80–81
lessons learned from, 81–84

Severely Injured Military Veterans: Fulfilling Their Dreams (SIMV) program, 85

sexual orientation demographic, peer support study and, 69

sexual violence at colleges and universities, 186

single parents, non-completion risk and, 150

single point of contact, for military-affiliated college students, 83

skills translation, as challenge or barrier to transition and, 11*t*, 12

Skocpol, T., 16

social media
communication with military-connected students with, 82–83
IVMF survey and, 5

social support. *See also* family support; friends support; peer support
military-affiliated college students and, 70–71
retention rate study participants and, 152

Society for Human Resource Management (SHRM), 184

socioeconomic factors
inequality and, 25–27
policy and practice implications and, 35–36

preservice, Korean War GI Bill academic outcomes and, 137

Spelman, J. F., 70

Spouse and Dependents Education Assistance (DEA), 13*t*

St. John, E. P., 151

staff
support for student veteran success by, 164
support for student veterans and, 180–181, 181*f*
training for, 36–37, 181–182

Stanford University, 186

Stanley, M., 136, 137

STEM fields
military service and preparation for, 20, 21*t*
racial and ethnic minorities and, 25–26
service background differences and, 32–35

stigma or stereotypes. *See also* identity and identification
California Community College System and, 167
faculty and staff training to reduce, 83
of identifying as disabled, 42–43, 51
PAVE implementation and, 106
PAVE training on, 100–101
power of peers and, 96
service to country and, 12, 14–15, 15*t*
student veterans concerns about peers and, 95

Stockton University, 118
case study, 127–129

student background. *See* demographics

student debt
  average loan amount and, 31–32,
  31f, 32f
  understanding, 36
Student Identifier List (SIL), progress
to degree attainment study and, 120
student veterans. *See also* disabled
student veterans; military-affiliated
college students; retention rates;
servicemembers; unfinished business
  general public's radar and, 179
  loan debt of, 188
  PAVE program and, 99
  peer support and, 95–96
  perspectives, importance of, 22
  rights of, California Community
  College System and, 164, 164t,
  170–171
  success in California Community
  College System for, 164
  use of term, 59
Student Veterans of America (SVA).
See also Peer Advisors for Veteran
Education
  matriculation patterns research
  by, 185
  Million Records Project and, 141
  PAVE development and, 96
  PAVE success and, 108
  on veterans earning postsecondary credential, 86
student veterans organizations
(SVOs), 125, 127–128
Student–Faculty Interaction (SF)
scale, 49
  disabled student veterans vs. other
  student groups and, 46t
  engagement patterns interview
  protocol, 57

students, training for, 36–37
substance abuse, traumatic brain
injuries and, 186–187
Success for Veterans Award Grants,
80
success rate, in progress to degree
attainment study, 120, 122
suicide ideation or suicidal behavior,
60, 101
Sulak, T., 150
support. *See* family support; friends
support; Peer Advisors for Veteran
Education; peer support; top-down
support
survey instruments
  demographics of responders, 5–6,
  6t
  development of, 4–5
Syracuse University social scientists,
3–4

T
Team Leaders. *See also* Peer Advisors
for Veteran Education
  Campus PAVE Teams and, 98
  implementation challenges for,
  107
  implementation support for,
  101–102
  PAVE success and, 108
  program evaluation and, 102–103
  training, 99–100
  training on support for, 101
  voices of, 106
The Telling Project, 128
textbook stipends (VA), data tracking
under, 139
Thomas Edison State University, 118
Thompson, L. W., 150

Time is the Enemy report (Complete College America), 26

time limits on education benefits
    out-of-the-classroom experiences and, 185
    in Post-9/11 GI Bill (2008), 123
    of U.S. Department of Education, 142, 147–148

time management, challenges for student veterans and, 94

time-to-completion, student veterans and, 142

Title IV financial aid, for student veterans, VA data tracking limits with, 139

Title IX enforcement, 186

Toolkit for Veteran Friendly Institutions, 81, 89

top-down support
    for military-connected students, 81
    servicemembers on helpfulness of, 7
    for student veterans in California Community College System, 164, 164*t*, 169–170

training
    for faculty and staff, 36–37, 69, 83, 126, 181–182
    PAVE challenges with, 107
    PAVE program, 99–101, 100*f*, 108
    servicemembers on goals for, 6*t*
    for students, 36–37
    veteran-specific, off- and on-campus communities and, 125
    web-based, PAVE program and, 109

transfers from one school to another
    data collection and, 140
    opportunities for, 152
    student veterans and, 143

transition from soldier to student. *See* postservice transition

Transition Theory, Schlossberg's, 148

traumatic brain injuries (TBIs), 41, 60, 83, 186–187. *See also* disabled student veterans

Tuition Assistance (TA) Program, 138–139, 140

Tuttle, T. J., 151

two-year institutions. *See also* California Community College System study
    student veterans and, 143

U

unemployment, struggling economy (2008) and, 117–118

unfinished business
    conclusion, 188
    educational equity, 187–188
    faculty and staff training, 181–182
    mental health and substance abuse, 186–187
    overview, 179
    related subpopulations, 185–186
    transfer credit for military schooling, 182–184
    workforce preparedness, 184–185

universal design (UD), 43–44, 52, 170–171

university administration. *See also* top-down support
    servicemembers on helpfulness of, 7

University Champions for PAVE, 97, 99–100

University Environment Scale, 64–65, 66*t*

University of Michigan, 96. *See also*
Peer Advisors for Veteran Education
 National PAVE Team and, 97
University of South Florida, 123
U.S. Department of Defense (DoD)
 dataset, 4
 education benefits, federal student
 aid and, 87
 education benefits, unmet financial need and, 29
 Executive Order 13607 on data
 sharing and, 141
 GI Bill as link between high education institutions and, 80
 Tuition Assistance (TA) Program
 database, 138–139
U.S. Department of Education
 Beginning Postsecondary Survey,
 26
 dataset, 4
 Executive Order 13607 on data
 sharing and, 141
 index of risk for non-completion,
 149–150
 six-year measure for completion
 of, 147–148
 surveys and data-reporting systems of, 139–141
 Veterans Upward Bound Program,
 87–88, 168
U.S. Department of Labor, dataset, 4
U.S. Department of Veterans Affairs
 (VA). *See also* GI Bill; Montgomery
 GI Bill; Post-9/11 GI Bill
 benefits, delays in, 14
 databases, 139
 dataset, 4
 on degree completion, 88

 education benefits, career track
 and, 168
 education benefits, federal student
 aid and, 87
 education benefits, unmet financial need and, 29
 Executive Order 13607 on data
 sharing and, 141
 Health Administration, PAVE
 and, 96
 health care crisis, 179
 Medical Hospitals, PTSD and
 TBI training and, 83
 Memorandum of Understanding
 on transfer credits, 183
 merging ED data with data from,
 140–141
 Million Records Project and, 141
 network, servicemembers on
 helpfulness of, 7, 9t
 networks supported by, 4
 student veteran retention or
 graduation rates and, 147
 VITAL initiative, 117
 work study positions, 41
 Yellow Ribbon program and, 124
U.S. Marine Corps' training philosophy, 159
U.S. Presidents' Commission on
Veterans' Pensions, 16

V

Vaccaro, A., 150, 158
Vallerand, R. J., 64
Van Dusen, R. L., 148, 157, 181
VET NET Ally (training seminar),
69, 83
Veteran Services Coordinators
(VSCs). *See also* Peer Advisors for
Veteran Education

Campus PAVE Teams and, 97–98
implementation support for,
101–102
National PAVE Team and, 97
PAVE role changes for, 107
PAVE success and, 107–108
program evaluation and, 103
training, 99–100, 101
veterans. *See also* military-affiliated
college students; student veterans
degree completion by, 88
as protected class under federal
law, 140
undergraduate STEM participation and, 33, 33*f*
unemployment (2008) for,
117–118
Veterans Access, Choice and Accountability Act (Choice Act), 124
Veterans Affairs (VA). *See* U.S. Department of Veterans Affairs
Veterans Benefits Administration
(VBA), data tracking by, 139
veterans centers, club, association, or
veterans resource centers
in California Community College
System, 163, 164*t*, 165–166
on-campus, 124
military-affiliated college students
and, 70
Operation College Promise on,
125
Veterans Educational Assistance Act
(2008), 117. *See also* Post-9/11 GI
Bill
Veterans Educational Assistance
Program (VEAP), 13*t*, 137, 138
veterans office with coordinator, 124

Veterans Readjustment Benefits Act
(1966), 137
Veterans Success Jam (2010), 80–81
Veterans Upward Bound, 87–88
veterans-serving organizations
(VSOs), 4
Vietnam War, GI Bill and academic
outcomes after, 137
vision loss, 41
VITAL (Veterans Integration to
Academic Leadership), 117
vocational certificates, student veterans and, 142
Vocational Rehabilitation Act
(1973), Section 504, 164
Vocational Rehabilitation and Employment (VR&E or Chapter 31),
105
vocationally useful educational goals
time limits on education benefits
and, 185
for veterans in California Community College System, 164, 164*t*,
168

W

Walmart Foundation, 80
Walter Reed National Military Medi-
cal Center, 85
warm hand-offs, use of term, 100
Warrior Champion program, 128
Warrior–Scholar Project, 88
websites. *See* online tools or sources
Welcome Week, Stockton University,
128
Wesleyan University, 186
Westat, 137
Whiteman, S. D., 61, 187
William Paterson University, 118

Williams, D. N., 149, 157
women
 in the military, misogyny and
 aggression against, 186
 STEM fields and, 26
women veterans
 California Community College
 System and, 171
 degree attainment study and, 120
 gender bias and, 185–186
work, balancing family and, 149
workforce preparedness, 184–185
working effectively with others,
engagement patterns interview
protocol, 55
World War I, Emergency Council on
Education and, 79–80
World War II
 GI Bill and academic outcomes
 after, 136
 servicemembers enrolling in
 higher education and, 16
wounded warrior, aversion to identifying as, 42–43

Y
Yelich Biniecki, S., 149
Yellow Ribbon program, 41, 124

Z
Zoli, C., 14